U1010448

CHECKMATE INVESTING

一击制胜

华尔街金牌投资人的99条忠告

[美] 江柏德（John M.Probandt） 著

Three Decades of Investment Tips Philosophy and Wisdom for Creating Wealth and a Happy Life

法律出版社 LAW PRESS·CHINA

Checkmate Investing: Three Decades of Investment Tips, Philosophy and Wisdom for Creating Wealth and a Happy Life
By John M. Probandt
Copyright © John M. Probandt
The English-Chinese edition is published exclusively by Law Press China.
All rights reserved.

本书英文版著作权归属于原作者。
本书中英双语版由法律出版社独家出版发行。
本书所有权利保留。

著作权合同登记号
图字：01–2018–6233

CONTENTS

目 录

第三章 基本业务操作

CHAPTER 4 Understanding Investment Principles

CHAPTER 5 Types of Investment Opportunities

第四章　了解投资原则

第五章　投资机会类型

第六章　当代世界投资

第七章　国际投资

CHAPTER 8 Maintaining Success

CHAPTER 9 Wall Street Options

第八章 保持成功

第九章 华尔街的融资途径

第十章 “将军投资基金”概要

附　录

Introduction **The Checkmate Investing Style**

This book will teach you to be in harmony with your surroundings in a way that creates consistent financial and personal success. The emphasis is on philosophy and the mental approach to investing along with excellent investment secrets.

Checkmate Investing is an exploration into the perceptions and intuition needed for a coherent method to investing. Success is not merely earning money. It is a mindset, a lifestyle, and an explicit way of dealing with the intricacies of the world;a process that if done correctly, can have the residual effect of making you very wealthy. Mental attitude is the key to discerning a winning investment from a losing alternative. Therefore, it is essential to have a rewarding and balanced life which enables you to see lucrative opportunities and capitalize on them. Success is a marathon, not a sprint, so you must prepare for endurance.

This manual provides insight which can be utilized immediately as opposed to a study course. Its lessons are not meant to be viewed in any specific order. As such, you can reread passages and continually uncover value by using it as a lens to view your evolving situations and attain a new and powerful perspective. In truth, every choice you make is an investment of time, energy, devotion, and money.

The principles herein are analogous to playing the game of chess where there is only total victory known as *Checkmate*. Thankfully, the real world is not a zero sum game, so dominating opponents is not mandatory. However,in business you will face a myriad of challenges and must surmount obstacle to realize a checkmate. To achieve such a financial victory, think strategically and plan several moves ahead.

前言 “将军投资”的风格

本书将引导你用与周边环境协调一致的方式，建立财务的连贯性与个人成功。我们的重点是用哲学和心理手段去投资，并提供卓越的投资秘诀。

“将军投资”是一种深入认知和直觉，并需要以连贯方法去探究的投资。成功并非仅仅是挣钱，而是一种心态、一种生活方式和一种应对纷繁世界的明确方法，这一过程一旦处理正确，剩余效应就能让你非常富有。辨别成功与失败的投资，关键在于投资者的心态。因此，拥有一个有益的以及平衡的生活是非常必要的，可以使你找到有利的投资机会并利用它们。成功不是冲刺跑而是马拉松，所以你必须要有长期备战的准备。

与课程学习不同，本书提供了立即就能采用的洞察力。所讲内容并不用按特定顺序来看。因此，你可以重读几遍，不断发现它的价值，并用它作“透镜”去观察你的进展情况，从而获得一个全新而强大的视角。事实上，你做的每一个决定都是对时间、精力、忠诚和钱财的投资。

本书的原则与象棋博弈类似，对弈中只有绝对的胜利，就是所谓的“将死”对方。值得庆幸的是，现实生活并不是“零和竞赛”，所以战胜对手并非是强制的。然而为了在生意中实现“将军”，你会面对无数挑战而且必须克服每道难关。想取得这样的财务胜利，需要运筹帷幄，提前规划。

Similar to chess, investing is not a static world and a move that paid dividends yesterday might not be a wise choice today. When thinking like a chess master, you have examined the future scenarios and already planned your options, regardless of what events transpire.

Included in the back of this book is a section titled,*Checkmate Checklists*. This compilation of pertinent information will properly prepare you for any potential investment opportunity and also serve as a helpful lexicon for both novice and experienced investors.

The *Checkmate Investing* style is predicated on the profitable results derived from meticulous guidelines over many years. This stratagem will empower you to reach new levels of growth and stability by maintaining a practical and simple approach to the complicated science of investing. Everyone will benefit from the wisdom and principles inherent in *Checkmate Investing*.

In addition, please visit our website which provides enlightening articles and germane resources: www.checkmateinvesting.com or email us at info@checkmateinvesting.com.

与象棋相似，投资世界并非静态世界，昨天得到红利的策略对于今天而言却并非明智选择。当你像一个象棋大师一样思考时，无论有什么突发事件，你已经想到了未来的情景并规划出了相应选择。

在本书附录部分收录了投资人必要的 14 个清单，所编的相关信息会让你在面对任何投资机会时都能做好准备，也是对初学者乃至资深投资者的一部有益辞典。

“将军投资”风格是源于多年一丝不苟的方针，并以成功范例为基础，通过保持一个实用的和简单的方法，使你快速达到一个成长和稳定的新高度，以此面对复杂的投资科学。每个人都能从“将军投资”固有的智慧和法则中受益。

此外，请访问我们的网站：www.checkmateinvesting.com 或发送电子邮件至 info@checkmateinvesting.com. 在那里会有启发的文章和相关的资源等待着你。

CHAPTER 1
Investing from the Inside Out

How do you become wealthy, stay wealthy, and enjoy being wealthy? There are countless inner aspects that must be in place to achieve affluence and happiness, including having realistic expectations, being well organized, presenting a successful image, treating employees fairly, sharing your prosperity, and much more. The importance of living a content, fulfilled, and balanced life with a network of relationships is often overlooked by investors. Success in life and investing depends on a plurality of circumstances.

第一章

从内到外的投资

你怎样才能富有，且一直富有，并享受富有？要达到富裕和幸福，有许多内在方面必须处置恰当，包括拥有切实的期望、组织有序、展现成功的形象、公平对待员工、分享成功等许多方面。在一个良好的人际关系网下，拥有一个满意、满足、均衡生活的重要性往往被投资者忽视。生活与投资的成功取决于一个多元化的环境。

Dreams vs. Realistic Expectations

It is imperative to believe in your dreams; categorical belief that you can accomplish your goals, obtain wealth, and enjoy a satisfying life.

Everything has to be in balance to assure enduring success. You need passion and a burning desire, but you must also possess a genuine attitude of appreciation, all tempered with patience and perseverance. There are very few overnight success stories. Most people work for years to develop a foundation of skills, experiences, and relationships, and then finally achieve prosperity.

In life and business, keeping perspective is always important. You must be able to control expectations and not imagine too much too soon or you will likely renounce a plausible idea and torpedo any subsequent dreams of success. All too often, people don't appreciate how much work and foundation are required before success becomes "overnight." Don't give up too soon!

An apposite analogy is the Chinese Bamboo tree. Normally, these trees take four years to sprout. Then six weeks later, they grow to a height of ninety feet! Envision planting the seed of your fledgling business, then watering and fertilizing it for four years and not seeing any results. Then, suddenly, like the tree, your idea becomes a towering success.

Growing a company starts with an idea waiting to blossom along with realistic expectations. With faith, tenacity, and persistence, you nourish this business, knowing the process will probably take more time than you initially imagined.

When I was in college, we were taught that it takes two years for most new enterprises to reach the point of profit. While this may be an apt rule of thumb, it could take less or more time. For example, when investing in biotech projects, it may take a full decade to earn a profit or even longer due to the extensive FDA process.

Marketing guru Seth Godin bewails, "It takes about six years of hard work to become an overnight success." Based on a sampling of household names, he is an optimist. Here are some supportive facts:

梦想与切实的期望

相信你的梦想是很有必要的；无条件地相信自己可以完成目标，获得财富并享受满意的生活。

要平衡周围一切才能确保经久不衰的成功。你需要热情和急切的愿望，但也要拥有诚恳的态度去领会，融合耐心和毅力。很少有一夜成名的故事，多数人都是工作很多年不断开发基础的技能、经验和关系，然后最终成功。

保持前瞻性在生活和事业中总是很重要。你必须能够控制自己的期望值，不能设想得太多并在太短时间内成功，否则你很可能会放弃一个貌似可行的想法并破坏随后的成功梦想。人们常常意识不到成功以前需要多少工作和基础，不要太早放弃！

中国的竹子是一个比较贴切的比喻，这些树通常需要 4 年时间发芽，然后 6 个星期之后会长到 90 英尺！想象一下你羽翼未丰的生意，就像播种下幼小的种子，4 年来不断浇水施肥并且看不到任何成果，突然之间你的生意就像竹子一样节节高升了。

一个公司的生长也要随同切实的希望而静待花开，要有信念，有不屈不挠和持之以恒的精神去滋养培育你的生意，明白这一过程可能比最初想象的时间要长很多。

我在大学读书的时候，老师告诉我们大多数新企业要达到盈利点需要两年时间，虽然这是一个恰当的经验法则，但是现实中所花费的时间或多或少。例如，当你投资一个生物科技项目，由于食品及药物管理局（Food and drug Administration，FDA）漫长的审批过程，可能需要十年或更久的时间才能实现盈利。

营销大师赛斯·高汀(Seth Godin)哀叹道:“要想成功需要大约6年的努力。”在这些家喻户晓的人物里，他是乐观主义者，下面是支持这一观点的一些实例:

Bill Gates founded Microsoft in 1975 to develop and sell BASIC interpreters for the Altair 8800. Six years later, he landed a contract with IBM to provide their IBM PC base operating system. It was another five years before Microsoft went public in 1986, making him an overnight success worth $350 million!

This youngster loved basketball and practiced day and night. When he tried out for his high school basketball team, the coach said he was not good enough to make the squad. This rejection drove him to practice harder and longer. Hall of Fame basketball player, Michael Jordan, later confessed, "I've failed over and over again in my life. That's why I succeeded!"

Steve Jobs established Apple in 1976. However, it took another eight years for Apple to gain market acceptance with the advent of the Macintosh in 1984. Even then, it struggled through the 80's and 90's until the introduction of the iMac and other consumer products which ultimately made him an overnight dot-com billionaire!

Larry Page and Sergey Brin started working on Google in 1996. But it took until 2004, when Google went public, for it to realize a market capitalization of $23B!

Mark Zuckerberg concocted "Facemash" to purge his mind of a lost girlfriend while a sophomore at Harvard in 2003. In 2005, he changed the name to Facebook which still showed a yearly net loss of $3.63 million. Within five years, it became an overnight success and continues to grow and expand!

Jeff Bezos founded Amazon in 1994 and took it public three years later, making him a multibillionaire. Amazon's initial business plan showed the company not expecting a profit for four to five years. This is a unique case where the strategy was actually more effective than his business plan predicted.

比尔·盖茨（Bill Gates）在1975年成立微软（Microsoft）公司，研发及销售用于微型计算机“牛郎星”的BASIC编译程序。6年之后他和IBM公司签下合同，并向IBM公司提供PC端的操作系统。又过了5年之久，1986年微软成功上市，比尔·盖茨一夜之间身价高达3.5亿美元。

有一位少年非常喜欢打篮球并且夜以继日地练习。当他在高中竞选篮球队的时候，教练认为他的能力还不足以进入球队。男孩被教练拒绝后增加了训练的强度和时间。他就是篮球名人堂获得者迈克尔·乔丹（Michael Jordan）！他后来坦承：“我这一生经历过无数次的失败。这就是我成功的原因。”

史蒂夫·乔布斯（Steve Jobs）在1976年创立苹果（Apple）公司，然而经历了8年之久的等待，随着1984年麦金塔电脑（Macintosh）的出现，才逐渐被人们所接受。即使这样，乔布斯在20世纪80至90年代也经历过挣扎时期，直至iMac等产品使他一跃成为计算机界的亿万富翁。

拉里·佩奇（Larry Page）和谢尔盖·布林（Sergey Brin）于1996年就在谷歌（Google）工作，但是直到2004年谷歌才正式上市，至此它的市值达到230亿美元。

2003年当马克·扎克伯格（Mark Zuckerberg）还在哈佛大学上大二的时候，就创立了“Facemash”，用来缓解和女朋友分手的烦闷心情。2005年他将之更名为脸书（Facebook），然而当时每年还在净亏363万美元。经过5年的努力，脸书成功了并且在不断的成长和发展。

杰夫·贝索斯（Jeff Bezos）于1994年创立的亚马逊公司（Amazon），3年之后家喻户晓，使他成为大富翁。亚马逊最初的商业计划显示公司并没有打算四五年之内会盈利。这是一个很独特的例子，因为他实际的商业策略比公司预计的更有效。

Let's closely examine the administrative policy that Checkmate Investing practices before investing in someone's dream. First and foremost, we take our time to thoroughly review all facets of the prospect. Expectations on time frames and future earnings must be realistic. We scrub the financial projections to determine when this opportunity will be self-supporting. If the current cash raise will only bring a few months of fiscal relief, which is often the case, we will ask relevant questions because raising money can be easy and fast, but in most cases it is slow and laborious. Additionally, seeking capital takes time away from all other company activities, so it is essential to determine how long the raised money will last. While projections of future earnings are not always accurate, at least they are a starting point.

Also, ramp up costs must be monitored as a company grows closer to liquidity. Enterprises that have been cash poor, and then receive an injection of funding, may decide to move to a nicer location, pay themselves higher salaries, purchase new equipment, and so forth. This happens again and again when cash begins to flow, many times causing the business to be right back where it started.

As investors, we avoid this type of situation and will often put ourselves in a position of approving such expenditures. In some industries, the physical address is key in building a brand image that requires status. In other businesses, staying the course and keeping costs low (including expenses for office space) are the best approaches until the company is totally self-sustaining. We have nothing against the executives and other employees becoming wealthy (in fact we want this to happen). However, we want them to prosper from the results of the underlying business and not off our invested money.

Remember the two year guideline when you make an investment or start a business and fully understand the time frame to turn a profit. Before investing, always look at cash in hand and receivables, if any, to calculate how much money is required to become profitable. Be realistic in your financial projections as running out of money in the middle of a deal is never a pleasant experience.

在投资某人的梦想之前，咱们不妨先近距离感受一下“将军投资”的执行方针是如何实践的。首先，我们应当花一些时间彻底地检查这项投资的所有方面。对时间规划和未来收益的期望值必须切合实际。我们从财务预测中确定何时该企业才能自给自足。如果目前筹集的资金只能缓解公司几个月的财务困难，而这也是最常见的情况，那么我们就需要问一些相关的问题，因为融资有可能很方便快捷，但是多数情况下融资都是很漫长且艰难的。加之公司需要费时筹措资金而无暇顾及其他正常工作，因此确定募集的资金能支持多久至关重要。尽管对未来收益的预测并不总是准确的，但至少它们是一个起点。

另外，随着公司不断发展，日益接近流动性，必须监控激增的成本。本来现款不足，然后获得资金注入的企业，可能会决定搬迁到更好的地点，或为他们自己支付更高的薪水，购买新设备等。于是现款开始大量外流，这种情况一次又一次地发生，导致企业又退回原点。

作为投资者，我们要避免这种情况的发生，但又经常把自己置于批准这种支出的情境。在一些行业中，地理位置是建立品牌形象地位的关键。在其他行业里，保持低成本（包括办公场所费用）是最好的方法，直到公司有能力完全自给自足为止。我们从不反对高管和其他员工变得富有（事实上这正是我们想要得到的结果）。但是，我们希望他们能够从有潜力的生意成果中创收，而不是花掉我们投资的钱。

当你进行投资或者创业时，请记住两年制法则（如果公司业绩连续两年表现不佳，就须抱以怀疑的态度），并且充分了解盈利的时间规划。在投资之前需要经常注意自己手头上的现款和应收款项，如果有，计算在实现盈利之前还需要多少资金。对自己的财务预测应该切合实际，因为在一项交易的中途发现没有资金绝对不是一次愉快的体验。

Successful Traits of a Dog

Man's best friend, the lovable dog, is a precise exemplar of sincerity, loyalty, respect, compassion, companionship, friendliness, forgiveness, trust, and enthusiasm. In Dale Carnegie's classic book, How to Win Friends and Influence People, he pointed out that dogs are loved because they are always interested in you. That's right; they only care about you and not themselves. Regardless of treatment, a dog is always excited to see its master because it is nonjudgmental and its affection is unconditional.

The entire social media phenomenon is built on this principle that people care more about themselves than anything or anyone else. Facebook and Snapchat confirm this fact with millions of people posting pictures about themselves, not others. With that in mind, make a conscious effort to take the time to pay attention and show respect to whomever you are dealing with, whether it is personal or professional. It is much easier to gain important and valuable information if you are liked by the person or people in a business relationship. Success begins with caring more about the other person than yourself.

This does not mean you will never fail. It does mean, even in the case of failure, your passion and desire must never wane. Unconditional excitement for your company or product will drive more sales than any other single factor. I must also emphasize that enthusiasm and caring about others must be sincere or you will never succeed. If you honestly do not believe in your product or service, then consider another investment.

狗的成功特质

可爱的小狗是我们人类最好的朋友，它们是集诚挚、忠诚、尊敬、同情、陪伴、友爱、宽容、信赖和热心于一身的典范。戴尔·卡耐基（Dale Carnegie）在其所著的《如何赢取友谊与影响他人》一书中指出，小狗之所以受大家喜爱是由于它们总是对你感兴趣，没错，它们总是对你感兴趣而非它们自己。不管主人怎么对待它，它总是一见到主人就兴奋不已，它的爱是无条件且不带任何偏见的。

整个社交媒体展现的都是以人们只关注自身，不在意其他任何人和任何事为基础的景象。脸书和色拉布（Snapchat）上数以万计的人贴出他们自己的照片而从不贴别人照片，就证实了这一观点。不管是从个人角度还是从职业角度，要考虑到这一点，下意识地多花时间，努力让与自己打交道的对方感受到你的关心和敬重。如果能让与你做生意的人喜欢上你，会使你非常容易获得重要的和有价值的信息。成功始于更在意他人而非你自己。

这样也不意味着你就不会失败，其核心意思是，即使万一失败了，你的热情和愿望绝不会衰退。无条件地热爱你的公司或产品，会比任何其他单一因素更容易增加销售额。我必须强调对别人的热心和在意一定是发自内心的，否则你永远不会成功。如果你真心不相信自己的产品或服务，那就考虑其他投资吧。

The Changing Landscape

There is an old adage, "If it isn't broken, don't fix it." This saying has a lot of truth to it. However for business, I have a substitute, "Even if it isn't broken, you better fix it or you will eventually go out of business."

The vast majority of people are drawn toward newness in the same way a powerful magnet attracts metal. People enjoy buying new things. The fashion industry relies on this and creates original designs every single quarter of every single year. The auto industry is the same. Even if the body style does not change, the engineers will at least add extras that create demand for the next generation. The consumer electronics business is entirely built on this idea as demonstrated by the phone industry which periodically launches new models with added features. In this way, the phone manufacturer is able to create fresh sales while also maintaining profit margins at a high level.

The longer something remains unchanged an interesting phenomenon occurs: a copycat competitor will arrive. New competition will force you to lower your prices and lose profit margin. To maintain your business, you must be innovative and periodically make subtle changes to your product to preserve your valued customers. Even establishments like McDonald's continually modify their menu to bring back old customers and attract new ones. For example, the McRib sandwich appears intermittently on its menu. At certain times of the year, McDonald's will have special types of pies or amend the flavors of milkshakes. They recognize that this is a balancing act and never want to lose loyal customers with dramatic menu changes. Conversely, the world renowned Big Mac and other such traditional items are never taken off the menu.

Not every enterprise adapts to the ever-changing environment and usually ends up regretting it. Kodak, founded in 1888, was an American manufacturer of photography related products, most notably the production and selling of camera film stock. They did a superlative job creating ways to encourage people to take pictures and, yes, buy more and more film.

风云变幻

有一个古老的谚语："要是没坏，就别去修。"此话不假，然而在生意场上我要把它替代为："没坏也要修，否则就歇业。"

绝大多数的人对新奇的事物都会像铁金属遇到强磁铁。人们喜欢购买新的东西，时尚业正是依赖于此，每年的每个季度都要推出新的原创作品。汽车业也是一样，即使车身设计没有变化，设计者也至少会加上一些附加功能，为推出新一代产品创造条件。家用电子产品更是完全以此为基础，以手机行业为例，厂家总是定期投放增加了新性能的新机型，通过这种方法，手机厂商总是能够既增加了销售额又保持了较高的利润率。

如果一种产品长期不变化就会出现有趣的现象：那就是山寨品牌竞争者会随之出现。新的竞争会迫使你降价甚至亏损。要维持你的企业，就必须创新并且定期对产品进行微妙的变化，以免重要客户的流失。就连麦当劳（McDonald's）这样的企业都会不断更新他们的菜单去迎合回头客并吸引新客户。例如，烤汁猪排堡会间歇性出现在他们的菜单中。在一年中某些日子里，麦当劳会推出特别类型的派或改良口味的奶昔。他们认识到这是折中的办法，绝不想因为变来变去的菜单而丢掉忠实的客户。相反，像世界驰名的巨无霸或其他类似的传统类别却永远不会从菜单中消失。

不是每个企业都会适应不断变化的环境，而且最终他们往往会后悔。柯达公司（Kodak）成立于1888年，是一家生产摄影相关产品的美国制造商，产品非常出名而且销售胶卷。他们曾经做过最棒的营销是鼓励人们去照相，没错，买他们的胶卷，然后去照相。

Then in 1975, a Kodak employee, Mr. Steven Sasson, invented the digital camera. Kodak was smart enough to file patents on this original product, but otherwise they buried the idea. The sales department was worried that such a novel product would cannibalize film sales. Of course they were correct; today almost no one buys film. However, they neglected to comprehend that the evolution of digital photography was going to happen regardless of their input. Eventually, Kodak decided to enter the digital world, but it was too late. In 2012, this once dominant company with 145,000 employees worldwide at its height and over 100 years of history filed for bankruptcy! This is a prime example of a powerful corporation that did not change with the times. What Kodak should have done back in 1975 was develop a futuristic plan to control a promising industry.

You do not have to embrace every technology on the horizon, but at least distinguish what they are. Most inventions never see the light of day. Even when a new product is market accepted, it normally takes years to gain sales momentum. So along the way, be prepared to make revisions to your product or service to survive.

然后在 1975 年有一个柯达公司的雇员名叫史蒂文·赛尚（Mr. Steven Sasson），他发明了数码相机，柯达公司当然很聪明地去申请了该原创产品的专利，但他们却雪藏了这一理念，销售部一度担心这种新奇产品会毁掉胶卷的销售。当然他们在这一点上是正确的，时至今日已经没有人再购买胶卷了。然而他们没有考虑到无论如何摄影数码化迟早会发生。最终柯达公司也决定进军数码领域，然而为时已晚。在 2012 年，这个一度叱咤风云，巅峰时期在全世界拥有 145,000 名雇员，有着一百多年历史的企业居然申请破产了！这是关于一个巨型企业不知随时代而变通的一个绝佳的例子，柯达公司在 1975 年的时候应该做的是开发一个长远计划以实现基业常青。

你没必要去迎合每一种即将来临的科技，但是至少你要辨别他们是什么。大多数发明都会自生自灭不见天日，即使一个新产品被市场接受，也需要日积月累才能增加销售量，所以在此期间，想好怎样对你自己的产品和服务做出改进以求生存。

Careless DNA

Being careless is a recipe for a train wreck. For whatever reasons, most people will not admit to their lackadaisical behavior and justify it with a lame excuse. Not good. Learn to fully accept the blame or you will continue to act irresponsibly. When using an ATM machine, I used to answer my cell phone. Once, I became so engaged in conversation that I left my card in the machine and had to order a replacement. The next time was more embarrassing. I left the ATM machine without even taking the money! Needless to say, now I never answer the phone or talk with anyone while using an ATM machine.

In business, carelessness can be a disaster. The mistake you make can either kill a deal or cost millions of dollars, if not hundreds of millions. In reality, if a careless blunder costs you even one dollar, that is a problem.

Here are a few helpful practices to avoid careless behavior. Periodically save and back up all documents, so you will not lose valuable work. When you obtain a business card, make notes on the backside, so you will remember that contact. Also, immediately scan it or take a photo and catalog with others.

Recalling people's names is another skill of magnitude as everyone loves it when a new acquaintance remembers their name. A smart habit is to repeat the introduced person's name and continue to repeat it in ensuing conversations. For some reason, all of us like hearing our names, which, in turn, unconsciously draws us closer to the new contact and helps develop a quicker relationship.

Also, slow down and proceed with caution when texting or emailing. Re-read every message before pushing "Send." The old dictum, "Think before you speak," has been around forever, so it must have significance. A pause in the narrative is often just enough time to regain intellectual acuity to best communicate your current situation.

天生粗心大意

列车失事的罪魁祸首便是粗心大意，不管出于何种理由，人们总是不愿承认自己的懒散行为并做出各种狡辩，这样很不好，要学会全面接受批评，否则会永远做事不负责任。我在用 ATM 自动取款机的时候总是同时接听着手机，有一次我过于专注通话内容而把银行卡留在了取款机内，为此不得不重新换卡，另一次更为尴尬，我在取款机取出钱后居然忘了把钱拿走！不用说，之后我再用取款机的时候，再也不接打电话或与他人闲聊了。

在生意场上如果粗心大意简直就是大祸临头，你犯的错误不是让你丢了买卖就是让你损失不说千万元，也是动辄百万元之巨。事实上，一个因为粗心造成的错误即使浪费了你一块钱也绝对不应该。

以下有几个有用的方法可以使你避免粗心的行为。定期保存和备份所有的文件，这样你就不会丢失重要信息。当你获得一张名片的时候，在背面作上标记，这样就可以记起那个联系人，另外立刻扫描或照相然后与其他的信息一起归档。

能记住别人的名字是另一项重要技能，因为要是有个新相识的人能记住自己的名字，是每个人都喜欢的事。一个聪明的习惯就是不断重复新结识之人的名字，并在后续联系中重复使用。由于某种原因，我们都喜欢听到自己的名字，也因此无形中拉近了彼此间的距离，有助于快速地发展彼此关系。

同样，在打字或写电子邮件的时候，也要小心翼翼慢慢来，在按“发送”键之前重读一遍，“想好再说”这句格言能流传四方一定有其道理。在叙述事情的时候停顿一下，可以给你足够的时间恢复心智，能够更好地表达目前的状况。

My aforementioned ATM debacles produced my favorite habit which is double-checking every little thing. If you dispute facts, double-check your research before insisting you are correct. Previous to this philosophy, there were numerous times when I was positive that my answer was correct, only to later find out I was wrong. Even the experts are occasionally inaccurate, so take extra time to double-check. It's a winning formula to evade carelessness.

Losing important items is common among careless individuals, so designate a particular place for things that you use on a regular basis. Checklists are useful in organizing your day. I travel frequently and routinely forgot to pack this or that until I finally wised up and started making lists. Managerial problems solved!

I am a huge fan of multitasking, but at the same time doing too many things at once can cause anyone to be careless. If you do multitask, occasionally stop and verify everything you initiated was actually completed. When you use spell-check, always go back and review the copy as words can be inadvertently changed to another word with a different definition. Do not just accept the suggested "computer" word until you have read and thought about its context. I have seen documents where a computer modified word altered the intended definition and caused disastrous results.

Sometimes careless behavior and sloppy work are due to apathy. Such errors will eventually give you a bad reputation. A worthy business ritual is to develop the attitude: "If other people think it is important, then I should think it is important, too." A substandard work ethic not only damages you, but it can also negatively impact your team's morale, goals, objectives, reputation, and productivity.

On the other hand, being a perfectionist is every bit as bad as the slacker. Such a purist can be too critical of others and soon be disliked by everybody. Worse yet, perfectionists are often slow on completing assignments and could cost the enterprise money by missing timely deadlines. Middle ground behavior is always best.

Mindfulness is the best way to assure you are on top of any situation. Always be completely present in what you are doing. Recognize that it is usually the small and unimportant things that will trip you up on the way to achieving the big and important things.

我前面提到关于取款机的灾难迫使我养成一个良好的习惯，凡事都检查两遍，如果你对这个事实有争议，那就请你在固执己见之前先复核一下你的调查结果。之前，我曾无数次认为自己是对的，直到最后才发现自己错了。即使是专家也会偶尔疏忽，所以一定要花时间复核，这是规避粗心的决胜公式。

在粗心的人当中，丢失重要物品的事很常见，所以要选定一个固定位置存放常用的物品。列出清单可以帮助你安排好一天的工作生活。我经常旅行而且总是丢三落四，直到后来我终于知道并采用了列清单的办法。一切混乱通通解决！

我本人特别喜欢多重工作，但是无论任何人如果同时做许多事都会粗心，所以如果你同时做好几件事，一定要定期停下来看看是不是每件着手做的事都已完成。当你使用“拼写检查”时，一定要返回原文看看是否正确，因为拼写检查往往会自动把一个词变成另一个意思完全不同的词。不要直接接受“电脑”自动建议的词，除非你已通读全篇并确定没有问题。我曾经遇到过文章里的词汇，被电脑自动更改以致意思全变这种灾难。

有时候粗心和懒散的行为是源于人们对工作的冷漠，这样的错误会给你带来不好的声誉。成功的商业惯例是要培养这种态度：“如果别人认为这个很重要，那么我也应该认为这个很重要。”不好的职业道德不仅会摧毁你，还会对你团队的士气、目标、宗旨、声誉和生产力带来负面影响。

另外，过于完美主义和懒散一样不可取。如此力求完美一定会对他人吹毛求疵并且不久就会被别人厌恶。更糟的是，完美主义者工作缓慢，会给企业由于错过截止日期而造成损失。中庸之道总是最好的。

处处留心是保证你立于不败之地的最好办法，要时时在意正在着手的工作，认识到在成就辉煌的道路上绊倒你的总是一些微不足道的小事。

Very few successful people have carelessness in their DNA. One thing they do have in common is their attention to detail. With this mindset, surround yourself with individuals who can reinforce your weak traits. If you are chronically careless and feel beyond repair, make sure someone you trust reviews everything you do or success will surely elude you.

很少有成功的人士天生粗心大意，他们之间的共同点就是都关注细节，要这么想，尽量和那些可以帮你改正缺点的人在一起。如果你是长期粗心大意根本改变不了，那就找一个你信赖的人，检查你做的每件事，否则成功永远不会属于你。

Future vs. Present

As mentioned previously, thinking ahead and preparing for the next move is vital. However, you must also be realistic about where you are today. People obsessed with the future forget about the present. It is unlikely you'll ever attain your next destination if you don't realize that today is the most important day in your life.

Each year when December arrives, it always amuses me how most people become sedentary and only focus on the upcoming year. And I ask, "What about the 31 days left this year?"

Never allow yourself to be caught up in this trap as every day, every hour, every minute is paramount. I have closed immense deals by remaining focused during December. Companies will often scale back in traditionally slow seasons to save costs. In contrast, sometimes the cut backs are excessive and new opportunities are missed, but perhaps not by your more ambitious competitors who thrive by stealing deprived consumers. Once a customer shifts to a competitor, you might lose that customer forever.

Embrace everyday as a chance to build your enterprise. Even on your day off, achieve a goal and recognize that each constructive move, like each day, is the only road to a Checkmate.

未来与现在

就如前面提到的，预见未来、提前考虑下一步是至关重要的，然而你也必须面对现实，明白现在所处的境地。人们更在意未来而忽视了现在，如果你认识不到今天在你生命中的重要性，你就永远实现不了下一目标。

每年当十二月来临时，让我好笑的是，大多数的人都在静等观望，他们只关注即将来临的新年。我就问他们："今年剩下的这三十一天怎么办？"

永远别让自己掉入这种陷阱，每一天、每一小时、每一分钟都很重要。我就曾经因为十分在意十二月而做成了大买卖。企业总会在传统上的淡季相应缩减以节省开支，相比之下，有时缩减过度会致使新的机会流失，可能并不是因为比你更有野心，带走了饥渴的消费者而兴旺的竞争对手造成的，但是一旦消费者投向你的竞争对手，你就有可能永远失去他们了。

要把每天都当成建设企业的机会，即使在你放假的时候，也要实现一个目标，并且认识到，就像你过的每一天，你的每一个建设性步伐都是在博弈中实现"将军"这一步的唯一途径。

Fairness vs. Success

Many people are perplexed on the subject of principles. It is fine to have a value system and to live your private life by principles of fairness. However, in business you must stay calm and focus on the standards of success. There are times when you must be assertive, but you can't let your anger or ego drive your decisions. You can't waste time and energy throwing tantrums over matters of principle that are unrelated to the bottom line.

A business executive should not be concerned with combating every minor injustice in life. For example, when a customer unfairly returns a product, a company may, as a matter of principle, be in the right to refuse the customer. But in the interests of building a brand, it might be better for an executive to bend and accept the return.

All business people are subject to everyday injustices. Consider if someone cuts you off in traffic. It is unfair, but you have the choice of either blowing it out of proportion, as a matter of principle, or letting it go. Road rage will distract you and taint the rest of your day. Turning a cheek will allow you to remain focused on the big picture which is being successful and making money. That's a good business strategy which is also good for your physical and mental health.

The idea of "It is the principle of the thing" is juvenile and has no place in the world of investing. The core belief is to stay within the boundaries of being an upstanding citizen who has integrity and simply strives to be more successful.

If you find yourself distraught over a trivial issue, move on and stop feeling sorry for yourself. When I was a teenager, I got a traffic ticket and became angry because I felt the policeman was in the wrong. My father merely said, "Suppose he was wrong. How about the thirty other times you broke a traffic law and didn't get a ticket?" I realized my father was right and never let such nonsense bother me again.

公平与成功

许多人一旦涉及原则总是很迷惘，有一套完整的价值体系并让自己按照公平的原则去生活，这样挺好，但是在生意场上你必须保持冷静并且关注成功的标准。有些时候你必须自主决断，但你不能让情绪影响决定，你不能浪费时间和精力为与底线无关的原则去发脾气。

一个企业主管在生活中不应该在意如何应对微小的不公，例如，当一个客户不按常规退货，按公司的原则规定，就有权利当场拒绝该客户，但是为了建立品牌形象，企业主管最好还是妥协变通一下接受退货。

生意场上的人每天都在面对不公，想想开车的时候要是有人故意别你车，这就不公平，但你有权选择，要不就按照原则以牙还牙，要不就放过他算了。开斗气车会分散你的注意力，而且会毁了这一天余下的时光。变通一下会让你把注意力放在能让你成功使你挣钱的大事上，这才是好的商业策略，而且也有益于身心健康。

“这是原则问题”这个想法是非常幼稚的，在投资行业里根本行不通。核心的理念是，做一名诚信的良好市民，并且只想通过努力而成功。

如果你发现自己因为一点小事而心烦意乱，先放手吧，别再为自己难过了。我十几岁的时候收到过一张交通罚单，我很生气，因为我觉得警察错罚我了，我父亲只是说：“就算他错了，要是你曾经违反过 30 回交通法规都没收到罚单呢？”我认识到我父亲说得对，以后再也不为这种没用的事烦心了。

Every time you become angry, step back and evaluate the situation from a different perspective. Once I was with a CEO who was trying to convince us to invest in his company. We were at the airport, headed to a site visit of his factory. The two hour flight was oversold, so we had to wait a couple of hours for the next flight. The CEO lost his cool and demanded to the ticket agent that we be issued seats on the oversold plane. I can still hear him yelling at the agent, "Do you know who I am?" The principle, he argued, was that he was a more frequent customer than the other passengers and should have priority. Instead, he should have taken that extra time to convince me to invest in his company.

It was very embarrassing and needless to say, we passed on the investment. His emotional behavior illustrated that he was not focused on success as his central principle. The only ethic he should have had in mind was to gain our confidence and ultimately our investment. This example demonstrates it is never sensible to lose one's cool. There are consequences for those who do.

Just to clarify, there is a major difference between throwing a tantrum and being assertive. There are times when being strong and firm are laudable to resolve a situation that ensures the success of the company. In such circumstances, the executive has the best interests of the company at heart and not his/her ego. I believe that the "principle of the situation" should never overshadow the bigger ethic of obtaining success.

每当你生气的时候，不妨退一步评估一下现状并换个角度思考问题。有一次我和一个公司的首席执行官在一起，他正试图说服我投资他们公司的项目，我们当时在机场，准备前往参观他们的工厂场地，两小时航程的机票已经全部卖光，所以我们要等几小时乘坐下一趟班机，这时该首席执行官失去冷静，非要让售票员从已经售光的航班上给我们挤出两个座位，我现在还能听到他对售票员的吼叫声："你知道我是谁吗？"他所争辩的原则，无非是他是飞机常客，理应优先对待。其实他本应该利用这个富裕出的时间来劝说我投资他的公司啊。

真是尴尬，不用说我们的买卖没做成，他的情绪化行为说明他没把成功当成他的主要原则。他唯一在意的应该是我们之间的信任以及最终达成投资，这个例子表明，情绪失控真的很不明智，会造成恶果。

这里只想表明乱发脾气和自主决断之间的主要区别，有的时候自主决断是值得称赞的，可以解决问题因此确保企业的成功。在这种环境下，在企业主管心目中，要摒弃小我，明白公司的利益大于一切。我相信"原则性的问题"永远不应该遮挡获得成功这个大理论的光芒。

Balancing Life and Wealth

Part of the inner game of achieving financial independence is to create stability in your life so you can enjoy your hard earned money.

Everyone assumes if they become wealthy, then all their problems will disappear. The truth is that unlimited money will make life easier in some ways, but you are still encumbered with many of the same dilemmas you had when you were not prosperous.

Wealth means living anywhere you want and affording more luxurious items. Money alone has never made anyone happy for a long period of time, but rather serves as a temporary fix. Once you are well-off, you are just like you were before as this is your new "normal." You just have more fiscal freedom.

Many people who quickly ascend to affluence find it is not what they perceived and often end up seeking more and more money, hoping it will fix the empty feeling in their life. In cases where enormous wealth is not satisfying enough, the next spiral is seeking more power to feel respected and admired.

Having said that, I do not believe the axiom, "Money is the root of all evil." Rather it is how people spend their money that can appear "evil." Some avaricious people become obsessed with power which can be very unhealthy. I know many billionaires, and the majority are very nice and down to earth people because their priorities are entrenched in well-rounded lives.

Each person has to define what a balanced life means to them but I would say that loving the people in your life and being grateful are certainly at the zenith.There is an abundance of scientific evidence that confirms habitually practicing gratitude is excellent for your health and well being. Some people keep a gratitude journal or perform a gratitude exercise once a week or month. I suggest counting your blessings on a regular routine.

I love earning money and always will, but adamantly refuse to let currency or any single issue knock me out of balance. Follow my lead by aiming for a stable life, and I believe in the end it will make you a better person and a more successful investor.

和谐生活和财富

要实现财务自主，心理策略的一部分就是要在生活中建立稳定的心态，这样就可以享受自己辛辛苦苦赚来的钱。

每个人都认为一旦他们有钱了，所有的问题就全部消失了。实际上如果真能有很多钱财，确实在某种程度上能让日子过得舒服些，但是那些你穷的时候就固有的一大堆问题，会依然困惑你。

富有意味着想住在哪里就能住在哪里，什么奢侈品都买得起，但是仅仅有钱从来不能让一个人快乐很长时间，不过是临时解药而已，一旦你过得好了，就又会和以前一样，认为这是你的新“常态”，你只是手头松快了而已。

许多快速致富的人发现富有和他们想象的并不一样，结果总是谋求更多的钱财，希望借此能填补生活中的空虚。在这些巨大财富满足不了内心欲望的情境中，下一轮就是寻求更多的权力以使他人景仰。

话虽如此，我仍不太相信这句格言：“金钱乃万恶之源。”不如说“罪恶”是人们花费金钱的方式所呈现的。一些贪得无厌的人沉迷于权力无法自拔其实很危险。我认识许多亿万富翁，大多数都是非常善良而实际的人，因为他们更在意的是守住自己的美满生活。

对于什么是和谐的生活，每个人都有自己的定义，但我想说，热爱和感恩你生命中的每个人，最是和谐。许许多多的科学实例都证实了习惯性的感恩对人的身心非常有益，使人感到幸福。有些人每天写感恩日志，每周或每月定期进行感恩练习。我建议应该长此以往常怀感恩之心。

我喜欢挣钱，一直都是，但绝不能让金钱或任何一物使我失去平衡，跟着我的步伐向着稳定的生活前进，我相信最终会使你成为一个好人乃至一个成功的投资者。

Trusted Friends and Associates

Loyal friends and a trustworthy business team form the foundation of an exultant personal and professional life. There are likely very few people in your life that can be trusted so entirely that you feel free to discuss any subject and can expect their honest opinion. These special confidants are an integral component of reaching and maintaining success.

During troubling times, I have found that talking to a trusted friend will instigate a resolution that seems to come out of thin air. Perhaps I only needed to slow down and envision another person's viewpoint to produce the most feasible elucidation. Life works this way, especially within the hectic investment world where everyone eventually needs external input which can be the difference between winning and losing.

Another benefit of trusted friends is that they can endorse you to others. You can brag about all your glowing qualities, but boasting is often ineffective and almost never believable. Most people become suspect if you must sing your own praises. Thus, a third party endorsement from a credible friend is extremely helpful.

Try to reconnect with old friends. Never be shy about calling someone even if you have not chatted for years. Trust is trust and a friend is a friend. Akin to the old expression, "Once you learn to ride a bicycle, you never forget," I have found this also applies to past acquaintances. I love hearing from them and maybe doing some business. So pick up the phone or use social media to reach out to estranged friends. Worst case scenario, you enjoy the pleasure of re-establishing a bond with an old crony. Best case scenario, you may just find your next billion dollar deal.

可信赖的朋友和伙伴

无论是在个人或者职业生活中，忠诚的朋友和可靠的商业团队是组成令人欣慰生活的基础。在你生命中可能没有几个人能让你全然信赖，随意和他们讨论任何话题，并期望他们给予坦诚意见，这些特殊的知己是你达到和保持成功的重要砝码。

在我烦恼困惑的时候，我发现和一个值得信赖的朋友聊天，可以忽然激发出解决问题的办法，可能我只是需要慢下来，从另一个人的角度去考虑问题，才能想到可行之路。生活就是以这种方式进行的，尤其是在狂热的投资行业，最终都需要外力去解决，这就是胜负之间的差别。

有可信赖的朋友还有另一个好处，那就是他在别人面前对你的支持，你也可以自吹自擂自己有多么优秀，但是自我吹嘘通常是无效且根本不可信的，大多数自我炫耀的人都会令人生疑，这种时候，让一个可信赖的朋友以第三方的名义支持你就非常管用了。

要尝试重新联络老朋友，即使你们好几年没联系了也千万别不好意思，信任就是信任，朋友就是朋友。就像俗话说的：“一旦学会骑自行车，就永远不会忘。”我发现这句话也适用于过去的朋友。我愿意和他们互通消息，也许还可以做点生意。所以拿起电话或用社交软件联系一下疏远了的朋友吧。最糟的情况，也还能和老友重拾旧谊，要是好的话，说不准你刚好找到了下一笔十亿美元的大买卖。

It is also judicious to maintain the friendship and trust of employees who leave your organization for another job. Sometimes loyal people are offered a better and faster opportunity to succeed. In such cases, I am happy for them and encourage them to pursue their goals. I tell them with sincerity that the door will always remain open if they wish to return. This policy is very beneficial in several ways. Firstly, this positive attitude allows you to rehire loyal individuals who departed for whatever reason. Secondly, the business world is small and having former devoted employees in other organizations can lead to all kinds of synergies and newfound prospects.

There is another benefit to maintaining the friendships of former employees. They know your aspirations and are more prone to pass along compliant opportunities. More than that, Checkmate Investing rarely invests alone. We welcome co-investors who can offer instrumental business contributions to assure success and help spread our financial risk.

While you endeavor to be build solid friendships, there are occasions when you have to end relationships. For example, those individuals who can't keep their ego in check must be replaced. Also, vindictive, mean-spirited people who hang around you, but are not loyal, can be a disaster. These "snakes" with legs tend to point out your flaws and seek to make you believe that you would be a failure without them. When you find such a person, it is best to disassociate as soon as possible since it will only be a matter of time before they cause you a major problem. However, always do this in a friendly and professional manner as burning bridges is never a recommended practice.

和那些从你身边跳槽去其他公司的雇员保持友谊和信任也是明智之举，有的时候忠诚的人会获得更好更快的成功机会，在这种情况下，我会为他们高兴并鼓励他们去追寻自己的目标，我真诚地告诉他们，如果愿意回来，我的大门永远向他们敞开。这个策略对各个方面都非常有益，首先，这种积极的态度可以让你重新雇用那些，不管何种原因离你而去的忠诚可靠的员工；其次，生意场毕竟是个小圈子，有个曾经为你忠心效劳的人在其他部门，可以带来各种协同效应和新的机遇。

和以前雇员保持友好关系还有另一个益处，他们知道你的志向，更愿意顺从机会而行，不仅如此，“将军投资”很少单独投资，我们欢迎共同投资者，他们既能提供有益而确保成功的商业贡献，也能帮助分散我们的金融风险。

当你努力想要建立稳固的友谊时，有的时候又不得不终止一些友谊。比如，那些不能保持自我而易受他人控制的人，你最好放弃，还有那些爱记仇、心胸狭窄的人，他们一点都不忠诚，如果这样的人在你身边，简直就是灾难。这些长着腿的“毒蛇”就想找出你的缺点，让你相信如果没有他们就会一败涂地。一旦发现身边有这些人等，要尽早避之，否则迟早有一天，他们会惹出大麻烦。当然，要以友好的、专业的方式令其离开，毕竟断人后路的做法永远不值得推荐。

Wealth and Giving

Many wealthy and happy people develop a habit of giving. This benevolent trait is another way to increase the odds that you, too, can become affluent.

You can begin by helping your family and/or local community. There are traditional institutions that assist others in need, like church associations, the Salvation Army, and numerous other charitable groups. Donate to a meaningful cause that is emotionally satisfying to you.

How big a commitment should you make? Find philanthropic role models to judge what action is best suited for you. Start small and gradually increase your involvement until you find the right level of dedication that enriches the quality of your life. Once again, it is really about finding more fulfilling balance in your life.

Giving back does not just mean monetarily, but time as well. For example, if you volunteer at a community food bank, you will see the plight of hungry adults and children. That puts your own luxuries and problems in context and increases your sense of gratitude and appreciation.

While it is imperative to have close relationships with industry people, such slanted affiliations can blur your thinking. By giving back to others, you will interact with individuals outside your trade zone that can share a broader perspective and open your eyes to becoming a smarter investor. Also, if you join the board of a charity, you will likely meet other remarkable and influential Samaritans.

And don't fabricate any time related excuses. Busy people still find ways to make a regular commitment to the less fortunate. Think charity and family, and discover the meaning of your life while appreciating the victory of being on top of the world.

富有和给予

许多富有和快乐的人养成了给予的习惯，这样的慈善之心是另一种方法，可以使你增加致富的概率。

你可以从帮助家人或社区开始这一实践，有很多帮助他人的传统机构，比如教会协会、救世军和众多的其他慈善团体。向一个有意义的项目捐款会让你情感上得到满足。

做慈善要做多大尺度适合自己呢，看看那些有博爱之心的榜样们怎么做的，以此断定哪种方式适合自己，先从小的开始，然后逐渐增加参与力度，直到找到适合自己的、能让生活质量充实的尺度，再次重申，这真正有利于你在生活中找到更加心满意足的平衡。

给予别人并不仅只限于钱财方面，也包括时间。比如，你在社区食物银行做志愿者，你会看到陷入饥饿困境的成人和儿童，相比你自己的奢侈品和自己的问题，就会增加你的感恩之心。

由于你与业界中人的紧密联系不可避免，身在其中而偏离社会多少会蒙蔽你的思想，通过给予他人，你会和生意场外的人打交道，能够分享到更广阔的视角，让自己眼界更宽，成为更精明的投资者。而且，如果你加入慈善机构的董事会，很有可能遇到其他卓越的、有声望的乐善好施之人。

不要编造任何与时间相关的借口，忙碌的人一样能找到方法服务于不幸的人，当你站在世界之巅，感恩成功的同时，想想慈善和家人，找出你人生的意义。

Net Worth Disclosure

Congratulations, you're finally rich and worth over a billion dollars! In my opinion, it is best not to needlessly disclose your net worth or you risk attractingthe wrong types of people. For example, if you reveal your imposing assets, you will become a magnet for con men, scam artists, and other swindlers seeking to make a quick buck. You can also become surrounded by shallow people who "like" you only for your money.I also advise taking precautions to protect your financial information from being revealed or hacked.

Everyone has seen the "Richest People in the World" lists published by Forbes and other magazines. I enjoy perusing these names, but hope I am never included. I want to be qualified, but not revealed. The truth is, these compilations are purely conjecture and do not define the cash position of the individual. I know plenty of very wealthy people who do not have as much liquid cash as you would imagine. I can't recount the number of times I have been solicited by a billionaire or multi-millionaire who is strapped for cash.

As such, it is adroit to invest in a way that does not reveal how prosperous you are. People trust us at CheckmateInvesting because we never disclose the identity of our investors. Many funds advertise their investors to create credibility. To me, this is unethical as we want our investors to be protected from such a breach of confidentiality. I strongly advise never disclosing your wealth to third parties, except for business purposes, like obtaining a loan.

净值披露

祝贺你，你终于富有了，并且拥有多达十亿美元的身家！以我之见，最好不要公开你的资产净值，这样做没有必要，会因此引起人渣们的注意，例如，你暴露出可观的资产，就会像磁铁一样吸引着那些寻求取得不义之财的骗子们。一些肤浅的人也会缠着你，他们“喜欢”你，其实只是因为你的钱财而已。我还建议你采取措施未雨绸缪，保护自身财务信息，以防泄露或让他人盗取。

每个人都看到过福布斯（Forbes）和其他杂志发布的“全球富人榜”。我喜欢仔细研究这些上榜名人，但是希望自己永远不要上榜，我希望自己能有资格，但不愿出名。事实上这种排行榜纯粹依靠推测，根本没有明确每个人的资金状况。我知道许多非常富有的人，他们的流动资金少到你不敢想象。我记不起有多少次了，一个亿万富翁或千万富翁由于资金不足而求我帮忙。

如此来说，不泄露自己财务状况，也是一种聪明的投资方式。大家信任我们“将军投资”，也是因为我们从不披露投资者的身份。许多基金依靠宣传其投资者身份来创造可信度，对我来说，这样很不道德，我强烈建议，永远不要向第三方公开你的财富，除非为了生意，如想获得贷款。

The Golden Rule of Employees

The art of human relations is crucial in running a profitable business. This should be called the Golden Rule of Employees: treat other people as you would like to be treated. It is an ancient adage, but many companies, large and small, fail at this practice.

Strive to create a healthy work environment where there is high morale and trust. If a company does not adhere to this philosophy and is not committed to improving a discontented situation, then reconsider investing. A poor work atmosphere will eventually decrease employee effectiveness, cause high employee turnover, and potentially lead to expensive lawsuits.

It starts with management. Beware of leaders who denigrate or yell at fellow employees for no reason, except to elevate their own egos. This conduct cannot be allowed as it will create a chaotic workplace and distrust will proliferate at every level. There can also be more serious employee issues such as discrimination or harassment.

Well run companies are proactive in creating healthy atmospheres. Methods must be in place to address problems with employees and management. This can be done privately with a committee that receives reports to uncover such difficulties. For example, if a company discovers a sexual harassment issue, it should be dealt with immediately. Such circumstances can cost the business exorbitant fees in legal settlements and wasted time in court. Also, consider scheduling human relationship seminars to eliminate bias in the workplace.

Alternatively, if a problem does not directly affect the company, such as an employee drinking too much after hours, then only intervene when it affects the employee's behavior at work or other business operations. Otherwise, allow that individual to make their own life's choices. This fortifies a copacetic work environment as most of today's employees would resent an employer needlessly interfering in their private life.

雇员的黄金法则

在经营一个营利的企业中，人际关系的艺术至关重要。这句话应该是被称作雇用他人的黄金法则："你想让别人怎么对待你，就怎么对待别人。"这是一句古老的格言，但是各种大大小小的公司却都败在了这件事上。

要努力营造一个健康的、有着高昂士气和信任的工作环境。如果一个公司不认可这个理念，也不想改善不满的状况，那就重新考虑是否投资吧。一个不好的工作氛围会降低员工的效率，引起频繁的人员流动，还有可能惹上花钱的官司。

要从管理开始着手，谨防那些领导无缘无故地贬低下属或对下属吼叫，除非是为了提升下属的自我能力，否则这种行为绝不允许发生，会给工作场所造成混乱，各级之间互不信任激增。当然还有更严重的雇员问题，比如歧视或骚扰。

运营良好的企业会积极主动营造健康的氛围，必须制定处理员工和主管之间问题的方法。可以通过成立一个委员会私下完成，委员会接受这些问题的举报。例如，如果一个公司发现性骚扰的问题，就要马上处理，这种情况可能让公司为了法律和解花费巨大，并且有可能会浪费时间去打官司。同样，要考虑安排人际关系研讨会，可以从工作场所驱除偏见。

或者，如果有一个问题对公司没有直接影响，比如，员工下班以后时常酗酒，那就直到其行为影响工作之后再出面干涉。如果没有影响工作，就应让该员工按其选择过自己的生活，这样会有助于营造良好的工作环境，因为现在大多数员工不愿意雇主无端干涉其私人生活。

That being said, a company can also provide options for employees to voluntarily make improvements to their private lives. This can include free classes in stress management and communication skills. It is also commendable to offer incentives and "opt-ins" for health related concerns, such as subsidized gym passes, nutritional lunches, confidential psychological counseling, and treatment for personal problems like alcoholism.

One of the secrets of smart investing is to scrutinize all aspects of human relations within a company and unearth what management is initiating to make improvements. Checkmate Investing always completes a thorough investigation into a company's personnel, in addition to the obvious financial factors. One thing is irrefutable; the attitudes of the current workers are clear indicators in predicting the future of a company.

话虽如此，公司还是可以提供一些选择措施使员工能自觉自愿地改善其私人生活，包括开设一些缓解压力和加强沟通技巧的免费课程，还提供推荐一些和健康相关、有奖励机制、自愿参加的项目，比如发放健身卡补贴、营养午餐补贴、私密的心理咨询以及像酗酒这种个人问题的治疗。

明智投资的秘诀之一是仔细研究公司各个方面的人际关系，发掘进行什么管理方法以求改进。“将军投资”除了要审查明显的财务因素以外，总是会通盘彻底调查公司内部的全体人员，有一件事不可辩驳，那就是当前员工的态度是清晰的指示灯，标示着企业的未来。

A Successful Image

Accept that other people will often judge you based on whether or not you project a successful and confident image.

A presentable appearance starts with personal hygiene and grooming. A shower before a meeting is compulsory, both for your cleanliness and confidence. Sparkling teeth and fresh breath are also mandatory. And no matter how long or short your head or facial hair, as long as it is neatly groomed, you will impress.

Confident people often smile as a way of conveying self-assurance. Smile as much and as often as is appropriate for the business you are in, and the country you are visiting. Don't overdo it, of course. In some countries too much smiling makes people take you less seriously.

Body language is another way to express confidence. Stand up straight. Don't slouch. Have a self-assured gaze and walk.

Speak confidently. That's partially a matter of the words you choose, coupled with an unassailable, yet pleasant tone of voice. Be cognizant of the reactions and feedback from your listeners and make adjustments accordingly to best communicate your message.

Some people do self-talk or affirmations to increase their confidence. Another useful tool is to visualize yourself in a mirror or on video to fine tune your positive presentation.

Clothes are also momentous in projecting an image of success. For example, suppose you met a presumably confident man seeking an investor partner, but he was wearing ripped blue jeans, a dirty old t-shirt, and worn out tennis shoes. Then you met another confident fund seeker who was wearing a nicely tailored suit, a pressed dress shirt, and polished leather shoes. Which gentleman would you feel more confident with doing a multi-million dollar deal?

成功的形象

其他人总是基于你是否展现出成功自信的形象来断定你是什么样的人，要接受这一观点。

良好的仪容仪表始于个人卫生和自我修饰，无论是为了清洁还是自信心，开会之前洗个澡是非常必要的，光洁的牙齿和清新的口气同样重要，头发和胡子长短不重要，但一定要修饰整洁，这样才能给人留下良好的印象。

自信的人总是用微笑表达他们的泰然自若，经常微笑也适用于正洽谈的生意中，以及正访问的国家中，但要适可而止别笑太多，因为在一些国家，你总是笑，会让当地人认为你做事不认真。

肢体语言是另一个表达自信的方法，要身材挺拔，不要蔫头耷脑，言谈举止要泰然自若。

说话的时候要自信，和你选择用什么样的词汇表达有相当的关系，加一些毋庸置疑的话，用动听的语调去说，察觉倾听者的反应，以此调整自己的接下来的话，以能够更好地表达自己。

有些人用自言自语或自我肯定来增加自信心，另一些人对着镜子或摄像头来调整自己以展现积极的形象。

要想展现成功的形象，服装也是非常重要的一环。例如，如果你遇到一个人，按理说是一个可信的正寻求投资伙伴的人，但是他穿着破牛仔裤、脏旧的T恤、磨破的网球鞋，然后你又遇到另一个想要筹措资金的人，他却穿着笔挺的西装、熨烫平整的衬衫和擦得锃亮的皮鞋。你觉得哪个人更可信，更愿意和谁做数百万美元的交易呢？

True, in some philosophical sense it should make no difference what someone wears. But often people make subconscious decisions about whether they trust someone based on their appearance.Of course there are always exceptions to the rule. For example, Mark Zuckerberg, the founder of Facebook, can get away with wearing t-shirts as he is a well known entity. But it is always wise to dress to impress if you are unfamiliar to the individuals you are pitching.

What people think of you can prey on your confidence. Never be embarrassed or feel unworthy when in the presence of revered people. Recognize that you have valid reasons to belong in any and all circles. Show respect, but also demand respect in return during your quest for acceptance.

As a side note, I emphasis that driving an expensive car does not guarantee an image of success. As a youth, I was impressed by someone driving a Rolls Royce or Ferrari. As I got older, I found that most prosperous people avoid such opulent possessions and do not care if you have an exotic vehicle or a gold Rolex watch and are often put off by such flaunting behavior. My years of experience confirm that only unsuccessful people are impressed by this type of materialistic showmanship.

Ingvar Kamprad, founder of Ikea, drives a very old Volvo 240. Similarly, Alice Walton, one of richest women in the world and daughter of Wal-Mart founder Sam, follows her father's lead and drives a Ford F-150 King Ranch.

As odd as it seems, if you drive an old car to a meeting with a successful person, there is no reason to be embarrassed and park three blocks away. I recommend the opposite; let the individual see your old car. Realize that this person only cares about accomplishments and not about pretentious status symbols. More likely, if you are broke, then you will be perceived as being motivated to work harder than someone who has no need for money. However, this strategy is not a reason to neglect dressing for success. Being well dressed and groomed shows that you respect the people at the meeting and will also make you feel as if you belong.

Also, keep your vehicle clean, inside and out, as this shows elements of your personal life. Besides, you never know who will see it at any given time. You can have a wonderful meeting and afterwards your host may ask you for a ride somewhere! Be prepared.

从哲学意义上来讲，确实穿什么衣服都一样，但是人们对于是否相信他人，总是基于他们的外貌做出潜意识决定。当然凡事都有例外，例如，脸书的创始人马克·扎克伯格，他穿T恤就没事，因为他是名人。然而要想游说不熟悉你的对方，穿着得体永远是明智之举。

别人对你的看法能够伤害你的自信心。在有威望的人面前千万别窘迫自卑，要认识到自己有正当的理由融入任何圈子。在你寻求被接纳的时候，要对别人表示尊重，并要让对方也尊重你。

附注一点，我要强调开一辆豪车并不能印证你成功的形象。我年轻的时候，对某人能开一辆劳斯莱斯（Rolls Royce）或法拉利（Ferrari）印象深刻，后来却发现，许多成功人士都回避这种奢侈品，他们不在乎你是不是开进口车或戴劳力士（Rolex）金表，总是对这种炫耀的行为不感兴趣。我多年的经验证实，只有不成功的人才会对这种物质上的炫耀感兴趣。

宜家家居（Ikea）创始人英格瓦尔·卡姆普拉德（Ingvar Kamprad），开一辆很旧的沃尔沃（Volvo）240，同样，沃尔玛（Wal-Mart）创始人山姆·沃尔顿（Sam Walton）的女儿爱丽丝·沃尔顿（Alice Walton）是世界上最富女人之一，听从她父亲的教导，只开一辆福特F-150国王牧场（Ford F-150 King Ranch）。

好像很奇怪，当你开一辆旧车去见成功人士的时候，没必要因不好意思而把车停在三条街之外。我的建议刚好相反，要让他们看到你的旧车，了解你这个人只在意成就而不是可炫耀的牌子。更有可能的是，如果你一文不名，那他们会认为你比那些不缺钱的人更有努力工作的动力。然而这个策略不是你不注意着装的理由。穿着得体、仪表堂堂表示你对与会人物的尊敬，也会使你能够融入其中。

而且要把车从里到外擦干净，因为这样可以展示你个人生活状况，另外，你永远不知道有谁，会在什么时候看到你的车。会议很完满，很可能散会后主持人想搭你的顺风车去什么地方，还是提早准备吧！

Your office is also an integral part of your image. A workplace that is too messy and cluttered can give visitors an impression that you are inefficient and unproductive. On the other hand, many of the most successful people I have ever met have extremely untidy offices, but they know exactly where everything is located. Of course, some people go overboard and make their office look impeccable before visitors enter. Personally, a space that is too neat with everything in order is a red flag to me. I find myself wondering if this person ever works or just cleans all day. There is a happy medium where your office looks "worked in," but still appears highly organized and efficient.

Image and perception can enhance your trustworthiness which is also important during presentations and due diligence. That doesn't mean you should hide problems, but instead disclose all weaknesses before they are uncovered. Investors can deal with issues as long as you are a competent problem solver. The fact that your company has problems, matched with plausible solutions, may be the reason you can obtain the capital. Potential investors will see that his/her money will add value to the company.

At all costs, avoid projecting the image of someone who wastes money on fancy toys. And stay away from expensive cars, luxurious yachts, private railcars, and lavish jets, as this is the quickest way to lose investors.

Sometimes you can do simple things to help create a positive perception. In China, we always take a picture with prospects and send it to them later, so they remember us. Shoot several photos and then edit the best image before sending it. You want the investor to visualize how good he or she looks beside you as a future long-term investor. In addition, you'll want to remember that person.

Do you have a simple phrase that describes your company? Sometimes a few carefully chosen words can create a memorable mental image. For example, there is a Los Angeles radio advertisement that has been playing for decades and promotes the "Smell Good Plumber." Their employees always wear clean uniforms and even carry extra uniforms in their trucks in case one gets dirty on the job.

In this instance, just three words are all it takes to form an indelible mental image and perception. You could hire any plumber in Los Angeles, and some might enter your home in dirty, stinky overalls. Or you could call the smell good plumber. Who would you rather employ?

你的办公室也是展现自我形象时不可分割的一部分。办公环境杂乱无章会使前来参观的人感到你做事没效率。相反，我遇到的许多成功人士，他们的办公室都特别凌乱，但是他们很清楚什么东西放在哪儿。当然有的人做得有些过火，在参观者进来之前，把办公室收拾的完美无瑕。就我而言，一个地方特别整齐，所有东西摆放有序，是一个危险信号，我会奇怪这个人是否工作，是不是每天只是打扫卫生。还是中庸之道令人愉快，让你的办公室看起来像“干事的”，又体现出组织有序效率高。

好的形象和认知可以提升你的可信度，在融资演讲和尽职调查的时候一样重要。这不意味着你应该隐藏问题，而是应该在问题没暴露之前就公开其所有不足之处。只要你是一个能够解决问题的人，投资者就能应对这些难题。事实上如果你找到了公司问题的相应解决方法，也许就是你得到资金的理由，潜在的投资者会看到其资金可以给公司增加价值。

无论如何，要规避一点，不要展现出你喜欢花钱购买昂贵的玩具，也要远离豪车、豪华游艇、私人轨道车乃至私人飞机，因为这是失去投资者的最快方式。

有时，你可以做简单的事帮助自己建立积极的认知。在中国，我们总是和潜在客户一起照相，然后发给他们，这样他们就能记住我们，拍几张照片，编辑出一张最好的发送出去，你要让投资者看到自己作为未来长期投资人站在你身边有多棒。此外，你也会想要记住那个人。

你能用简短的一句话描述你的公司吗？有时候几个精心挑选的词可以造出难忘的精神意象，例如，有一个洛杉矶电台广告已经播放了几十年并成功推广了“气味好的水管工”。他们的员工总是穿着干净的工作服，而且居然在他们货车里放着一套备用的工作服，以防在工作中弄脏了可以替换。

在这种时候，仅三个词就足以形成一个难忘的精神意象和认知。在洛杉矶你可以雇用任何一家的水管工，有些人可能穿着又脏又臭的工作服进入你家，你也可以雇气味好的水管工，你愿意用谁呢？

Image and perception are particularly relevant if you intend to list your company on the stock market. Listed companies within the same industry can often trade at very different P/E (price-earnings) ratios. This means, if you have a better image with analysts and investors, your P/E ratio may be bigger than that of the competitors which translates into a higher market cap. This phenomenon happens frequently. Of course this is not solely due to how you dress, but the amalgamation of every little detail of imagery previously outlined.

Whether it is a small business or trillion dollar corporation, I covet investing in companies that go the extra mile to achieve a breathtaking image that even smells good. We have invested in disorganized ventures, but not blindly. As a prerequisite of the investment, we require they hire a consulting firm to enhance or recreate their visual impression. Perception and imagery are not everything with investing, but they are instrumental in building a billion dollar brand.

如果你的公司想要上市，形象和认知尤为重要。同一行业内的上市公司经常会按全然不同的 P/E 率（市盈率）交易，这意味着如果你在分析师和投资者那里拥有良好的形象，你的市盈率就会大于竞争对手，进而转化为更高的市场价值。这种情况经常发生，当然这绝不仅仅因为你怎么着装，而是融合了之前描述的每种形象的细节。

无论是小公司还是万亿级大企业，我渴望投资于那些通过加倍努力实现惊人形象的公司，而且闻起来“气味好”。我们也投资过那些杂乱无章的公司，但不是盲目的投资，作为投资的先决条件，我们要求他们雇用咨询公司来加强或重建自身视觉形象，认知和形象在投资中并非全部，但是有助于树立一个价值十亿美元的品牌。

Referrals

Networking is one of the most vital skills on your road to prosperity. Don't let shyness or a quiet nature stop you from reaching your financial goals.

You must develop a habit of continually making contact with other people and building friendships and business relationships.But you also have to learn to be bold in asking for help, particularly in regards to referrals.

A referral is one of the most natural and easy business connectors. All you must do is ask! Most people will not object to giving you a recommendation, so make it a routine to ask everyone you meet. And never be embarrassed or act offended when someone says "No." Instead, move on to another subject to ease any stress that may be related to the rejection. Everyone is connected to someone else and referrals are a direct conduit for uncovering new opportunities.

Even the poorest of people may have a rich and powerful childhood friend or relative. Unfortunately, I have excluded some prospects and later heard them say, "I wish I had known" or "If you had only asked, I could have helped." Do not count on someone helping you unless you take the time to ask.

I stress that you solicit anybody and everybody for leads. It is human nature to want to help others. Sometimes the very affluent are reluctant to give referrals, but when they do, it is usually worth the time. Of course, ask obvious brokers, like lawyers, accounting firms, investment houses, but do not stop there—ask everyone for help! You will be gleefully surprised at what you will receive in return.

Attending seminars, schools, conferences and other events are ideal venues to ask and learn of new opportunities. When someone gives me a lead, I follow up with progress reports. I have also found superlative employees when asking for referrals. The power of a personal recommendation is an amazing tool you should exploit every day. For instance, at an altitude of 35,000 feet, a flight attendant referred me to a person who invested 75 million dollars in our fund! I have many such stories, so please do not be shy and routinely ask for referrals.

引　荐

沟通联络是走向成功的重要技能，别让羞怯或安静的天性阻挡你想要达到财务目标的脚步。

你必须养成一种习惯，要不断联系他人以建立友谊和业务关系。但是也要学会大胆地向别人寻求帮助，尤其涉及帮你引荐给他人这种事。

引荐是最自然和简单的业务连接器之一，你所需要做的就是请求！大多数人都不会拒绝帮你引荐，所以作为日常，请求所有你遇到的人帮忙。即便有人拒绝你时，也不要感到尴尬或受到冒犯，转移话题来缓解被拒所带来的压力。每个人都和别人有着千丝万缕的联系，引荐是发现新机遇的一种直接的渠道。

即使是最穷的人也可能有一个有钱有势的童年玩伴或亲戚。遗憾的是，我就曾经忽视过潜在资源，之后听他们说“我要知道就好了”或“你要提一句就好了，我早就帮忙了”。你自己不花时间去求人，就别指望别人主动来帮你。

我要强调的是，你要恳求任何人帮你引荐，乐于助人是人类天性。有的时候特别富有的人不情愿引荐他人，但一旦他们帮你，花点时间就太值得了。当然寻求显而易见的经纪人，比如律师、会计师事务所、投资公司是应该的，但是不要止步于此，要找所有人帮忙！你会欣喜地惊讶于之后得到的回报。

参加研讨会，上课，开会和一些其他的活动都是求人引荐和获悉新机遇的理想场所。当某人帮我引荐时，我会紧紧把握机会后续跟进。在寻求引荐时，我还找到过顶级雇员。强大的个人推荐是绝佳的工具，你应该每天利用它。例如，在 35000 英尺高度的航班上，一个空乘给我引荐一人，此人之后在我们的基金投资了 7500 万美元！我有很多这样的例子，所以请你别害羞，经常性地请求别人的引荐。

Business and Pleasure

It is often said not to mix pleasure and business. That implies you should always be grimly serious and never have any fun. However, this ignores the importance of building relationships.

Many business deals emerge after people converse over a meal. Some agreements are formulated during a round of golf. You have to be serious about business and investing, but also recognize that entertainment plays a fruitful role.

Even if you don't formally entertain others, it is still valuable to make your interactions as pleasurable as possible. You are cultivating relationships. Be as likable as you can while still projecting a refined professional image. In some situations a simple smile, joke, or kind word can be the impetus for a business liaison.

The thought that business and pleasure should not be confluent is ignorance at best. Ideally, all business deals should include an element of enjoyment. Trust is built, not just by a business transaction, but by people interfacing with each other. This does not mean entertaining everyone you do business with, but make an effort to discuss other matters besides the business at hand. If you care about the individual, not just the business angle, then you will find other wonderful objectives will surface.

One Christmas night, I took a contingent of Chinese guests to dinner. I had recently arrived in Los Angeles and was suffering from jet lag, so I chose a nice restaurant that served until 10:30 PM. When my group arrived, the eatery was winding down. We patiently sat there for twenty minutes, but no one approached our table. Understand that my guests were extremely important to my business and future revenue. Being from China, they had never experienced a Christmas dinner and didn't know what to expect.

After another ten minutes passed, I made a decision not to let anything affect the camaraderie we were all enjoying and politely summoned a waiter. Five more minutes passed, and the same server returned and apologized because the two waiters assigned to our table had departed! He kindly offered to take their place and immediately took everyone's order. I was elated and said, "This is Christmas, and it is a blessing to even be here!"

生意和快乐

人们总是说别把快乐和生意混在一起，意思是说你应该总是冷酷严肃而不能欢乐。然而这就忽视了建立人际关系的重要性。

许多交易都是人们饭局之后聊出来的，有的协议是在打高尔夫的时候规划出来的。你要认真对待生意和投资，但是也要认识到娱乐在这当中扮演着重要的角色。

即使你不正式招待他人，也要让你们之间的互动尽可能的欢乐。你正在培养友好关系，正在展现精干的职业形象，这时候要尽量讨人喜欢，在有些场合，一个简单的微笑、一个小玩笑或者好听的话都可以成为商业联系的动力。

认为生意和快乐不能融合在一起的想法顶多是无知而已。最理想的状态是，所有的生意都应该包含欢乐的元素。信任的建立，不只是靠业务往来，而是靠人与人间的相互配合。这样不是说你应该招待所有和你做生意的人，而是除了手头上的业务外，想办法再谈些别的话题。如果你在意一个人，不能只是从生意角度上在意，然后你会发现其他意想不到的好事随之出现。

一个圣诞夜，我带一队中国客人去用餐，我刚到洛杉矶正在忍受时差，所以我选了一家不错的餐馆，他们通常晚上十点半就打烊了。当我们到达那里的时候，小餐馆已经客人不多了，我们耐心的坐着等了 20 分钟，但没有人来我们餐桌点餐，我明白这些客人对我的生意和未来收入有多重要。他们来自中国，从来没体验过圣诞晚餐也不知道该有怎样的期待。

另一个十分钟过去了，我决定不让任何事影响我们正沉浸其中的友情，我礼貌地叫来一个服务员，又 5 分钟之后，同一个服务员回来并向我们道歉，因为两个分派给我们餐桌的服务员已经走了！他好心地提出替代他们，并立即为我们点餐，我很兴奋并说道：“今天是圣诞节，能来到这里是我们的福气！”

Next I ordered white wine, but he mistakenly brought red. He apologized and offered to return the wine for the desired vintage. I assured him not to worry. After all, he was tired, having worked more than twelve hours that day. We kept the red wine, then I reassured him that the group would keep any of the served dishes, even if they were wrong. In the end, I must proclaim that was the best Christmas dinner ever.

All those dinner guests are now long-term friends with Checkmate Investing. They witnessed me keeping my cool, and appreciated how I did not waver in my concentration on them. Normally, a person in my position would have felt embarrassed and gotten upset. This story illustrates how mixing business with pleasure can develop personal relationships on another non-business level while making life that much more enjoyable.

之后我点了白葡萄酒，但他拿错了，变成了红葡萄酒，他道歉并提出换成我们想要的酒，我让他别担心，毕竟他那天已经工作了超过十二小时，很累了。我们留下了红酒，我还让他放心，上来的所有菜品我们都要，即使错了也不用退。最后我必须宣布，那顿饭是我曾经以来吃过的最好的圣诞晚餐。

和我一起吃饭的所有客人现在都是我们“将军投资”的长期朋友，他们见证了我保持冷静，并感激我一直专注他们。通常一个人如果处在我当时的场面，会感到万分尴尬和恼怒，这个故事阐明了在与生意无关的情境下，让生意和快乐融为一体可以发展人际关系，同时使生活更加愉快。

Emotions and Wealth

Emotions are a controversial subject as most people will advise you to keep your feelings completely out of investing. Once again, I believe just the opposite. Emotions create passion which can inspire a curiosity that induces you to learn more about an investment opportunity. Conversely, you can't let emotions cloud your judgment and control your investment decisions.

Avoid falling in love with a deal until you have reviewed similar opportunities in the same space. By seeking out comparable ideas, you keep everything in perspective and won't fall head over heels over a prospect unless it has true merit.

Always push yourself to learn everything about the particular situation. When I use emotions constructively, I am driven to ask more intelligent questions and drill down in a more enthusiastic manner to clearly uncover the company's existing merits and flaws.

With most investments, a time will arrive when it is best to sell and move on. By being emotional in the curious way, you will have learned not only about your company, but about competitors and other businesses that effect this investment. Often, the future winning prospect is the one that you discovered by owning the current investment.

情感和财富

情感是一个有争议的问题，因为大多数人都会建议你在投资的时候千万别动感情。再一次，我认为恰恰相反。情感可以创造激情，因而激发人的好奇心，促使你更多地了解投资机会。反过来，你不能让情感影响判断以及控制投资决策。

不要轻易认定一笔交易，除非你在同一领域中考察过相似的情况，通过找出可以比较的理念，看清每方面，不要陷入一个景象中，除非真有价值。

总是迫使自己学习特定情况的每一方面。当我积极地运用情感的时候，总能带动我去问一些有独特见地的问题并且以更加热情的方式深度钻研，清晰地去发现该公司目前存在的优势和不足。

对大多数投资来讲，会有一个最好的时机将其售出并继续前行，通过拥有感性的好奇心这种方法，你不仅会了解自己的公司，还能了解竞争对手和影响这项投资其他公司的情况，未来美好的发展景象就是从目前投资中发掘出来的。

Quid Pro Quo

"You do something for me, and I'll do something for you" is the old decree of quid pro quo. In reality, it is unhealthy to operate a business if you expect a quid pro quo.

I follow a different set of rules and often do things for others and expect nothing in return. I do hope if I need a favor in the future, maybe that person will lend a hand. Generally, it does come to fruition that doing good deeds for others will result in good things happening in my life. Again, business favors, without strings attached, will develop a network of positive relationships.

I believe in helping others because it is true, "What goes around comes around." Occasionally, I will find appealing deals, but pass them on to friends. In several instances, the investments panned out exponentially. Even though my friends made millions, I expected nothing in return. Hopefully, I will always have those people's trust and friendship, but I sought nothing more.

I also believe in the concept of Karma; sending out good vibes brings back good things. The chief problem with those who demand a quid pro quo is that eventually it will create unfair or unethical decisions.For example, if I am to be paid a commission, I want this percentage to be fully disclosed beforehand. With quid pro quo that amount is not normally divulged.

Appreciate that you are alive and well, and that sometimes you can help others with nothing expected in return. And always remember, you are forging relationships of trust and friendship that will ultimately be rewarded in unforeseen ways.

对等交换

“你为我做了什么事，我也要为你做什么事。”就是旧法令里面说的对等交换。在现实中，运营一个企业的时候，如果你总期待对等交换，那就不太好。

我遵循一套完全不同的法则，总是为别人做事并不求回报，我当然希望如果将来有一天真需要别人帮忙之时，那个人有可能会帮我。通常，我对别人做好事，将来会有好事发生在我身上，好人确实会有好报。再说，没有附加条件的业务上的支持，将是建立良好关系的网络。

我相信帮助他人，因为我相信这是真的：“善有善报，恶有恶报。”偶尔我会找到不错的买卖，然后转给我的朋友们，其中有几次，投资大获成功。虽然我的朋友们挣了数百万元，我却不求回报，我有望能永远得到他们的信任和友谊，除此之外我别无他求。

我也相信因果报应的观点，发出好的旋律会得到好的共鸣。那些要求对等交换的人，他们最主要的问题在于，最终会产生不公平或不道德的决定。例如，要付给我佣金，我希望提成比例可以事先彻底公开，而按照对等交换的原则，这个数目通常是不能公开的。

感恩你现在活得不错，你还能不求回报地帮助他人，并且永远记得，你正在建立的信任与友谊的人际关系，终会以不可预见的方式回馈于你。

CHAPTER 2

Investing in Yourself

It is essential to invest in yourself by improving all aspects of your life. Your motto should be continual growth privately, professionally, and in your various investments. Attending industry conferences, paying attention to details, perfecting listening and communication skills, trusting business instincts, learning from mentors, and of course maintaining good health and a positive attitude are some of the ways to invest in yourself. Such self-improvement will advance you beyond the average investor.

第二章
自我投资

通过改善你生活中的各个方面来自我投资是非常必要的，你的座右铭应当是不断地成长，个人的、职业的以及从各种投资中不断成长。参加行业会议，注重细节，修炼倾听和沟通的技能，相信商业直觉，向导师学习，当然保持良好的身体和积极的态度也是你自我投资的一些办法。这种自我改善会使你超越普通的投资者。

Attending Conferences

One way to improve yourself is by attending conferences related to your business. In addition to meeting a bevy of eager referrals and innovative people, you will be privy to the latest industry updates. Be aggressive and approach as many leads as you can. The more diverse individuals you communicate with, the greater the pool of resources available to you.

This is particularly true if you become a conference speaker and are the center of attention which will draw attendees to you. Even if you are not a speaker, you will still learn much from these sessions and perhaps meet an entrepreneur who can provide an entree into previously unknown investments.

Use an app to expedite the process of gathering people's information. Besides taking a photo with them, I pass out business cards. When I receive a business card, I immediately scan it with my phone in case it's misplaced.

Some conferences have breakout groups which offer more flexibility to ask out of the ordinary questions and elicit more unusual information. Sometimes the pertinent questions others ask are ones that you should be asking, but never thought of previously. And always arrive early for every breakfast and event. Those are opportune times to productively and individually socialize.

Conferences often cost money to attend, but it's generally worth every penny. The more a seminar costs, the more likely the attendees are serious about investing and aren't there just for a free lunch.If you can afford to sponsor the event, others will perceive you in an elevated light.

If you can't attend a trade symposium, send associates from your company, but try your best to be there. I go to as many such events as possible, and it's always time well spent. Keeping in touch with the investing world around you is of utmost value. You will undoubtedly experience synergistic results.

参加会议

通过参加与业务相关的会议是一种改进自我的方法。除了见到一帮渴望引荐和富有创意的人以外，你还能了解到最新的行业动态。要有进取心，尽量多找门路，你越和各种各样的人交流，有效资源就越多。

如果你成为会议发言人，并成为与会人员注意力的中心，这样尤为如此。即使不是发言人，你依然可以从这些会议中学到很多，也许遇到一个企业家，能够提供一块敲门砖，让你进入之前不知道的投资项目。

利用应用软件来加速收集他人信息的过程，除了和他们合照以外，我还发名片。而我要是收到一张名片，就立即扫描到手机里，以防错放找不到。

有些会议会分成小组，这样更方便去问一些平常的问题并从中抽取不平常的信息。有些时候别人问的相关问题正好是你应该问的，但却事先没想到。每次去吃会议早餐或参加其他活动的时候，一定要早到，那些都是有效的以及可以单独社交的最佳时机。

为了参加会议常常会花掉很多钱，但是通常你花的每一分钱都是值得的，研讨会的费用越高，与会之人就会越认真对待投资，而不只是去吃免费午餐。如果你可以赞助发起这个活动，其他人会对你另眼相看。

要是你不能参某个贸易座谈会，就派你公司的同事去，但是你最好亲自去。我会尽量多参加这种活动，而且总是值得花费时间参加。和你身边的投资行业保持联络是最高的价值。你会毋庸置疑地体会到协同合作的成果。

Conference schedules and locations can be found by subscribing to industry magazines and searching the Internet. All the prominent investment houses sponsor enlightening seminars. I have both identified and invested in many flourishing enterprises as a direct result of attending these instructive gatherings. The list of benefits is endless, so make it a routine to go to as many as possible.

会议日程和地点可以从订阅的行业杂志里或上网查到，所有著名的投资公司都会赞助这种启发性研讨会。参加这种有益的集会的直接结果，就是从中接触到许多大企业，我既得到了他们的认可，也参与过他们的投资，所以要作为日常尽量多参加这些活动。

Detail Oriented

Details are imperative to any successful business. This does not mean being so precise that you diminish your accomplishments. Instead, pay attention to specifics for the sake of understanding and not missing opportunities. To overlook a minor detail is often the difference between profit and loss.

My most beneficial attributes are being a quick thinker and energetic doer which allow me to swiftly assess a favorable opportunity when presented. However, those same traits can also cause me to hastily pass over a crucial detail, so I surround myself with people who can shore up my weaknesses.

Checkmate Investing adheres to this equilibrial method of evaluating an investment. I employ team members to double check every aspect of the transaction and never become agitated when someone points out a factor I overlooked. I am very much the opposite and encourage my team to always challenge my reasoning. The same is true when I reject an opportunity and an associate thinks I am wrong. I urge him/her to try and resell me on what was ignored and why we should invest.

I put detail and being organized in the same boat. Do everything viable to stay organized as it will be easier to notice minutiae if you are systematized. Take notes and do not merely rely on your memory or you will indubitably forget critical details.

Never put off what you can do today until tomorrow. Go that extra mile while still keeping balance with your time. Set schedules that are workable. I can write and exercise more efficiently early in the morning as nothing else is on my mind. It is also my alone time to regain perspective.

I always complete a "to-do" list each evening before retiring. Then every morning, after exercising, I review the file again to see if anything has been neglected. I also take time everyday to visualize my objectives for success by writing down my goals in the form of achievable versus dreams.

注重细节

对于任何一个成功的企业来讲，细节都是至关重要的。这并不是说由于特别细致就会减少你的成就，反而，注重细节是为了更好地理解并且不会错失良机，忽略一个小细节往往是盈亏之间的差别。

我是一个脑子转得快、精力充沛的实干家，这是我最大的优点，当一个有利的机会摆在我面前的时候，我可以快速地评定出来，然而，这些优点也可以让我匆忙中忽略掉一个关键的细节，所以我总是与能帮我改善这一弱点的人一起共事。

“将军投资”在评估一项投资时遵循这一平衡的方法。我雇用团队成员去仔细检查交易的每个方面，如果有人指出我忽略了某个因素，我绝不起急。正相反，我会鼓励我的团队总是去质疑我的论证。同样如此，当我拒绝一个机会，而同伴认为我想的不对时，我会要求同伴设法说服我，到底是忽略了哪方面，为什么我们应该投资。

我把细节和有条理归为一类，要想尽任何办法使得做事有条有理，因为如果你凡事系统化，就会很容易察觉细枝末节。凡事要做记录，别只是靠自己的记忆力，否则毋庸置疑你会忘记关键的细节。

千万别把今天能办的事推到明天，多努力一些的同时又让你的时间保持平衡。设置一些切实可行的日程安排。我在清晨的时候写作和锻炼的效率最高，因为那时候脑子最为清醒，也是我独自一人能够重新高瞻远瞩的时候。

我总是在每晚休息之前完成“任务清单”，然后每天早上，锻炼身体之后，我再检查一遍文件，看看是不是忽略了某件事情。我也会每天找时间把设想的成功目标，以切实可行的和梦寐以求的相对比的方式写下来。

Best of all, I appreciate every day and all that surrounds me. This practice energizes me as paying attention to detail requires fortitude. Make it a habit to thoroughly examine the particulars of your work. Details are one of the keys to intelligent investing.

重要的是，我感恩每一天和我拥有的一切，这个习惯激发我注重细节所需要的毅力。彻底检查你工作中的所有细节，使之成为一个习惯，细节是智慧投资的密钥之一。

Listening Skills

Read books. Take courses. Brainstorm with experts. And practice your listening skills.

Being a great communicator is central for any company. Clearly articulating your vision is the path to efficiency. Motivating others on your team or investors or bankers can lead to extensive recognition and enduring success.

Some people will pontificate merely to show how worldly they are. Others will focus on selling their idea and won't listen to constructive feedback. The best way to expand your knowledge is to stop talking and thinking and just listen. Turning a deaf ear is often a road to disaster. For example, what good is brainstorming with colleagues if you are the only speaker? You should throw out ideas, then stop and hear the opinions of the others. Even when you strongly disagree, do not speak, but continue listening. It is human nature to get excited over your ideas and tune out others who may suggest unimagined alternatives. Don't be myopic.

When you are seeking an investor, anything he or she asks is important to them, even if you think it is off topic, so simply listen. After the investor poses a question, respond with direct answers without going off on a tangent. Sometimes just listening will show that you sincerely care and induce an investor to develop trust in you.

The entire psychology industry is based on the two principles of trust and listening. A proficient psychologist will not talk much, but instead draw words and emotions from the patient. In turn, the patient will talk up a storm and divulge everything because of their trust in this professional. Similarly, skillful salesmen articulate their pitch and then listen. They draw the consumer out with unrelated stories, then listen, evaluate reactions, and succinctly respond. Before long, the prospect just buys the product because the salesman has gained the person's confidence.

If you learn to listen and care about what others have to say, you'll acquire many new friends because most people love to talk. If you are giving a presentation to investors, carefully listen to all audience feedback and you'll be able to overcome just about any objection.

聆听的技巧

看书、修习课程、和专家一起集思广益并且训练你的聆听技巧。

一个善于交际的人是任何公司的核心。清晰地表达你的愿景是最有效的途径。激发你团队中的其他人或者投资者又或者银行家，可以让你得到广泛的认同和持久的成功。

一些人武断地发表意见只能显示出他们有多世俗。其他人只关注于推销自己的想法，不去倾听有益的反馈。不说话、不思考，只是去聆听，是扩展自己知识的最好办法。不听别人说话往往会导致灾难发生。比如，和同事集思广益的时候，就你一个人发表意见，能有什么用处？你应该把自己的看法说出来，然后就先停下，去倾听别人的意见。即使在强烈反对的时候，也先别说，而是继续听下去。兴奋于自己的想法而不理别人的观点是人类的天性，而别人的观点很可能是你从来没想到过的想法。千万别目光短浅。

当你寻求一个投资者的时候，所提问的问题，即便你觉得偏离话题了，对他们来讲却很重要，所以只是倾听就好。当投资者提出一个问题之后，直接回答不要离题。有时候，只去聆听会显示出你真诚地在意投资者，并使其渐渐相信你。

整个心理学都是基于两大原则：信任和聆听。一个资深的心理学家不会说很多，而是引导患者说话和情绪表达。反过来，患者由于信任这个专家，会滔滔不绝地说出并暴露出所有问题。同样，高明的推销员清晰地说出他们的意图之后就去倾听，他们用不相关的事情吸引消费者，然后倾听、评估反馈，并简短回答，没多久，由于推销员得到了信任，客户自会购买他的产品。

如果你学会聆听并关注别人必须要说的话，你会得到许多朋友，因为大多数人喜欢聊天。当你向投资者演讲的时候，仔细倾听所有观众的反馈，这样你就能赢得所有的异议。

I always enter a meeting or presentation fully expecting to be challenged by the prospects. Being confronted shows their interest and allows me to respond with solutions to win them over. On the contrary, when I am being pitched and the fund seeker talks incessantly, not allowing me to ask any questions, then I seldom make the investment.

If the audience continually asks questions, go with the flow and answer them. Do not get flustered and insist on completing your spiel. Just answer the questions. Your goal is to convince them to invest, not to applaud your dog and pony show. Maybe they are fully cognizant of your needs, but have a few more reassuring questions before investing.

The main purpose of the presentation is to introduce you and your idea to prospects. It also gives you the capacity hear what you're up against, so you can then revise your game plan for the next pitch meeting. Listening is the primary faculty to either making or receiving an investment.

我进入会场的时候，总能充分地想到来自客户的质疑，有异议说明他们感兴趣，也能给我机会说出解决方案而赢得他们的信任。相反，如果别人找我筹钱，而寻求资金的人不停地说话，不允许我问任何问题，我基本不会给他们投资。

如果观众不断提出问题，就顺其自然地回答他们，千万别慌，别固执于自己的高谈阔论，直接回答那些问题，你的目标是说服他们投资，而不是让他们为你的盛大表演喝彩。可能他们已经完全认可了你的需求，只是在投资之前有一些能让人更加安心的问题。

演讲的主要目的是把你的和你的想法推荐给潜在客户，也会使你能够倾听别人会怎样质疑，这样你就可以为下次推介会修改策略。不管是投资别人还是得到投资，聆听是最主要的能力。

Incessant Learning

There are both direct and intangible benefits to habitually seeking knowledge related to investing. There is also a value to learning about advances in health, fitness, and current events. If nothing else, reading books, magazines, newspapers, and online reports broadens your edification, making you more informed, interesting, and appealing to eclectic individuals. Many immensely successful people regularly read to rejuvenate and expand their awareness.

Of course, many people have other priorities and are too busy to spend hours reading. In particular, active business people tend to eschew anything unrelated to their work environment which makes them one dimensional.

However, modern technology has made it more convenient to learn. Listening to audio files while commuting or traveling or even exercising has made education available to everyone. You can hear a wide range of topics such as recordings of conferences, investing, health, etc. Just about every book today is accessible on audio.

Many of us spend lots of time in a car. If you drive two hours a day commuting back and forth to work, that equals 10 hours each week which amounts to 40 hours a month or 480 hours each year. Based on a 12 hour day (due to sleep and relaxation), that is a total 40 days or more than 10% of the year lost sitting in a car. Imagine how much can be learned during that idle time, decade after decade!

Audio files can also be very relaxing. I used to be frustrated and bored while in transit, but now I love driving, even when unexpected delays slow me down, thanks to audio information. Another benefit of listening to audio pep talks en route to a meeting is an ever-present and powerful "can do" attitude when I arrive.

An unanticipated benefit from audio files is I'm now a better listener! Take advantage of any down time in your life by finding ways to enhance your knowledge on any number of subjects, personal or professional.

不断地学习

习惯性地寻求有关投资的知识，既有直接效益又有无形效益，了解健康、健身和时事的发展也很有价值。如果别无选择，看书、看杂志、看报纸以及在线报道都能提高你的修养，使你自己见多识广、风趣幽默，能够吸引不拘一格之士。许多特别成功的人士经常看书以使自己焕发青春并扩展自己的认知。

当然，许多人有更重要的事做，过于忙碌无暇看书，尤其那些活跃的商人，他们更愿意避开与其工作环境无关的任何事，使自己生活在单一维度。

然而，现代科技使学习更方便。在上下班时、旅行中、甚至锻炼身体的时候，收听音频文件可以使每个人接受教育。你可以听到包罗万象的话题，如会议录音、投资、健康等，现在几乎每本书都能以音频形式收听。

我们许多人都花很长时间坐在车里，如果你每天上下班开车 2 小时，相当于一周 10 小时，一个月 40 小时，一年就是 480 小时，一天按 12 小时来算（除去睡觉和休息），那就是 40 天，或者说一年中超过 10% 的时间都浪费在车里了。10 年又 10 年过去了，想想在这个空闲时间里能学多少东西啊！

收听音频也能让人放松心情，我以前坐在车里时总是觉得沮丧而无聊，但是现在我喜欢开车，感谢有音频信息伴随我，即使由于意外的原因而耽误了时间也没关系。在去开会的途中收听鼓舞士气的话是另一个好处，当我到会的时候拥有的，是一个始终存在和强大的“能做到”的态度。

收听音频文件的一个意料之外的好处就是我现在是一个更好的聆听者了！利用你生命中的工休时间，找到能提高学识的方法，个人或职业的各种科目。

Learn By Doing

School has its place. A formal education can teach you life-long skills. But the most significant aptitude is learning how to troubleshoot.In many businesses you have to ascertain specifics on your own. This is predominantly true in developing a startup company or devising technologies, so embrace the creative challenge of educating yourself.

Most people would say the purpose of school is to learn a career. To me this is not the singular function. Instead, I look at the point of higher education as twofold:

1) Learn to socialize properly by dealing with people.

2) Learn how to problem solve by creating solutions to challenges.

Gaining knowledge is not limited to books. You will always be in "school" because real education comes from doing. Hands-on experience teaches you how to solve problems as you constantly face the impending obstacles in life.

I was talking with a PhD friend about business school. For 17 years, he was a professor at a major university and then retired to become a businessman. He admitted learning much more by actually running a company than in a classroom. Reality presented a far greater creative challenge than he ever imagined. Remember, a guy with a PhD in Physics and Business was making this statement.

School provided an excellent base and taught him many valuable lessons. He learned how to research and find answers, how to interact with others and listen, how to socialize, how to solve problems, how to be patient, and how to be clearly understood by others.

But in business, he had to learn by doing. He now believes there is no question or confrontation in the real world that he cannot resolve. Your own base of knowledge may be limited, but if you embrace whatever education is needed to achieve your objective, you will.

边干边学

学校自有它的意义。一个正规的教育能教给你终身的技能。但是最重要的能力是学会怎样排除困难。在许多企业里，你只能靠自己查明情况，在发展新公司和发明新科技的时候尤为如此，所以要接受自我学习这一创造性挑战。

许多人都会说学校的目的就是关于职业的学习，对我来讲并不只是单一功能；相反，我认为高等教育的重点是双重的。

1. 通过与人交往学会得体的社交。

2. 通过创造应对挑战的解决方法学会解决问题。

要获得知识不只限于书本，你会永远在“学校”里，因为真正的教育来自实践，由于你在人生中要不断面对即将来临的难题，实践经验可以教会你怎样解决问题。

我和一个博士朋友谈起过有关商学院的问题，他在一所重点大学当了17年教授，然后退休成为一名商人。他承认通过实际经营一个公司学到的东西要比课堂上多很多，现实呈现出的创造性挑战要远比他曾经想象的大得多。要记住，一个拥有物理学和商学双博士学位之人居然得出如此结论。

学校提供一个绝佳的环境，并教给他许多有价值的课程，他学会了怎样去研究并找到答案，怎样与他人互动和聆听，怎样社交，怎样解决问题，怎样拥有耐心，怎样让别人清楚地了解自己。

但在商业活动中，他必须边干边学，他现在相信现实世界中没有什么他不能解决的问题或冲突。你自己的知识基础可能是有限的，但是如果你接受为达到目标所需的任何知识，那就会是无限的。

Teaching Lessons

Another way to grow intellect is by teaching. You improve your mastery of a subject, learn to better explain issues, and have a chance to enrich the lives of others. Additionally, you meet new acquaintances and have a platform to network.

To teach is to learn by experience. The teacher often learns more than the students who ask questions on various and unexpected topics. This obligates an instructor to decelerate and thoroughly research all aspects of the matter at hand. I have taught courses at several colleges and found the experience to be very educational, stimulating, and enjoyable.

You can teach subjects related to your business or choose material disparate to your industry. For example, if you have a passionate interest or hobby, you can pass along that knowledge. Regardless of the topic, teaching helps you learn how to speak to an audience, and it offers a forum to build your network.

If you have an opportunity to teach, even as a guest lecturer or Sunday school teacher, do it. You will find it to be a gratifying and worthwhile experience. When you give, you always get something back in return. Teaching is giving.

授 课

给别人讲课是另一种让自己变得更加智慧的方法，你能让自己对一个科目更加精通、学会怎样更好地解释问题，并且有机会使别人的生活更加充实，此外，你还能结识新人，有一个联络他人的平台。

给人讲课是在实践中学习，老师永远要比学生学习得更多，因为学生总是会问各种各样的、意想不到方面的问题，这就强迫老师慢下来并彻底研究手边问题的所有方面。我曾经在几个学院授过课，发现这一经历非常有教育意义、令人兴奋并享受其中。

你可以讲授一些和自身业务有关的科目，也可以讲授无关的方面。比如，如果你对某一领域有强烈的兴趣或爱好，就可以传授这些知识。不管是什么课题，授课会帮你学会怎样向听众讲话，也能提供一个平台以构建你的关系网。

如果你有授课的机会，即使作为客座教授或主日学校的老师，也一定要去，你会发现那是一个令人欣喜的、值得去做的体验。当你讲课之后，你总会有所收获。授课就是给予。

Popular Culture Value

One of the traits of an accomplished investor is being synchronized with the world around them. Many investors don't place enough value on the ever-changing cultural trends. In my opinion, this is a grave mistake if you are seeking copious wealth. Among many others, movies, fashion, and food preferences are forecasters of what consumers will be buying in the future.

It's easiest to track music. You can listen while commuting, exercising, working at non-business tasks, and in your hotel room during business trips. Regularly listen to radio stations that play contemporary music to access present-day issues and inclinations.

I also recommend exploring music from other nations and cultures, particularly if you are engaged in international investments. For example, if you are an American doing business in China, listen to that country's modern music. What types of songs do Chinese youngsters tune in? What does it tell you about their hopes and dreams? What sort of creative energy does the music reflect? More precisely, what does it tell you about the future of business in China?

Of course, this is true for music everywhere. If you listen to current music in a local region, it will tell you something about the hopes, dreams, tastes, preferences, and creative energy of its residents that will affect future business tendencies.

It may seem bizarre for music to influence the investing world, but such untapped trends keep you in touch with reality. Restricting investment analysis to only dynamics that can be measured limits your imaginative options.

Schools often ignore such cultural alternatives and only teach a strict set of investment rules. I met a fund manager who had such a calculated mindset and checklist driven approach that he was inflexible, robotic. He had lost the ability to see beyond the page he was reviewing. People like that are useful to perform the analytical part of due diligence and situation evaluation, but I would not include them in any final decisions.

流行文化的价值

资深投资者的特点之一就是能与其周围的世界同步发展。许多投资者不重视不断变化的文化潮流，在我看来，如果你想要寻求成功，这样做就大错特错了。在众多潮流中，电影、时尚、饮食喜好等，是消费者购买趋势的预报员。

最简单的就是追随音乐的潮流，你可以在上下班时、锻炼时、非业务时，以及在出差时的宾馆房间里听音乐。时常收听电台播放的当代音乐能让你了解到最新发行的和最受欢迎的音乐。

我也建议探索其他国家和文化中的音乐，如果你正从事国际投资尤为如此。比如，如果你是一个美国人，正在中国做生意，就听听他们国家的现代音乐。中国年轻人喜欢收听什么类型的歌曲呢？什么是他们的希望和梦想呢？这个音乐反映的是哪种创作能量呢？更准确地说，是关于未来中国的商机，你能了解到什么呢？

当然，音乐确实无处不在，如果你聆听本地区的流行音乐，它会告诉你当地居民的希望、梦想、品位、偏好和创作能量，而这些都会影响未来商业的发展趋势。

音乐能影响投资领域，这似乎很奇怪，但是这种尚未开发的趋势可以让你和现实保持联系，将投资分析只限于可测量的动态范围内，会限制你的想象力。

学校总是忽视这种文化影响，而只会讲授一套严格的投资规则。我遇到过一个基金经理，他就有这种教条的心态和靠规则驱使的方法，顽固而机械化，除了他看到过的资料之外，看不见别的东西，像这样的人适合在尽职调查和形势评估时执行分析部分，但在最终决断时，我绝不让他们参与。

Checkmate Investing takes the time to assess all the external factors surrounding a venture. Winning investments are found through analysis first and then appraising cultural trends, management, the market vibe, and enthusiasm for the project.We will never make any investment based totally on a written analysis.

For example, I hired a major consulting firm to analyze the China market for a company we were buying; the Asian side of a major American entertainment company with more than 5000 characters in its IP (Intellectual Property) library. Our goal was to generate money on the IP and also build a theme park. The consultants came back with a well executed report that could not have been more wrong. They concluded that China would never protect IP and only the theme park had value and advised us to pass on this risky deal. These specialists disregarded the growth of cinemas in China and failed to research that China was beginning to create their own IP. Once a country crafts their own product, they want it protected and will protect other countries' products as "a reciprocal arrangement." This paradigm demonstrates that even the "experts" will sometimes arrive at the wrong conclusions and miss the mark.

Nevertheless, such analytical reports are more often right than wrong. I still believe in hearing a third party's opinion in addition to our internal review, but I never solely rely on external information for the final decision. Checkmate Investing strategizes on many levels to uncover all possible valuations and sometimes going against the grain will produce the biggest returns.

In the example above, concerning the large consulting firm that did such a horrendous job, I later scrutinized my mistakes. The biggest error was in the hiring process when I chose the firm solely based on its prestigious name. At that time, I deduced that a well known, branded business only employed upper echelon professionals who would add credibility to their commissioned report. However, what good is credibility if the individual you enlisted is incompetent? As a result, I concluded you should always hire the "person," not the "firm." Next, explore the experience and relationships of this lead individual and his/her support staff. You must be comfortable with the people you are hiring and have utmost confidence in their abilities to help you attain your goals.

“将军投资”会花时间评估一个企业周围的所有外部因素，成功的投资都是先从分析开始的，然后评估文化趋势、经营手段、市场氛围以及对项目的热情。我们做任何投资都绝不会只基于书面分析。

例如，我雇用了一家专业咨询公司为我们分析中国市场，目的是当时正在收购的一家公司，该公司是一个美国大型娱乐公司的亚洲分部，在IP（知识产权）库里有超过5000个经典角色。我们的目标是在IP上赚钱，并建一个主题公园，咨询顾问拿来一份极其错误的可行性报告，他们推断中国永远不会保护IP，而只有主题公园有价值，并建议我们放弃这一有风险的投资。这些专家不顾中国电影院线的增长趋势，也没研究出来中国正在开始创作自己的IP。一旦一个国家制作自己的产品，他们会让产品受保护，因为“互惠原则”也会保护其他国家的产品。这一范例论证了即使是“专家”有时也会得出错误的结论，并错失良机。

然而，这种分析性报告总是正确的多。我依然相信，除我们内部检查外，还要听取第三方的意见，但我从不只依赖于外部信息来作最终决定。“将军投资”在许多层面上制订策略，去发现所有潜在的评估因素，而且有时“背道而驰”会产生最大的回报。

在上例中，关于那个做了极大量工作的大咨询事务所，后来我细致审查并发现了我的失误。当我选择公司时，最大的错误就是在招聘过程中，仅仅以其享有的声誉为基础。当时，我推断一家知名的品牌企业只雇佣那些会为委托报告增加可信度的上层梯队专业人员。然而，如果你所征募的个人不称职，那么可信度有什么用呢？因此，我得出结论，你应该是雇用“人”，而不是“公司”。然后，调查这个领导个人以及其他支持人员的经验和关系。你必须对你正在聘请的人感到满意，并且对他们协助你达成目标的能力充满信心。

I do not make mistakes more than once, so when it came time to find a competent Chinese lawyer, I focused on the person, not a team of attorneys. The person I hired, Zhang Ting, had previously worked with a very large firm for nearly 12 years, then moved on to a smaller, Beijing based and very prestigious legal partnership, "DOCVIT." Without question, she is a star when it comes to lawyers. She is well organized, punctual, speaks perfect English and Mandarin, and has outstanding communication skills that prevent misunderstandings. She is knowledgeable in both Chinese and Western law in addition to being an excellent and relentless researcher who has solid relationships to call upon should there still be unanswered questions.

I learned a long time ago how to evaluate a person's character. When I visit a professional's office, I observe how this individual interacts and is perceived by fellow employees. In the case of Zhang Ting, she is favorably regarded at all levels: respected, admired and recognized as acutely intelligent. I also watched her congenially interacting with the staff on assignments that required a team effort.

As a final note, Zhang Ting has more than a high Intelligence Quotient "IQ." She also has a high Emotional Quotient "EQ." When you possess both, the world is yours, and we are pleased to have such a fine person as Zhang Ting representing Checkmate in China.

我不会多次犯错误，所以当发现一个称职的中国律师的时候，我关注的是这个个人，而不是一个律师团队。我聘请的律师张婷曾在一家非常大的律所工作过近 12 年，她后来转到了一家规模较小、总部位于北京、声名远扬的合伙制律所“Docvit”。毫无疑问，作为律师，她是个明星。她井井有条、守时、能够讲流利的英语和普通话。她还有着很强的沟通技巧，能防止误解。此外，她对中西方法律都深有造诣。她既是一位优秀的、坚持不懈的研究者，又有着坚实的人脉，使她在面对未决问题时能够求助于这些人。

我很久以前就学会了如何评价一个人的品格。当我访问一个专业人员的办公室时，我会观察这个人与同事互动的方式以及同事对她的评价。在对张婷的观察中，她在各个层面都得到了好评：受人尊敬、欣赏并且被认为非常聪明。我还注意到在需要团队合作的任务中，她与同事的互动非常默契。

最后一点，张婷不仅具有高智商（IQ），她还具有很高的情商（EQ）。当你拥有这两者时，这个世界就是你的。我们非常荣幸有这样一个杰出人物——张婷——“将军投资”在中国的代理。

Healing Old Wounds

Most people don't associate emotional healing and forgiveness with attaining wealth. But they should. As the aphorism goes, "Holding a grudge is like drinking poison and hoping the other person dies."

Any emotional wounds that might interfere with your success must be healed. Consequently, it is worthwhile reconnecting with disgruntled people from your past. There is always a possibility that a healthy relationship can be restored.

As probed in the previous chapter, achievement often hinges upon a strong network of business relationships and friendships and reconnecting with past associates. If you had a disagreement with another person, reflect and examine that discrepancy. Typically such differences are born from frustration. Often a person from your past can be helpful for your current quest, and reliable people and resources are so very hard to find. It's not worth jeopardizing your future journey over a past issue. So clear the air with former displeased colleagues and communicate by calling or sending a social media message.

In most cases, old wounds can be easily healed. Generally, eight out of ten disagreements have been forgotten long ago. Oftentimes, the relationship the second time around is much stronger. Trust is earned and with old friends, even ones with incongruities, you will frequently find an enduring bond of loyalty. Time does not erode legitimate trust, but you have to be more proactive than merely leaving your door open. You must take that leap of faith when restoring old acquaintances.

It is always best to be upfront and specifically inform the other person why you are contacting them. Perhaps you are seeking new opportunities or raising money for an imminent venture. Do not prevaricate and prattle nonsense about your concern for the individual's welfare and family. Be professional and respectful, after all, time is valuable. The prior collaborators who are energized by hearing from you make the effort worthwhile.

Naturally, some people will not be receptive and not every broken relationship can be mended. Toxic people must be avoided. Nonetheless, I believe in forgiving, so at least once per week reach out to a long-lost ally and make an attempt to rekindle your affiliation.

治愈旧伤

许多人都不会把情感治疗和宽仁之心，与获得财富联系到一起。但是确实应该联系起来，就像格言里说的：“心怀怨恨就像一边喝着毒药，一边期待着另一个人的死亡。”

任何可能会干扰你成功的情感创伤都必须治愈，因此，重新联系以前和你有旧怨的人是非常必要的，总会有重新恢复健康关系的可能性。

正如我们上一章所探索的，成就取决于业务关系、友谊和过去同伴，这一强大的关系网络。如果你曾经和那些人不和，反省并检查那个矛盾，通常这种分歧都是源于失败。你以前的朋友很可能对你现在的问题有所帮助，而且可信赖的人和资源都非常难找。因为过去的问题而危害你未来的旅程就不值了，所以打个电话或发个信息联系他们，和以前有过不和的同事消除误会。

大部分情况下，旧伤都容易治愈，通常 80% 的分歧早都已经被忘掉了。常常第二次的友谊会更牢固。从老友那里赢得了信任，即使是有过不和的老友，你总会发现紧密联系的忠诚。时间不会腐蚀真正的信任，但你不要仅仅敞开大门，还要积极主动一些。在重拾旧谊的时候，你必须放手一搏。

最好事先并且明确地告诉对方，你想联系他们的目的。也许你正寻求新的机会或为一个新项目筹集资金，千万别闪烁其词、废话连篇，光说那些你对他个人幸福和他家庭的关心等没用的话。要专业并恭敬，毕竟时间宝贵，以前的合作者因听到你的消息而欢欣鼓舞，会让你的努力没有白费。

理所当然的，有些人不会那么容易接纳别人，也并不是每一个破碎的友谊都可以修补完好。要远离恶毒之人。尽管如此，我仍相信宽容之心，所以至少每周一次，联系一个失散多年的同伴，并想办法重新点亮你们的友谊之光。

Communication Skills

Prominent investors are generally excellent communicators. Honing your communication skills takes precedence in facilitating relationships and clarifying investment decisions.

Always communicate straight forwardly. If there's a problem, I want investors to know early on. If there is good news, I want to share that as well. Never exaggerate the facts, as so many investors do, because that only leads to tribulations.

Send out updates on a regular basis, not just when there is an event. Investors love being informed even if there is no new intelligence. We want our financial partners to feel confident about being in the loop at all times just like we expect quarterly reports for our investments. Communication is another way to assure everyone that the company is committed to their goals. However, all announcements should only be done through official channels to avoid the spreading of misinformation.

Part of being a great communicator is being able to definitively say "Yes" or "No." Many people have trouble making decisions. Sure, you may not want to hurt someone's feelings by rushing to a conclusion, so diplomacy and sensitivity must be considered.

The ability to make a positive or negative verdict is crucial when investing.Never allow yourself to be talked into making a poor investment. Sometimes the answer must be "No" when everyone else is saying "Yes."

This sounds simple, but there are countless variables that can make decisions difficult. For example, I never want to be accused of an inside deal for a friend. A friend's venture may get priority, but it will also receive even more scrutiny than others, and I will only invest if it passes our due diligence and evaluation process.

Also, I want to be able to impart solid reasons why we choose not to invest in a friend and why we will or won't help them find another possible financier. Furthermore, I always notify the rejected people as soon as possible.

沟通的技巧

杰出的投资者通常都是卓越的沟通者。磨炼你的沟通技巧，可以使你在促进人际关系和明晰投资决策时，占得先机。

在与人沟通时要直截了当地说出来，如果有什么问题，我愿意投资者从一开始就知道，如果有什么好消息，我也愿意一早分享。不要像许多投资者那样夸大事实，因为这样只会带来苦难。

定期发出最新动态，不要非等到出现事故的时候再说，即使没有新消息，投资者也希望知道进展。我们想让我们的金融合作伙伴，因为置身其中而感到自信，就像我们投资的时候希望得到季度报告一样。沟通是另一种方法，可以向所有人保证，公司正致力于他们的目标。然而，所有的公告都只能通过官方渠道发布，以防错误信息的传播。

作为一个优秀沟通者的一部分就是能果断地说“行”或“不行”。许多人都难以决断。确实，你可能不想由于草率的决定而伤害某人的感情，所以交际手段和敏感程度都是必须加以考虑的。

在投资的时候，做出肯定的或否定的结论，这种能力至关重要。永远不要让他人说服你去做糟糕的投资，有时候，当其他人都说“行”的时候，你也必须说“不行”。

这个听着简单，但是现实中有数不清的变量，使你难下决断。例如，我从来不愿意为了朋友进行内部交易而被指责，朋友的项目可以优先考虑，但也会比别人接受更多的审查，而且我也只有在其通过了我们的尽职调查和评估过程后，才会为他们投资。

而且，我希望能够告诉他们确凿的理由，为什么我们不选择为一个朋友投资，以及为什么我们会或不会帮他们找其他可能的投资人。此外，我总是尽快告知那些被我们拒绝的人。

At Checkmate Investing, we might say "No" for now, but recommend returning later when the project is further developed. Perhaps an element is lacking and with time the investment may be more attractive. On many occasions, after second review, we do invest. Always persevere, improve on your product or service, and revisit financiers who showed initial interest. We believe in evaluating the same opportunity multiple times as it matures.

We encourage all potential entrepreneurs to talk with other funders, not just us. We never want to be responsible for holding someone up and having them miss another source. Fund raisers seek us out because we are more than the traditional investment group and can also add value to their company.

On opportunities we turned down that later became successful, we examine what we missed and why we passed on the proposition in order to improve our investment process. This type of appraisal helps us become even better investors. I would always rather miss a good prospect than make a losing investment. Losses are not easy to recover from, so be conservative and never invest unless you are convinced. New opportunities always pop up.

One communication trait I learned from my mother was repetition. She used to drive me crazy by constantly repeating herself at least three times, telling me the same message a little different each time. Now I have that same trait and can proudly admit this attribute is accountable for much of my success. People are not always listening the first time they are told something. How often do you hear, "you told me that before?" Explicit communication cannot be repeated enough in the world of investing.

No matter how close you listen, sometimes you will misunderstand or misinterpret what is being conveyed. Additionally, there are too many distractions today with Smart Phones and other gadgets, so listening can be an exigent task. Occasionally, people get annoyed with me repeating myself, but I am never offended by this complaint since it confirms that I am being heard and understood. Think about it, the basis of the advertising world is to repeat the message over and over again so eventually everyone hears it. The investing world is no different.

在“将军投资”，我们也许现在说“不行”，然而随着项目进一步发展，之后我们又建议他们回来，也许先是缺乏某一元素，而随时间推移变得更有吸引力了。在许多情况下，二次复查后，我们又决定投资了。一定要坚持这一点，改进你们的产品或服务，再次拜访那些最开始就对你们有兴趣的投资人。我们相信，随着它的成熟，要多次评估同一项目。

我们鼓励所有想筹资的企业家，不要只与我们洽谈，也和其他资助者谈谈，我们从来不愿承担垄断别人、让其失去其他资源的责任。筹资者寻求我们，是因为我们不仅只是传统的投资团队，我们还可以让他们的公司增值。

有的投资项目，我们拒绝了，但是后来他们成功了，要检查我们错过了什么，以及我们为什么不做这一项目，以此来改进我们的投资程序。这种评估能帮我们成为更好的投资者。我宁愿错过一个好的项目，也不愿做一笔糟的投资。损失不容易弥补，所以还是要保守一些，除非你被说服了，否则不要投资。新的机会总是会随时出现。

有一个沟通的特点是我从母亲那里学来的，那就是重复。她常常不断重复至少三遍，简直把我逼疯，同一个消息每次说的稍有不同而已。现在我也拥有这一特点，而且能自豪的承认，我的许多成功都要归功于这一特性。当你第一次说什么的时候，人们一般不会去听，你听到过多少回“你之前告诉过我吗？”在投资领域，详尽的沟通重复多少遍都不够。

不管你听地多仔细，有时你也会误解或曲解别人要表达的东西。此外，现今时代智能手机和其他小应用在手，分心的东西太多，倾听可能成了苛求的任务。有时候，我总是重复要说的话，很烦人，但当我听到他们抱怨时，从来不觉得冒犯，因为这证明他们听到我说什么了，并且听明白了。想想看，广告界的基础就在于不断重复信息，这样最终每个人都听到了，投资界也一样。

When a point of discussion is especially important, I will also send an email or phone message repeating what I said orally. Conversely, when I do not understand what is being said, I will ask the speaker to repeat it until I fully comprehend the connotation. Take the time to develop these communication skills and watch your investment results improve.

当讨论的一个要点特别重要时，我也会发电子邮件或短信息，重复一下我口头说的话，相反的，当我不明白别人所说话语时，我会让此人重复一遍，直到我完全理解其内涵。多花时间训练这种沟通技巧，守候自己投资效益的提高。

Business Instincts

Many investment counselors ignore the concept of instinct. In my opinion this is a costly mistake.Of course, always perform vigorous due diligence before finalizing any investment decision. But also develop the power of your sixth sense in order to make the best conclusions.

People use different words to describe the same thing. First, there is the analytical part of the brain. But human beings also have instincts, sometimes called intuition or gut feelings. In the context of investing, it is referred to as business instincts or business intuition.

Some scholars believe intuition is merely the ability to gain a wider understanding by accessing knowledge and experience locked away in our subconscious minds.

Others believe intuition is the ability to gain a different perspective of the same information. We have portions of our brain that function quantitatively. But there are also sections that process qualitatively.

Most people believe our instincts are part of a survival mechanism. Like animals, our brains are wired to quickly automate safe responses to life threatening situations. It's as if there is no time to think, just react. The impetus is not from our brain, but our body or gut feelings.

In the end, it doesn't matter how instinct works, just that it does. We must recognize the relevance of our instincts in determining the merits of an investment.

It takes a conscious effort to learn to trust your instincts to assure a prosperous future. Keep a journal and write down what logic tells you, then what instinct tells you. You'll see that instincts provide a different angle on evaluating the investment. How many people have buyer's remorse and complain: "I had a gut feeling that I shouldn't buy the property!"

There are also courses and books that describe how to develop and get in touch with your intuition. While instinct cannot be learned, as it is already there, additional knowledge will help you trust this valuable tool.

商业本能

许多投资顾问忽视直觉的概念，在我看来，这是一个极大的错误。当然，在最后定论之前，一定要有力地执行尽职调查，但是为了做出最好的决定，也可以开发你的第六感觉。

人们在描述同一件事情的时候，会用不同的词。首先，在人的大脑中有一个分析的部分，但是人类也有本能，有时称作直觉或直感。在投资的背景下，是指商业本能或商业直觉。

一些学者相信直觉仅仅是为了获得更广泛的理解的能力而已，而这一能力是通过获取贮存在潜意识中的知识和经验实现的。

其次，一些人认为直觉是对于同一信息，获得不同观点的能力。我们的大脑中有一个部分是负责处理信息的数量方面，但还有另一部分，是负责处理信息的质量方面。

许多人相信我们的本能是生存机制的一部分，就像动物一样，在有生命危险的情况下，我们的大脑连接着快速自动安全反应，就像是根本没时间思考，直接反应，这种动力不是来源于大脑，而是身体或直觉。

最后，本能如何运作并不重要，但它确实起作用了，我们必须认识到，本能与决定是否值得投资的关联性。

需要有意识地努力，了解并信任你的本能，它能给你一个繁荣的未来。写一个日志并记下来，看看从逻辑角度你了解到了什么，再看看本能又告诉你什么，你会发现，在评估投资上，本能提供了一个不同的角度。有多少人听到过买家的懊悔和抱怨："我的直觉告诉过我，当时就不该买这个财产！"

也有一些课程或书本讲解怎样开发和运用你的直觉，然而本能不是学会的，而是本身固有的，额外的知识可以帮助你信赖这一有价值的工具。

No matter how much research and due diligence is put into appraising an investment, I still draw on instinct as the final decision maker. In almost every deal I have been correct. Trust your instincts.

评估一项投资时，无论做多少研究或尽职调查，我依然利用本能作为最后决策的制定者，几乎在每次交易中，我都是正确的，所以要信任本能。

Mentors

I advise experienced and inexperienced people to find a mentor to assist in your quest for success. A mentor can be anyone who knows the ropes, will share relevant advice, and can introduce you to influential contacts.

Mentors are indispensable and do not have to be retired, gray-haired men. To that point, an older, experienced person can benefit from a younger mentor. The elderly person may have tried to launch a product in the past that was not quite ready for the consumer market and failed. The younger mentor can show why it might be time to try again. Without the current input, the venerable person might have completely dropped the idea because it was previously rejected.

Corporate executives can also benefit from a mentor. By having a trusted confidant, who is not part of the company, the decision-maker can discuss a plethora of ideas with this independent counselor and arrive at more intelligent decisions.

Sometimes executives take on too much responsibility and don't have a trusted team member who will offer autonomous opinions. CEO's usually have committees, but due to office politics, they might not listen closely to such groups. In many companies, subordinates are always lurking who want to take over the boss' job, so the executive might be reluctant to share his intimate objectives with potential rivals. In some ways this is healthy, as you want ambitious people, but normally this is more harmful than good.

I believe in conferring with trustworthy associates on all investments. But I always employ external mentors to add unbiased viewpoints along with years of wisdom that induce me to consider other factors before moving forward. With this approach, I often regain perspective on the matter at hand.

Finding the right mentor only requires the temerity to ask. You do not have to know the person ahead of time, just research who you admire and respect, then reach out to him/her. If you are turned down, don't be offended just seek someone else.

导 师

我建议不管是有经验的还是没经验的人，都要找一个导师，帮助你去追求成功。不管是谁，只要懂行都可以成为你的导师，可以和你分享相关的建议，也能把你推荐给有影响力的人。

导师是必不可少的，不必非是退休的、白头发的老年人。在这一点上，一个年长的人、有经验的人，反而能从较年轻的导师那里受益。年长者过去可能在消费市场不太成熟的时候，曾经投放过一种产品，但失败了。而年轻导师可以说明为什么现在有可能是再试一次的最好时机。没有当前的建议，年长者可能会因为以前被拒过，而完全放弃这一想法。

企业高管也能从导师那里受益，决策者可以和不在同一公司，可信赖的知己，讨论许多想法，通过这个独立顾问，能够作出更智慧的决断。

有时候高管们承担太多责任，而没有一个可信赖、能提供独立观点的团队成员。首席执行官通常会有委员会，但是由于办公室政治，他们可能不会仔细倾听这些团体的意见。在许多公司内部，下属总是觊觎接手老板的工作，所以高管可能不愿和潜在的对手分享他的私密目的。在某种程度上，这是有益的，因为你想要有抱负的人，但是通常是弊大于利。

我相信可以和值得信赖的同伴协商所有的投资，但是我总会雇用外部的导师，来形成公正的观点，随同他们多年的智慧，可以引导我考虑其他因素后再继续前进，利用这一方法，我常常能重新审视手头事情。

找到一个合适的导师只需要去请求的勇气，你没必要之前就认识其人，研究你欣赏和敬重谁，然后直接去联系此人。如果你被他们拒绝，也别生气，可以再找别人。

Remember, you are asking very successful people to help you. Sometimes these people genuinely do not have the spare time and will balk. Thank them, as they will likely remember your audacious admiration and might even help you at a later date.

Where do you find a mentor? I advise asking someone who is reliable that you have known for a long time. Candidates can be a retired person from your industry or a young person with fresh ideas. Most former executives are bored when they retire and relish the opportunity to have purpose again. I love having retired CEO's as friends and mentors as they give worthy advice, precious insights, and insider skills that can only be learned after decades of experience.

There is no rule stipulating that you are only allowed one mentor. Why not enlist multiple trustworthy sounding boards? And always treat a mentor with respect, be grateful for their advice, and remain gracious.

记住，如果你正寻求特别成功的人来帮助你，有时这些人确实没有空闲时间，因而会推诿，要谢谢他们，因为他们很可能会记住你出于敬佩的胆大行为，甚至可能在之后的日子里帮到你。

应该去哪里寻找导师呢？我建议去找那些可以信赖、相识长久之人。候选人可以是你们行业的退休人员，或者有新鲜理念的年轻人。多数以前的高管退休后很无趣，盼望着有机会能重出江湖。我喜欢和退休的首席执行官做朋友，或请他们当导师，因为他们会给出有价值的建议、宝贵的见解和内行人的技巧，而这些只能从几十年的经验中学到。

没有规定限制你只能有一个导师，为什么不多招纳几个可信赖的参谋？要始终尊敬导师，感恩他们的建议，并对他们保持亲切的态度。

Good Health and a Positive Attitude

It is difficult to formulate meritorious investment decisions if your physical being is not sound or your mental attitude is deficient. Your body and mind must be in sync to perform at a high level.

I do not believe that you must workout two hours a day and never drink alcohol, eat rich food, or party. If you subscribe to that sort of spartan health regime, without any fun or joy, hats off to you. But most people can't maintain such a regimented lifestyle.

I believe in healthy moderation. It is more realistic to adhere to a daily physical routine that is sustainable, not overwhelming. For example, jogging, walking, swimming, and planking allow you to simultaneously exercise while reflecting on business transactions.

Investing in yourself begins with a candid assessment of your health. How do you really feel? What was the result of your last medical exam?What needs to alter in your physical condition for you to be successful? Everyone is different.

Science has unequivocally proven that everybody must get enough sleep to have a clear mind. We all have different sleep timetables, so determine how many hours a day you require. Do everything you can to optimize the quality of your sleep.

A nutritious diet will improve your physical and mental well-being. You will have more energy and think more clearly. Even modest changes in your diet can have health benefits.

Doctors and dieticians recommend eating more fruits and vegetables, especially green, yellow, and orange varieties. Refrain from digesting starchy vegetables, processed food, and greasy junk food. Also renounce white flour and white sugar. You don't have to retain a "perfect" diet, but the above suggestions will indubitably improve your health.

People respond to specific diets differently, so establish one that is best suited to your metabolism. You may want to keep a journal of what you eat for a couple of months, along with tracking your weight to observe how your body and mind are reacting to your consumption.

健康的身体和积极的态度

如果你的身体状况不好，或你的精神状态欠佳，就很难制定有价值的投资决策。你必须同时保持身心健康，才能发挥最佳水准。

我不认为你必须每天锻炼两个小时，也不能喝酒、吃油腻食品或参加派对。如果你真愿意克制自己过那种清苦的健康生活，没有任何乐趣和快乐，那我向你致敬。但是大多数人不能坚持这种受约束的生活方式。

我认可适当的健康方式。坚持每天按时锻炼身体，会更实际一些，可以接受而不太过分。例如，慢跑、步行、游泳和平板支撑，使你在锻炼身体的同时还能思考商业交易。

自我投资要从公正的评估自己的健康状况开始，你感觉如何？你上次体检结果怎样？在通往成功的道路上，你需要怎样改变身体状况去适应？每个人都有所不同。

科学已经明确证明，每个人必须睡眠充足才能有清醒的头脑。我们都有自己的睡眠时间表，所以确定你自己每天需要睡多久。一定要想尽任何办法优化你的睡眠质量。

营养配餐可以促进你的身心健康，你会精力更旺盛，思路更清晰。即使只是稍微调整一下你的食谱，也能有利于健康。

医生和营养师建议吃更多的水果和蔬菜，尤其绿色、黄色和橙色类别的，少吃淀粉类的蔬菜、加工食品和油腻的垃圾食品，最好也不要吃面粉和白糖，你不必执意于一份“完美”的食谱，但是上面的建议无疑会改善你的健康。

人们对特定的饮食反应不一，所以制定一份适合你自己新陈代谢的食谱，你可以记个日志，按一种习惯吃几个月之后，看看体重怎样，以及身心的反应如何。

Have realistic goals about your weight. In a perfect world, everyone would be at their ideal poundage all the time. Unfortunately that is not the case, and most people's weight fluctuates, especially during the holidays or while on vacation. Those individuals with a slow metabolism will never look like a fashion model without endlessly starving themselves. Don't beat yourself up if you are a few pounds overweight. You must love and accept yourself.

For an investor, there are very practical reasons to keeping your weight in check. If your body mass gets too heavy, you are more likely to feel sluggish and have less physical and mental energy which will directly affect your capacity to make clear, focused judgments.

This brings me to attitude, in particular anger management. When younger, I was quick to lose my temper until I saw another person, who I greatly respected, lose his temper and go ballistic. I forever lost respect for him and scorned such inappropriate behavior. I then reflected on my anger, which was even worse at times, and decided never to lose my cool again. This conscious change in attitude took much effort and discipline.

I dug deeper into my psyche and concluded that my pessimistic thoughts or hurtful words made me angry and irritable. For example, I thought a hotel clerk had purposely lost my reservation which upset me to the point of retaliation. But I caught myself and realized I was the one responsible for allowing anger to creep into my mind. Our thoughts drive our reactions, so maintain a positive attitude and deal with matters in an intelligent way. That does not mean you should push the situation aside, just do not lose your temper.

Exercise is also an antidote for anger because it gives you a natural outlet for venting. Rigorously working out redirects your mind from antagonism to the physical task at hand and displaces the negative thoughts. If you feel pessimism littering your psyche and are not in a location for an exhaustive workout, then take a walk, meditate, count to 100, etc. There are plenty of means to combat anger and stay focused on your career.

Your attitude can either destroy you or serve as a powerful tool for finding success. For instance, most of us are in constant mental chatter, talking to ourselves all day long. Unfortunately, this "self talk" is usually negative, so make a concerted effort to practice positive self talk which will bring greater rewards. I also read books on the power of an optimistic attitude. As an investor, I advise you to do likewise.

对你自己的体重要有一个现实的目标。在完美世界里，每个人都会永远保持自己的身材，可惜现实并非如此，许多人的体重都会起伏不定，尤其在节假日或度假期间，那些新陈代谢缓慢之人，如果不是天天节食，永远不会像时装模特那样苗条。就算你有点胖，也别折磨自己，你必须喜爱和接受自己。

对于一个投资者而言，控制住自己的体重有着非常实际的意义。如果你过于肥胖，就有可能感觉行动迟缓，体力和精力不足，会直接影响你清晰地作出重要判断的能力。

这让我想到了态度的问题，尤其是克制自己的脾气。当我年轻的时候，特别容易发脾气，直到我看到自己特别敬重的一个人，他乱发脾气直到暴怒，我从此不再敬重他，而且看不起这种不恰当的行为。我然后反省自己，有时情况甚至更糟，因而决定以后绝不再失去冷静。这种态度上有意识的转变，需要付出很多的努力和自律。

我挖掘自己的灵魂深处，发现是我的悲观想法或伤人的话语，令我生气发怒的。例如，我认为酒店服务员故意弄丢我的预订，这让我很生气，并有了报复心理，但是我发现并认识到，其实都怪我自己，才会让怒火在心中蔓延。我们的想法决定了我们的反应，所以要保持积极的态度，以聪明的方法去处理事情。这不是说你就对事情听之任之了，只是你别发脾气就好。

锻炼身体也是平息怒气的解药，因为它能让你将怒火自然地排放出去。严苛的体能锻炼可以使你把与人争执的怒火，转换成眼前的身体训练，因而取代负面想法。如果你觉得内心充满了悲观情绪，又处于不方便体能锻炼的地方，那就考虑散散步、冥想、数数等方法。有好多办法能平息怒火，转而专注于自己的事业。

在寻求成功的道路上，你的态度既可以摧毁你，也可以成为一个强大的工具帮助你。比如，我们当中大多数人都常常是精神上的话唠，一天到晚自言自语。可惜这种“自我谈话”通常是负面的，所以要努力训练正能量的自我谈话，这会给你带来极大的回报。我也会读一些富有乐观态度的书籍，作为投资者，我建议你也这样做。

Throughout the day, use self talk as your own personal GPS system by reinforcing:

• I am a likeable person.

• I am perceived as sophisticated, intelligent, and humble.

• I am liked and trusted because I am good at my profession.

• I am respected by others because I respect them.

• I am a success because I care about other people.

• I am a good speaker because I am a good listener and take the time to learn a subject.

• I know there is always more to learn.

• I make prudent decisions because I take the time to understand the situation.

• I always trust my instincts.

• I always keep my cool and develop a winning solution.

• I have common sense.

• I have loyal friends because I am loyal.

• I am good at making money because I am always in touch with my environment and the details of the opportunity.

Make self talk even more powerful by writing it down and reciting out loud at least once each day. Regardless of your age, healthy self talk should be part of everyone's daily life.

Self talk can also be used to increase the sense of peace and calm in your life, so constantly remind yourself:

• I am at peace within myself.

• I will always keep calm, regardless of external circumstances. If I am late due to traffic, I will maintain my cool and still achieve my goal.

• I know how to relax and enjoy life in my free time.

• I am a good spouse and take the time to make my partner feel special every day.

通过加强以下方面，全天候的，用自我谈话作为你的个人定位系统：

- 我是一个和蔼可亲的人。
- 我在别人眼中，是一个富有经验、智慧并且谦逊的人。
- 因为我在自己的专业领域中，能力很强，所以我受人爱戴和信任。
- 因为我尊敬别人，所以别人也尊敬我。
- 因为我在意他人，所以我是成功的人。
- 因为我善于聆听，所以我善于表达，而且我会花时间去学一门知识。
- 我知道总是有许多东西要学。
- 我要谨慎地做决定，因为我要花时间了解情况。
- 我始终信任我的本能。
- 我要时刻保持冷静，找到最优解决方案。
- 我有基本常识。
- 因为我忠诚，所以我也拥有忠诚的朋友。
- 我很会赚钱，因为我时刻与周围保持联系并关注细节。

每天至少一次，通过把自我谈话记录下来并大声背诵出来，以加强其作用。不要在意你的年龄，健康的自我谈话应该是每个人日常生活的一部分。

自我谈话还能使你在生活中更加平和、安静，所以要不断提醒自己如下方面：

- 我内心很平和。
- 不管外界环境怎样，我要时刻保持平静，即使由于交通堵塞而来晚了，我也要保持冷静，去实现自己的目标。
- 在闲暇的时候，我知道怎么放松自己，享受生活。
- 我是一个好的伴侣，会花时间让我的同伴感到每天都是特别的日子。

- I take time to spend time with my family.
- I notice and comment on small things.
- I take the time to listen instead of always talking.

Relaxation is imperative for mental and physical health. This can include soaking in a bathtub or hot tub, attending a movie, concert, or ballgame, taking a leisurely walk, working on a hobby, spending a few moments in silence or meditating. Set a routine that you enjoy and can do on a regular basis. Even a few minutes a day of a relaxation can improve the quality of your life.

- 我会花时间陪伴家人。

- 我会注意并评论小的事情。

- 我会花时间聆听而不是自己唠叨不停。

放松自己，对身心健康是非常必要的。包括泡个热水澡、看电影、听音乐会、打棒球、悠闲地散步、从事业余爱好、安静一会儿或冥想，这些都可以。安排一个日程，做一些自己喜欢的，且天天都能做的事，放松自己，即使是每天只花几分钟，也能改善你的生活质量。

CHAPTER 3
Basic Business Operations

There are basic fundamentals that are indispensable in protecting and operating a successful business. Different types of insurance, complicated contracts, state and federal taxes are some of the external concerns. Assembling your executive team, determining their wages and salaries, payroll procedures, and other internal issues must be smoothly coordinated. Each of these topics can and should be further researched in the future when they become pertinent to your company or investment.

第三章
基本业务操作

在保障和运作一个成功企业时，有一些基本原理必不可少。不同种类的保险，复杂难懂的合同、州税和联邦税，这些只不过是一些表面上需要注意的事情。招募你的执行团队，制订他们的工资薪金、工资单规程，和一些其他内部问题也必须协调一致。将来当这些话题与你的公司或者是投资项目相关时，都可以也应当深入研究。

Crypto Currencies / Blockchain

Technologies are now so advanced that "Crypto Currencies" have come into existence. Since the inception of BitCoin in 2009, currently there are over 1100 cryptocurrencies being exchanged and in the future there will be new ones and some of the existing ones will fail. There will be scandals, fraud, litigation and new legislation but they will find a way survive and become an integral part of monetary exchange, futures trading and the financial system. We know technology is why crypto currencies exist but really there are other reasons. Let us look at the landscape and review a little history to understand the reason crypto currencies came into being.

Fundamentally, cryptocurrencies exist to offer a peer-to-peer transaction based on an open-source code. Open-source code means it is viewable by anyone who wants to see it. The peer-to-peer aspect of cryptocurrency means that third parties can be removed from core monetary transactions and offers greater financial freedom. It also places cryptocurrency assets technically beyond current limits of regulation and possible confiscation as the verification of funds, transfer of funds and generation of units operate independently from any central bank. Unlike early digital currencies in the 1990s that relied upon a "Trusted Third Party" approach, cryptocurrencies today have no centralized controlling authority. In addition, cryptocurrency mining is deployed to validate the cryptography behind each transaction and record fully confirmed transactions in the distributed public ledger known as "Blockchain". The fundamental value behind cryptocurrency lies in the Blockchain's existence and its extraordinary benefit associated with preservation of transactional integrity. The more of a cryptocurrency is mined, the more complex the cryptographic puzzles become and this contributes to an upper limitation on the total volume of cryptographic coin that can be produced, thereby increasing scarcity value of the coin.

加密货币 / 区块链

如今科技高度发达，加密货币已经出现。自从 2009 年比特币首次引入，目前已经有超过 1100 种加密数字货币正在流通，并且将来还会有一些新的种类出现，而原有的一些则可能会衰退。这其中会伴随着丑闻、诈骗、诉讼和新的立法，但是它们会找到生存下去的方法，并且会成为货币交易、期货贸易以及金融系统不可或缺的一部分。我们明白加密货币是依靠技术而存在的，但事实上其中还有其他的因素。让我们来看看它的情况并回顾其历史，以此了解加密货币出现的原因。

从根本上讲，基于开源代码的加密数字货币，提供了点对点交易的可能。开源代码的意思是，任何人想看都能看到。加密数字货币中的点对点方面意味着，可以移除核心货币交易中的第三方，并且提供更大的金融自由度。这同时也让加密数字货币资产，处于在技术上超越了当前管理限制，而不会被没收的位置，因为资金核实、资金转移以及虚拟货币的产生，这些操作是独立于任何中央银行的。不同于早期 20 世纪 90 年代的数字货币，需要依赖“可靠的第三方”的方法，今天的加密数字货币没有权威的中央控制机构。另外，加密数字货币挖矿已经开展起来，去验证每一次交易背后密码学的有效解，并且将完全确认的交易，记录在分布式的公共总账，我们称为“区块链”中。加密数字货币的基本价值，就在于“区块链”的存在，并且其极大的利益与保护交易的完整性紧密相连。越多的加密数字货币被开采出来，密码学难题就会越复杂，然而这会导致加密数字货币产生的总量提升受限，因此增加其稀缺价值。

At a macroeconomic level, Cryptocurrency has come into existence with as a response to national policies of various countries in Asia and North America, including China. The Chinese economy has grown at an unprecedented pace since early 2000. Great wealth has been created in China. China operates under a closed currency policy which restricts the free movement of money. Due to this closed currency policy it is hard to get money out of China. This has led to crypto currencies being a popular alternative within China. People use these Crypto currencies to move wealth from China to other countries. The Chinese closed currency policy has been a good policy internally for many important state objectives. However, these reasons would comprise an entire book so we will not get deep into this subject. Just let it be known that the closed currency policy of China of one of the reasons that Crypto currencies exist.

More interesting is the American side of why crypto currencies have taken off and become popular. Let's look at some American history to understand this comment. Many people blame problems in America for under-regulation. Sometimes this has been the case often creating abuse and improper behavior. However, the opposite has also been a problem. Too often over-regulation has created a disastrous result. There are so many examples but I will briefly discuss only two of these.

The first example is prohibition which was made a law and ratified on January 29, 1919. Prohibition in the United States was a complete disaster. The ratification of the 18th Amendment to the U.S.A Constitution which banned the manufacture, transportation and sale of intoxicating liquors was the beginning of a black mark in American history.

Prohibition was the result of a widespread temperance movement during the first decade of the 20th century in America. Prohibition proved to be difficult to enforce as many people opposed this law. Companion legislation known as the Volstead Act was meant to help with the enforcement of prohibition but it failed miserably. The increase of the illegal production and sale of liquor "bootlegging", the proliferation of illegal drinking spots and the rise in crime was unprecedented. Gangsters that never existed before were commonplace during prohibition. People like Al Capone came into prominence due to prohibition. Gangsters were glamorized and even idolized by the public. Violent crimes and killing sprees were common in many USA cities like Chicago. By the end of the 1920's people were openly revolting against prohibition. In early 1933, Congress adopted a resolution proposing a 21st Amendment to the Constitution that would repeal the 18th amendment. The 21st amendment was ratified by the end of that year, bringing the end to prohibition.

在宏观经济的层面上，加密数字货币的出现，是对多个亚洲和北美等国国家政策的一种回应，其中自然也包括中国。自2000年年初以来，中国的经济正在以史无前例的速度发展。并且创造了大量的财富，而中国采用了封闭式货币政策，来限制资金的自由流通。正因为这个封闭式货币政策，导致中国的资金很难外流，致使加密数字货币这种方式在中国流行，人们运用加密数字货币将财富从中国转移到其他国家。中国的这一封闭式货币政策，对于实现许多国内的重要目标来说，是一个好政策，而其中缘由则需要一整本书来详说，所以在此我们不再深入探讨。只需要知道，中国的封闭式货币政策，是导致加密数字货币出现的众多因素之一。

更有趣的是，为什么加密数字货币能在美国腾飞并流行起来。让我们回顾一下美国的历史来理解个中缘由。很多人把问题归结于美国的监管不足，有些时候这样做，确实会产生滥用和不当的行为，然而与之相反，也一样有问题。因为有太多时候，都是由于过度监管，而造成灾难性的结果。这其中有太多的例子，但是我只是简短地讨论其中的两个。

第一个例子，是在1919年1月29日批准并作为法律颁布的《禁酒令》。《禁酒令》在美国简直就是一个彻底的灾难。当时通过的美国第18条宪法修正案，明令禁止制造、运输、销售任何烈酒，这便是美国历史上污点的开始。

《禁酒令》就是20世纪初期第一个十年中，广为流传的戒酒活动的产物。由于很多人反对这一法律，《禁酒令》被证明难以执行。随之颁布的《沃尔斯特法案》（禁酒法案）旨在帮助实施禁酒令，但是它也惨遭失败。非法生产和销售“私酒”的数量激增，快速蔓延的非法饮酒据点和直线上升的犯罪率都是史无前例的。以前从来没有过的街头暴徒，在《禁酒令》期间也变得司空见惯了。像艾尔·卡彭（Al Capone）这样的人因为禁酒而出名。暴徒被美化了，甚至被当时的公众所崇拜。暴力犯罪和屠杀事件在芝加哥等很多美国城市都很常见。在20世纪20年代末期，人们开始公开反对《禁酒令》。1933年年初，国会通过了一项决议，提议通过宪法第二十一条修正案，并废除第十八条修正案。第二十一条修正案在当年年底得到批准通过，《禁酒令》终于结束了。

The USA Patriot Act is law passed after the September 11, 2001 terrorist attacks. It was reactionary to the attacks of 9/11 and not well thought out. Its goals were to strengthen domestic security by identifying and stopping terrorists. The passing and subsequent renewal of the Patriot Act has been extremely controversial. Although the early existence of the Patriot Act scored victories against then-known terrorist networks, since that time, the terror networks have adapted to the legislation and its effectiveness has been greatly diminished. Even worse, the Patriot Act has made it very hard for Americans to do simple things like open bank accounts overseas. Legitimate business is always questioned thereby causing delays or stoppage. Challenges and questions are detrimental to all Americans who wish to move money they have legally earned. Everyone is treated as suspect and assumed to be a criminal when they purchase things, deposit money or move funds.

Crypto currencies owe much of their existence and success to The Patriot Act. Instead of stopping terrorism and illegal movement of money The Patriot Act has caused currencies like Bitcoin to exist and thrive. Crypto currencies are now used in the illegal drug industry, arms industry, moneylaundering and terrorism movements, thereby propelling the illegal activities into a realm that is not regulated by any central bank. Everyday new crypto currencies are being started. Prohibition was easy to fix as it only had to be repelled. However, the crime families that came into existence as a result of prohibition are still operating. The Patriot Act is a true Pandora's box and probably will never be fixed. It appears crypto currencies are here to stay and with that once again over regulation has created a nightmare not just for USA citizens but people everywhere in the world.

The moral of the story is that regulations are needed but over-regulation can be a fertile ground for crime and the disaster of unintended consequences. The blockchain aspect of cryptocurrencies ultimately will aid regulators and justify the existence of such currencies but the range of governments responding either harshly or with tolerance to cryptocurrencies ensures that the cryptocurrency market will remain volatile and unstable for some period of time before its blockchain benefits ultimate establish a stable equilibrium for hopefully lightly regulated cryptocurrency existence.

2001 年 9 月 11 日恐怖袭击后，美国通过了《爱国者法案》。颁布这项法案本来是为了反对“9 · 11”恐怖袭击，然而并没有经过深思熟虑。其目的是通过识别和阻止恐怖分子，来加强国内的安全。《爱国者法案》通过后，以及之后的补充法案，一直备受争议。虽然早期《爱国者法案》的存在，对当时已知的恐怖主义网络取得了胜利，但从那时起，恐怖网络已经适应了这项立法，使其效力大大削弱。更糟的是，《爱国者法案》让美国人在面对一些简单的事情时，也变得困难重重，比如在海外开设一个银行账户。合法的企业总是受到质疑，从而导致延误或停工。这对所有美国人来说都是极其不利的，因为只要他们想挪动自己的合法收入时，就会遭受到质疑和询问。当购物的时候，存钱的时候，移动资金的时候，所有人都会被视为犯罪嫌疑人或者假定成罪犯。

加密货币的存在和成功很大程度上归结于《爱国者法案》的存在。《爱国者法案》非但没有阻止恐怖主义和非法资金流动，反而导致了比特币这种货币的存在和繁荣。加密货币现在被用于违禁药品行业、军需工业、洗钱和恐怖主义运动，从而将非法活动推入不受任何中央银行监管的领域。每天都有新的加密货币出现。《禁酒令》很容易修复，因为它只需要被抵制即可。然而，由于《禁酒令》而产生的犯罪家庭仍在运作。《爱国者法案》真是一个潘多拉的宝盒，而且可能永远都不会被修复。看来加密货币会长久存在了，如果再这样过度地监管，会给不仅仅是美国公民而是全世界的人民制造一个噩梦。

这个故事的寓意是，监管是必要的，但过度监管可能是犯罪的沃土，也会出现意想不到的灾难性结果。加密数字货币的区块链方面最终会帮助监管部门，并且证明这种货币的存在，但是在政府的监管范围内，他们对加密数字货币要么采取严厉的方法，要么采取宽容的态度，这就使加密数字货币市场，仍会在一段时间内动荡不安，直到在区块链的作用下，使加密货币有望在一种宽松的监管下存在，而最终建立一个稳定平衡的市场环境。

Insurance

Developing and procuring the proper business insurance is a challenge. There are so many types of plans that must be reviewed before you can decide which is best suited to your company's needs. These include Directors and Officers (D&O), general liability, data breach, workers compensation, errors and omission, property, commercial auto, and more than imaginable.

For example, key man insurance covers a top executive in case of death or other health related reasons that cause termination. Such key man policies are mandatory with technology investments as many times the leader is the whole company. Although there are likely other competent employees, without this one chief person the company will stumble and possibly fail.

Each layer of insurance will protect your investment. We cannot and would not buy insurance for every possible catastrophe, but we definitely require protection against accidents, fire, earthquake, errors and omission, employee accusations, health, various disruptions, and more.

For the novice, it is impossible to identify what policies to buy beyond basic coverage. I recommend hiring an experienced insurance consultant to review your entire business and offer suggestions. Large agencies like Marsh, AON, Arthur J. Gallagher, Jardines are solution based risk management firms and experts in categorizing hazards you may not have considered. They will thoroughly educate you and help establish which insurance options are relevant to your particular company.

You must have insurance that covers legal costs lest your company is ever sued. Policies vary and only cover certain circumstances. For example, intellectual property insurance reduces the financial risk of being sued by other companies for IP infringement.

保　险

开发和购买适当的商业保险是一项挑战。在决定哪一款最适合你公司的需要之前，有很多类型的方案必须进行审查。其中包括董事和高级职员险（董事责任险）、一般责任险、数据外泄险、劳工补偿险、错误和遗漏险（职业责任险）、财产险、商业汽车险，以及超出想象范围的其他保险。

例如，核心人员保险涵盖一名高管，以防由于死亡或其他健康相关原因导致合同终止。这样的核心人员政策在技术投资中是强制性的，因为多数情况下，领导者就代表整个公司。虽然可能有其他有能力的员工，但是没有这个首席人员，公司会踌躇不前或者可能会失败。

每一层保险都会保护你的投资。我们不能也不会为每一场可能发生的灾难购买保险，但我们绝对需要防范事故、火灾、地震、错误和遗漏、员工指控、健康、各种干扰等。

作为新手，很难确定除了基本险以外，还要购买哪一种保险。我建议聘请一位有经验的保险顾问来审查你的整个业务，并提供建议。像 Marsh、AON、Arthur J. Gallagher、Jardines 这样的大型代理机构，都是可以提供解决方案的风险管理公司，而且他们擅长对危险进行分类，而这些危险你可能从来都没有考虑过。他们会对你进行全面的培训，帮助确定哪些保险品种与你的公司有关。

你必须有包含诉讼费的保险，以免你的公司被起诉。保险单千变万化，但只能在特定的情况下管用。例如，知识产权保险只能降低被其他公司起诉侵犯知识产权的财务风险。

Also, obtain multiple quotes to assure you are not overpaying. On each policy, take the time to understand the language, such as knowing the procedure on how to collect. If you have business interruption insurance, you want the ability to file a claim and be paid out quickly. Insurance is expensive, which is another reason to engage a top agency that can help control costs and offer comparison quotes along with their recommendations. The tip is to have a solid insurance program from day one.

Keep in mind, insurance companies are in business to earn money, and they have a tendency to increase premiums aggressively. The only way to guarantee you are not overpaying is to perform a yearly review and have your policies re-quoted from competitors.

此外，获取更多的报价来保证你不会超额支付保险费。对于每一个保险单都应该花一些时间来理解内容，比如要了解理赔的程序。如果你买了业务中断险，你希望知道怎样提出索赔，并迅速收到赔付。保险费是昂贵的，这是另一个要雇用顶级机构参与其中的原因，可以帮助控制成本，提供各报价之间的比较信息，并提供建议。小窍门就是，从第一天开始，就要有一个可靠的保险计划。

记住，保险公司做这门生意就是为了赚钱，而且他们倾向于想方设法地提高保费。唯一能保证你不会超额支付的方法，就是每年进行一次检查，让其他的保险公司对同一保单，也给出报价。

Contracts

When faced with contracts, I advise hiring a specialized attorney. There are too many legal intricacies to represent yourself, including cultural discrepancies. For example, in China binding contracts are nothing more than an initial step or guideline to doing business and far from assurance that trade will actually occur. In the USA, I believe in simple contracts, but often this is not possible due to complexities.

The main purpose of a contract is to define and align the expectations of the various parties. A contract can help avoid misunderstandings and define solutions in case of disputes. Often, two people think they understand each other's motives, but are really far apart. Making and passing out notes after meetings can help avoid confusion. On complicated deals, it might be wise to start with short, non-binding, interim agreements that can be the precursor for the formal binding agreement. As business is discussed and agreed upon, write it down in bullet points where both parties sign off. This way, misunderstandings can be reduced significantly.

On licensing contracts, be careful that the time frame is long enough to protect both parties. It could take longer than anticipated to complete the licensing ramp up, and you will likely spend significant money on the promotional aspects. There are many examples of licenses expiring just when the product begins to show a profit.

On the contrary, I have observed protracted exclusives with no performance clauses. Sometimes the licensee is not pushing the market hard enough which could result in profits being lost. Thus, make sure performance clauses, such as reaching a certain number of sales over a period of time, are embedded into the contract. If the targeted agenda is not met, then the licensor can cancel the contract.

合 同

当面对合同时，我建议聘请一位专业的律师。有很多法律方面的复杂性与你自己有关，包括文化差异。比如，在中国制订合同只不过是一个初步的计划，或者是做生意的一个指导方针，距离确认这笔交易是否会真的发生还相去甚远。在美国，我信任简单的合同，但多数时间因为错综复杂的各种事情，根本不可能。

合同的主要目的是定义和调整各方的期望。合同可以帮助避免误会，并且一旦出现争议时，可以明确解决方案。很多时候两个人自认都很了解彼此的动机，但是事实却并非如此。会议结束后，做笔记并分发笔记可以帮助避免容易混淆的事情发生。在复杂的交易中，最好先从简短、非约束性的临时协议开始，作为正式、具有约束性协议的前身。随着业务的讨论和商定，将其写进要点，让双方签字认可。这种方式，可以大大降低误会的发生。

在许可证合同中，注意它的时间范围是否长到足以保护双方。通常延长许可证会花费比你预期更长的时间，而且很可能在宣传方面上花费很多资金。像某件商品刚开始盈利的时候，但它的许可证到期了，这样的例子数不胜数。

相反，我观察过一些没有履行条款的长期许可特例。有些时候，拿到许可的人没能大力推动市场，因而导致利润流失。因此要确保履行条款被写入合同中，比如在特定的一段时间内，要达到一定的销售额。如果最终没有达到目标议程，那么许可方可以终止合同。

I cannot stress enough the importance of hiring an experienced lawyer when negotiating and drawing up any and all agreements. Yes, the lawyer's job is to protect you from the diverse risks that contracts can cause. Still, it is your job, as the businessman, to assess the lawyer's advice and then make your own decisions. Sometimes it is prudent to go against counsel's suggestions, as certain risks must be taken if the deal is to be completed. If you resist a legal authority, be sure you recognize and have options for the perils that might lie ahead.

Contracts can be instituted for just about every situation like having your executives always sign an employee contract. We want documentation that this person is 100 percent committed to the job. Employment contracts can vary from a simple one pager to being very convoluted, so once again, hire a top notch attorney.

当谈判或者起草任何协议的时候，雇用一个经验丰富的律师非常重要，这一点我怎么强调都不够。是的，律师的职责是保护你免受因合同所引起的各种风险。不过，作为商人，你的工作就是去考虑律师的建议，然后作出自己的决定。有时候和律师的建议背道而驰也是一种精明的体现，因为为了促成一笔交易，必须要承担一定的风险。如果你违抗了某一法律权威，你一定要认识到未来可能发生的危险，并有备选方案。

在任何情况下都应该签订合同，比如一定要让你的主管们签署劳务合同。我们需要文件证明此人百分之百地投入工作。劳务合同可以简单到只有一页纸，也可以变得非常错综复杂。所以再次重申，要雇一个顶级的律师。

Intellectual Property

Intellectual Property (IP) includes a work or invention, such as a manuscript or design, to which one has rights, patents, trademarks, copyrights, and trade secrets. Patents generally protect ideas in terms of products and processes. Trademarks protect words and symbols related to the source of goods or services. Copyright protects creative expression of ideas, such as audio files, video, movies, pictures, software programs, etc. Trade secrets protect confidential information that provides a business advantage.

Business newspapers expound on companies that spend millions of dollars to purchase patent portfolios, license copyrights to content, or acquire licenses to trademarks.

IP law is highly specialized and often compulsory to defend a company from copycats. In some situations, a business may be built around licensing IP. (e.g., licensing technology, knowhow, content, etc.)

Once again, hire the best lawyers when it comes to protecting IP. In some cases, the IP is a major part of the valuation of a business. In others, IP is only a small segment. A competent IP attorney can advise you on how to assemble an IP portfolio to increase the worth of your company.

IP is more vital for some investments than others. There are business niches that compete solely on the cost of identical products for which there is no need to develop IP. Due to costs, other companies do not take IP seriously enough to be patented and the results are usually disastrous.

I look at the IP of a potential investment and factor it into my decision. Is there IP that could help prevent "copycats" from undercutting the company? Does the enterprise's business model include licensing IP? Has the company done enough to protect its IP?

知识产权

知识产权（IP）包括一项作品或者发明，比如手稿或设计，作者对其拥有权利、专利权、商标权、版权和商业机密权。专利权通常保护产品及其工艺的创意。商标权是用以保护与商品或服务的来源有关的文字和符号。版权是用以保护思想的表达形式，如音频文件、视频、电影、图片、软件程序等。商业机密权则是保护带来商业利益的机密信息。

商业报纸对那些花费数百万美元购买专利组合、内容版权许可，或者获得商标许可权的公司进行了详细的说明。

知识产权法律是高度专业化的，并且通常是强制性的，以保护一家公司不受盗版的侵害。在某些情况下，可以围绕知识产权许可（如授权技术、诀窍、内容等）开展业务。

再次重申，当面对保护知识产权问题时，你应雇用最好的律师。在某些情况下，知识产权在评估一个企业中占主导地位。而在其他的企业中，知识产权只占一小部分。一个称职的知识产权律师，可以建议你如何组成一个专利组合，来增加公司的价值。

对某些投资而言，知识产权至关重要，而对于其他投资就没那么重要。在有些商业领域中，对于无须开发知识产权的相同商品，只是单纯地比拼成本价的高低。由于成本的原因，一些公司并没有给予知识产权足够的重视，因而不去申请专利，然而结果往往是惨痛的。

我将知识产权看作一项潜在的投资，是最终是否决定投资的一个因素。是否有知识产权可以防止“模仿者”削弱此公司？企业的业务模式是否包括知识产权许可？此公司是否已经尽力保护其知识产权？

A classic example of a short-term license involves the sports industry. Up until 1959, the National Football League relied primarily on attendance for revenue. At this point, merchandising did not exist in any manner. A year earlier, the Los Angeles Rams were the first team to put their logo on their uniforms. The archaic assumption was that merchandise could never be sold, only given away to promote the various teams.

Along came television and movie star, Roy Rogers, known as the "King of the Cowboys." He was very popular with all age brackets and adored by the entire American population. At one point, his Roy Rogers enterprises sold more than 400 products, including western wear, toys, lunch boxes, flashlights, and much more. He was earning considerably more from his licensing and merchandising sales than from his television show and movie roles. This is incredible since his TV show was always in the top ten ratings.

After seeing the logo on the Rams' uniforms, Rogers had an extraordinary vision and applied his business acumen to the NFL. In 1959, he convinced the league to sign an agreement where he would develop and sell merchandising and licensing for them. The profit sharing deal was fifty percent to Rogers and fifty percent to the NFL. Within one year, Rogers was producing over 300 NFL products and earning gigantic profits.

Then the roof caved in on Rogers. He had made two critical mistakes. The first was that he only signed a two year contract that expired as NFL product sales were sky rocketing. Of course, the NFL decided not to renew his contract. The lesson is to always have long term contracts when signing licensing agreements. I suggest 25 years with automatic rollover provisions.

The second mistake Rogers made was not signing his key employees to protracted contracts. One reason he lost the deal was because his key employee jumped to the NFL side during negotiations. If that employee had been locked into a long term agreement, this debacle would not have happened and most likely the contract would have been renewed. On an annual basis, the NFL generates 3.2 billion USD in sales as the result of merchandise and licensing.

有一个关于体育行业经典的短期许可例子。直到1959年，美国橄榄球联盟主要依靠门票挣钱。那时，文化衍生商品还没有出现。在此一年之前，洛杉矶公羊队是第一支将自己队徽印在球衣上的球队。按照当时的想法，衍生商品根本卖不出去，只能宣传各个球队而已。

随之而来的就是影视明星，被称为“牛仔之王”的罗伊·罗杰斯(Roy Rogers)。他受所有年龄段人欢迎，并受到了全美人民的喜爱。罗伊·罗杰斯的企业一度销售过400多种产品，包括西部服饰、玩具、午餐盒、手电筒等。他取得许可并销售的产品使他挣了一大笔钱，甚至超过了他从电视节目和影视角色中所挣的钱。这真是不可思议，因为他的电视节目收视率总是排在前十。

当看到公羊队队服上的队徽后，罗杰斯有了非凡的远见，并将他的商业头脑应用到了NFL（美国橄榄球联盟）。1959年，他说服联盟签署了一项协议，使他可以进行衍生商品的开发和销售，并取得经营许可。利润按照五五开分配，其中50%归罗杰斯，另50%则归NFL。在一年之内，罗杰斯生产了超过300种NFL的产品，并获得了巨额利润。

接着罗杰斯遇到了重大危机。他犯了两个严重的错误。第一个是他只签署了一份为期两年的合同，当该合同到期之际，正值NFL的产品销量直线飙升之时。NFL当然不会跟他续签合同。这个教训是，在签署许可协议时一定要签订长期合同。我建议用25年的自动滚续条款。

罗杰斯犯的第二个错误，是没有和核心员工签订长期合同，而导致他在这笔交易中失败的原因之一，正是他的核心员工在谈判期间跳槽到NFL那边了。如果这名员工被绑定在一个长期协议中，这种灾难就不会发生，而且很有可能成功续签合同。之后由于衍生商品和经营许可在手，NFL每年都能产生32亿美元的销售额。

Paying the Workforce

When investing, it is crucial to compute how much to pay your employees. Is each employee worth the affect his/her salary has on the bottom line of the company?Your decision process should include these factors:

- How much will the entire workforce cost every month?
- How many actual employees will you need?
- What level of employees will be needed?
- How will you pay for these people?
- How will you retain loyalty?

We execute a thorough employee compensation study before every investment. Wage amounts will determine whether to hire part time, permanent or to outsource. Wages in the service industry are the majority of the costs as opposed to product expenditures in manufacturing. You also need to know what the ratio of executives to hourly employees is and how much you will compensate them. Furthermore, employee benefits and payroll taxes must be added to the salaries to calculate the real cost to the company. When considering an investment in a business where costs are more than you think appropriate, then ask why and find those answers.

Executives, in addition to a salary, will probably seek stock options and other benefits. If so, consider a more lucrative bonus package or a higher income.

Take care of your employees fairly, but at the same time, have enough capital to expand the business. Again, such analysis is the Checkmate Investing stratagem. We want to win, we want satisfied employees, and we want the company to grow and prosper.

支付员工

当你做投资时，计算出要付给员工多少薪水是至关重要的，对于每名员工，将其薪水写进工资单是否值得，你的判定过程应该包括如下方面：

- 每月全体员工的薪酬总共多少？
- 你实际需要多少名员工？
- 你需要什么水平的员工？
- 你怎么支付给这些人？
- 你怎样保持员工的忠诚度？

我们在每项投资之前，要实行全面的员工薪酬研究。全部薪金的多少，决定了是雇用临时工、长期工，还是外包公司。在服务业里，薪金支出是主要成本，而在制造业里正好相反，产品支出是主要成本。你还需要知道高管和时薪员工的比例，以及要支付他们多少钱。此外，员工福利和工薪税必须算在薪酬里，以便计算出公司真正的成本。在某一行业中考虑投资的时候，如果成本远远高于你的预期，那就要问问为什么，并找出答案。

高管除了得到工资以外，很可能要求股票期权或其他福利，如果这样，就要考虑更划算的奖励计划或更高的收入。

要公平地关爱你的员工，但与此同时，要有足够的资本去扩展你的业务。再说一下，这种分析结果就是“将军投资”的策略。我们要赢，我们要让员工满意，我们希望公司繁荣昌盛。

Seasonal Earnings

Many investments are subject to seasonal earnings. This means that sales will be higher during certain times of the year, like Christmas or Valentine's Day. There are many retail companies that have big earnings across the span of one year. However, when broken down, they lose money for eight or nine months annually and only show profits for three to four months. For this type of business, you must look at cash reserves and other sources to pay the bills in the down months.

Maybe the company can obtain a line of credit to survive the slow months. The problem with this approach is that occasionally even the best of companies will have a slump in sales for one reason or another which will jeopardize the ability to pay back the creditor. For this reason, it is best to build up cash reserves and use the line of credit sparingly.

An investor must stringently inspect each previous year's seasonal earnings to assure past sales can be repeated or even improved upon. You must understand what factors were in place that accounted for those sales. Were sales created by fad buying or will they recur year after year? Seasonal businesses can be tricky, so scrutinize closely.

季节性收入

许多投资项目都受季节性收入的影响，意思是说在每年的特定时间里销售额较高，比如圣诞节或情人节。有许多零售企业全年的总收入很高，然而买卖不好的时候，他们一年中有八九个月都在赔钱，只有三四个月能有利润。对于这样的企业，你要考虑现金贮备和其他来源，以备萧条月份时可以支付开销。

也许有的公司会依靠获得信贷额度来拯救萧条期，这种方法的问题在于，即使最好的企业，也会偶尔出现由于某种原因而致使销售额下降的情况，这就会影响还贷的能力。基于这个原因，最好还是增加现金贮备，谨慎使用信用额度。

一个投资者必须严密地审查之前每一年度的季节性收入，以此确保能够达到或超越以往的销售额。你必须明白是什么原因导致这样的销售额，是不是源于一时流行而创造的销售业绩？以及这种情况会年年重复吗？季节性企业可能会非常棘手，所以要严密审查。

Taxes

Suffice to say, every dollar paid in taxes is money deprived from your company. From day one, proper tax planning is prudent if you expect your business to grow and prosper. Top consultants, accountants, and tax attorneys are expensive, but will ultimately save you money.

Also, never be overly aggressive when calculating taxes as it may come back to haunt you. I tend to stay away from all tax shelters, especially buying tax shelters which can be a scam that could result in repaying the written-off money, plus excessive penalties well after the fact. I love tax holidays which will often be given for various reasons such as relocating to a specific geographic region.

On the other hand, always take advantage of tax savings that are clearly legal to reduce your tax liability. For example, tax laws continually change, which can create confusion about how to safely reduce your legal responsibility. Again, a tax attorney is invaluable when there are gray areas in the law.

There are many other taxes beside federal, so develop a strategy for all of them. There are also Value Added Taxes (VAT) and other tariffs. All of these potential levies will deplete profits. At least once per year, revisit your tax plans to reassure you are in compliance with any/all updates. Taxes must be paid, so plan ahead, have a clear strategy, and seize as much of your earned profit as is legally possible.

税　务

可以说，你用于支付税金的每一元钱都是从你公司拿走的。如果你想让自己的公司繁荣昌盛，那么从一开始，就要筹划好适当的纳税计划。顶级顾问、会计师、税务律师都很贵，但最终会为你省钱。

还有，当计算纳税的时候不要过于激进，否则你会陷入其中，我倾向于不用任何避税手段，尤其不要购买所谓可以避税的方法，很可能是一个骗局，结果往往是，事后要重新上缴避开的税款，外加大量的罚金。我喜欢免税期，会因为各种原因给予优惠，如迁移到特殊地段。

另外，要利用节税这一明显合法的方式来减少税务负担。例如，税法经常变化，怎样才能安全地减少法律责任，会给你带来困惑。再次强调，当法律中存在灰色地带时，雇用一个税务律师是非常重要的。

除了联邦税以外，还有许多其他税种，所以要为纳税制订一个策略。还有增值税（VAT）和其他的关税，所有这些潜在的税费都会削减利润。每年至少一次，检查你的纳税计划，确认符合任何或所有的税务更新变化。税款是一定要缴纳的，所以要提前规划，有一个清晰的策略，只要是合法的，就尽量节省你挣来的利润。

Control Costs

Managing expenses is a balancing act and compulsory in both our personal and business life. Every dollar spent without at least earning another dollar in return is a step in the wrong direction. I am not parsimonious, but realize unnecessary costs are dangerous. For instance, I normally fly coach class to save money and send a message of frugality to others in my company.

Also, I regularly take flights of six to twenty plus hours which can be tiring. If money is tight, I would rather balance the expenses by enjoying a nice dinner or sleeping at a better hotel than to waste money on an airplane seat. If you search the Internet, you can often find a five star hotel for a similar price as a less accommodating alternative. This should not be construed as being miserly, but rather as being a penny-wise businessman who cares about investors by not squandering money. When you factor this across hundreds or thousands of employees, the fiscal impact is significant.

When looking for office space, compare options and save money. I have occupied sublets that have been as much as 75% below the existing market. If you are like most companies and pay for employee parking, try to negotiate a combination price. When you purchase raw materials, always get multiple quotes especially as you grow. All of these tips are applicable whether the company has three employees or several hundred thousand employees.

As a company expands, you must continue this habit of prudent spending. For a small company, overspending is relatively easy to keep in check. For a larger company, costs are harder to analyze, but such an examination must be done with regularity to reduce expenditures without diminishing quality. I am always amused by the employee who complains of cost cuts. Yet, that same employee will earn a larger paycheck or receive a bonus as a direct result of trimming unnecessary company spending. There is a profound difference between being prudent and stingy.

控制成本

不管是个人生活中，还是在业务中，费用的管理既是必要的，也是平衡的做法，每花出去一元钱，而没能至少挣回一元钱，就是往错误的道路上前进了一步。我并不吝啬，但是认识到不必要的花销是危险的。例如，我通常为了省钱而买经济舱的机票，同时向公司里其他同事传递节俭的信息。

另外，通常我的飞行航程都在 6 小时至 20 小时之间或更长时间，会感觉很累，如果手头不宽裕，我宁愿花这个钱享受一顿美餐，或住一家条件较好的宾馆，也不愿把钱浪费在飞机舱位上。如果你上网搜索，总能找到一家五星宾馆，用同样的钱来弥补飞机上的不适。这一行为不应被认为是吝啬，而应理解为一个省小钱的商人，因为在意投资人，所以不浪费钱财。当你把这个因素计入成百上千的员工中，会有可观的财政影响。

当寻找办公地点时，多比较几家，尽量节省开支。我曾经在转租的房子里办公，能比市场价低将近 75%。如果你和大多数公司一样，为员工支付停车费，就要试着谈一个批发价。当你购买原材料的时候，一定要多方比较报价，尤其在公司刚起步时。无论你的公司只有 3 名员工，还是有几十万名员工，这些小窍门都很适用。

随着公司的扩大，你必须延续这一精打细算的习惯。对于小公司而言，避免超支会相对容易一些，对于大公司来讲，成本开销很难估算，但还是要尽量时常检查一下，在不降低质量的情况下节流。当有的员工因降低成本而抱怨时，我觉得很好笑，对啊，要是减少了那些不必要的开销，省钱的结果，就能让该员工挣得工资更多，或者收到额外奖金。精明和吝啬之间差别巨大。

Occupying a very inexpensive office space is rarely a good idea as image and perception are also significant in most businesses. Your office has to project success when clients visit. For example, if you lease a rundown space in a seedy part of town, you will save money, but will also risk scaring off customers with an inferior working environment.

On the other hand, for some types of businesses, the cheapest working space is the best choice, especially if you do not rely on walk-in customers. Telemarketing companies do not require fancy addresses because all their business is conducted by phone, mail, or the Internet.

There are advantages to having an office near stylish restaurants or other facilities to conveniently entertain guests. If your business is a forty minute drive from any nice restaurants, it is almost impossible to take clients out for lunch.

Being close to a major transportation hub, such as an airport, can be of value when selecting office headquarters. It might be easier for clients, customers, and consultants to visit.Public transportation access is another relevant issue, making the commute easier for your employees and customers. When choosing your office location, compromise between cost, image, and other business specific considerations.

Drive your cost management programs with detailed budgets and line items. Written guidelines are a must, so executives can differentiate between what expenses are and are not acceptable. Cost analysis is fundamental to every company.

选一个特别便宜的办公地点，并不是一个好主意，因为对于大多数公司而言，企业形象和认知也是非常重要的，当客户来访时，你的办公地点是需要展现成功形象的地方。例如，你在城里最脏乱的地方，租了一个破旧的房子，你是省钱了，但也会有因为劣等的工作环境而吓跑顾客的风险。

另外，对于某些类型的企业，最便宜的工作地点反而是最佳选择。尤其是不需要顾客上门的那种。电商就不需要豪华的店铺，因为他们的业务都是靠电话、邮件、网络实现的。

把办公地点选在邻近时尚饭庄或其他设施周围，可以便于你招待顾客。如果你的公司距离任何一家高级酒楼都要40分钟车程，就连带客户吃个午饭都不太现实。

要比邻大的交通枢纽，比如机场，其周边就很适合选为办公总部，可以方便顾客、客户和顾问来访。邻近公共交通是另一个相关问题，让你的员工上下班更方便，客户也易于来访。当选择办公地点时，要综合花费、形象和其他商业方面来考量。

利用详细的预算，并排列出各项，来推动你的费用管理，必须书面写出指导方针，这样高管就能区分哪些花费可以，哪些不能接受。成本分析是每个公司都必不可少的环节。

Cash Management

A major concern with all companies is cash management. Sales proceeds in most industries are not immediately transferred into their business bank accounts. Normally, there is a time lag of thirty, sixty, even ninety days that can be enormously disruptive if cash supervision is not in step with cash needs. When bills are due and employees are to be paid, the cash must be available.

Constantly plan ahead, identify what future sales to expect from your business, and review your receivables history on a monthly basis. Most companies function in cycles and cash needs are not equal every month. In some industries, it makes sense to have a working capital credit line or to factor receivables.

There are other solutions to acquiring money, such as accounts receivable management, offering a discount to unpaid receivables if they pay without delay, or contacting suppliers to negotiate your dilemma. Perhaps the supplier will extend you credit, affording you more time to resolve financial issues.

If you are a company with an abundance of cash, you must have a proper investment strategy for placing excess capital.

Checkmate Investing closely monitors cash management and flow as part of our sophisticated investing process. Perhaps 50% of the cash on hand will not be needed for two years which enables you to be more aggressive with investments. If you suddenly need to access cash quickly, there are few such investments, and the only alternative is an interest bearing checking account. A higher return on your cash means losing liquidity of that capital.

Investing cash also has tradeoffs. The longer the cash is invested, the higher the return. But the longer the term, the lesser the liquidity. So be assiduous and clearly understand the associated risks and factor in your liquidity needs.

现金管理

对于所有的公司来说，现金管理都是一个需要特别关注的问题。在大多数行业中，销售收入不会立即转入其商业银行账户。通常情况下，销售收入与实际到账会有 30 天或 60 天甚至 90 天的时间间隔，如果现金监管和资金需求之间没有协调一致的话，会造成极大的破坏。当账单到期，或者需要支付员工时，必须拥有足够的现金。

应不断提前做好规划，确定公司的预期销售额，并且以每月为基础，检查之前的应收账款。大多数公司是按周期运营，需要的资金每月都不同。在一些行业中拥有运营资本信贷额度或者将应收款项计入其中，也存在一定道理。

还有其他的方法可以获取资金，例如应收账款管理，给那些能立即付账的应收款项提供一定的折扣，或者联系供应商来帮助你度过困境。也许供应商会延长你的还款期限，给你更多的时间来解决财务问题。

如果你是一家拥有大量现金的公司，必须拥有一个合适的投资策略来解决资本过剩。

“将军投资”密切监控现金管理和流动，以此作为我们富有经验的投资步骤之一。可能大约要有 50% 的手头现金，在将来的两年内都不会被用到，才会使你可以更大胆地去投资。如果你突然需要快速取得现金，其实很少有这种投资项目，唯一的选择就是带息存款账户。而为获取更高的回报，意味着会使你失去资本的流动性。

现金投资也需要权衡。投资的时间越长，回报就越高，但是投资期限越长，流动性就越小。所以要努力地清楚了解与你的流动性需求相关的风险和因素。

Maintain a cash reserve account for emergencies, future costs, and unexpected predicaments. For example, assume that in three years your factory will need to spend ninety-five million dollars on new equipment. Accordingly, it is best to start preparing for that immense expenditure now. Consider these factors:

- Are you planning to pay cash for these machines or lease them or seek a loan?
- Where will the money come from?
- How early should you prepare?
- Are there tax advantages coinciding with the various options to purchase the equipment?
- Can the old equipment be sold to decrease the costs?
- How about costs to train employees to operate the new equipment?
- How will new equipment and related dangers affect your current insurance needs?

Brainstorm all possibilities to solve cash management problems. When approaching others for either funding or to extend your credit with suppliers, prepare a presentation illustrating your predicament and provide a viable solution that includes answers to the above bullet points. If they are not convinced of a low risk, then a new supplier must be found. It would also be sensible to revamp your original presentation and make it more compelling to convince any newfound suppliers to work with you.

要有一个现金储备账户以防突发事件、未来成本和意想不到的困境。例如，假设你的工厂在 3 年之内，需要花费 9500 万美元购置新设备。因此，最好现在就开始准备这笔巨大的支出。要考虑如下因素：

- 你打算用现金购买这些机器，还是租赁它们，抑或寻求贷款？
- 钱从哪来？
- 你应该提前多久着手准备？
- 在购买这些设备的众多选择中，是否有符合税收优惠政策的？
- 能出售旧设备以降低成本吗？
- 培训员工操作新设备的成本是多少？
- 新设备和相关的危险会不会影响你当前的保险需求？

多动脑子去想所有可以解决现金管理问题的可能性。当你向其他人寻求资金或向供应商要求延长还款期限时，准备一份说明困境的情况报告，并提供一个可行的解决方案，其中包括对上述要点的回答。如果他们没有被说服确认风险较低，那么就必须找新的供应商。改进原来的报告，是一个明智的选择，使它更有说服力去说服任何新的供应商来与你合作。

Executive Management Team

The management team of a potential investment is just as important as the actual enterprise and can be the difference between earning a profit and losing money.

The leader of a company is the captain of the ship, and we don't want to hire a drunken sailor. We ascertain if this skipper can navigate rough waters, keep the crew calm, and guide the business to the gold. Like every prominent leader, there are good and bad captains, pilots, quarterbacks, coaches, politicians, and of course, CEOs.

Ultimately, the character of the leader and his/her ability to make hard decisions is the number one attribute. We assess the principal's business instincts, commonsensical judgment, attention to details, and coherent answers to industry questions. We also interact with fellow employees to gauge their respect for the chief officer.

If we feel the management is weak, we will either not invest or ask if they object to us hiring a new CEO.Normally, convincing a founder or CEO to step down is complicated as most cannot imagine someone else knowing more about operating their enterprise.

When reviewing the top management of a company, look at their age, experience, past failures and accomplishments. Also scrutinize the team around them, and how they relate to each other.

- What is their management style?
- Do they have any bad habits? If so, do their good traits outweigh the bad? What is the character of the company leader?
- What traits have made them a success or failure in the past?
- How balanced are their lives?
- Do they respect the budget?
- Are they fully engaged in the business or do they have hobbies or other interests that distract them?

高级管理团队

要做一项投资，管理团队和企业实际上一样重要，团队管理水平直接决定了盈利还是亏损。

一个公司的领导就像航船上的船长，而且我们也不想雇用一个喝醉的水手，我们要弄清这个船长是否能够在波涛汹涌的水域上航行，能够让全体船员保持冷静，并且引领企业找到财富。就像每一个著名领袖一样，总有称职的和不称职的，船长、飞行员、橄榄球四分卫、教练、政客，当然首席执行官也一样。

最终，领导人的性格和作出艰难决定的能力是最主要的因素，我们评估当事人的商业本能、常识判断、细节关注和对行业问题能连贯应答这些因素。我们也会与员工互动来衡量他们对首席执行官是否尊敬。

如果我们感到管理薄弱，就会放弃投资，或者征求他们的意见，换一个新的首席执行官，看他们是否反对。通常说服一个创始人或者首席执行官辞职是很复杂的，因为多数人都不能想象，除了此人还有谁能更了解该企业的运营。

当评估一个公司的高级管理层时，要看他们的年龄、经验、过往失败与成就。也要仔细审查他们身边的团队，以及他们之间的关系。

- 他们的管理模式是什么？
- 他们有恶习吗？如果有，他们的优点能胜过缺点吗？公司的领导人是什么性格呢？
- 是什么特质导致他们过往的成功或失败呢？
- 他们的生活和谐吗？
- 他们看重预算吗？
- 他们是全心投入工作了吗，以及他们有什么容易分心的爱好或兴趣吗？

- Do they have a business plan and how dynamic is it?
- Do they follow the game plan?
- How are they dressed and groomed?

In the end, the leader of the company must possess many sterling qualities. Otherwise, a business with a rudderless commander will most likely fail and your investment will be naught.

- 他们有经营计划吗？计划是否有活力？
- 他们是否遵循计划了？
- 他们的仪容仪表如何？

最后，公司的领导人必须拥有许多优秀的品质，否则，一个无能指挥官运营的企业，结局很可能是失败，而你的投资也会化为泡影。

Hiring and Human Resources

Every hire must be carefully thought out.Sure, firing unproductive employees can alleviate some problems, but hiring the wrong person in the first place can create collateral damage to the organization. Dismissing any worker can also positively or negatively impact the morale of the entire company.

Whenever you are forced to terminate someone, try to minimize any hard feelings. A few nasty words from disgruntled former employees can impinge on your company's reputation and make hiring new workers troublesome. I believe in helping discharged people find a new job regardless of the reason you let them go.

During the hiring process, you must weed out anyone who has a propensity toward vindictiveness, the worst of all human traits. Such a person can cause severe internal and external consequences to your enterprise.

A malicious former employee can file unjustified lawsuits, such as groundless discrimination or sexual harassment grievances. Potential claims can waste company time for many years, even after the person is discharged. Throughout the interview process, this unsavory trait can often be uncovered by asking precise questions.

While experience is advantageous, in many circumstances people can learn on the job. But to change a person's character is impossible, so examine more than an applicant's CV. Study the individual's overall temperament during the hiring process.

Sometimes hiring an inexperienced person is a good thing. It might be arduous at first, but you might create an appreciative and loyal employee who is a bastion for many years. Loyalty is one of the most telling traits, so find ways to determine the allegiance of a candidate.

Furthermore, be open to rehiring former employees. Usually an employee leaves a company voluntarily to pursue a better opportunity and to improve his/her life. In some cases, people have to be released during a recession which has nothing to do with their work habits. Such rehires are very loyal and already trained, so there is no downtime.

人才招聘和人力资源

招聘每名员工时，都必须考虑清楚。当然，开除不称职的员工能解决一些问题，但是如果从一开始就没招对人，会给公司造成间接伤害。开除任何一名员工都有可能对整个公司的士气造成影响，这种影响有可能是积极的，也可能是消极的。

当你被迫开除某人时，想办法让怨气最小化。从心怀不满的前雇员嘴里说出的几句难听的话，能影响你公司的声誉，从而在招聘新员工时困难重重。我愿意帮那些被开除的人找到新工作，不管当初让他们离开是出于何种原因。

在招聘的过程中，你必须排除那些有怀恨心理倾向的人，这是人类最大的缺点，这样的人，会给你的企业内部和外部造成严重的影响。

一个恶意的前雇员可能会提出不正当的诉讼，比如毫无理由地告发遭到歧视或性骚扰，公司会为这种潜在的索赔耗时几年，甚至到当事人都离开公司之后。整个面试过程中，一般通过问几个精确的问题，就能发现这种令人讨厌的品性。

虽然工作经验是有利的条件，但在许多情况下，人们可以在工作中学习。而要改变一个人的性格就不太可能了，所以别只看应聘者的简历，在招聘过程中，要全面考察这个人的整体气质。

有时候雇用一个没有经验的人是好事，开始的时候可能有点费劲，但是你可能会造就一个感恩和忠诚的员工，会对你忠心耿耿很多年，忠诚是一个最显著的优点，所以要想办法判断应聘者的忠诚度。

此外，要愿意接受重新雇用以前的员工。通常一个员工自愿离开公司，是为了追寻更好的机会，并改善其生活。有些时候，公司由于不景气，被迫开除一些人，而这与他们工作习惯无关。这样重新雇用的是非常忠诚且训练有素之人，可以直接开工，无缝衔接。

Your human resources team must be trained on preparing and evaluating the company's application form/questionnaire, which if satisfactorily completed is followed up with an oral interview. For certain jobs, I also believe in role playing to see how the prospective employee handles hypothetical situations and problems. The more time spent with the aspirant, the better chance of hiring the right person. And don't forget, some qualified people are shy, but a competent interviewer can make them feel comfortable and elicit their true character.

Use all techniques to locate qualified candidates, including referrals, headhunters, Internet sites, campus recruitment, trade shows and conferences, anywhere your industry does business.

As mentioned earlier, have your new employees sign employment contracts before they begin working. This action binds everyone to the team effort and sets down basic guidelines to follow.

It makes sense to include stock options for even the lower level workers. If you give an employee a stock that vests (is redeemable) a few years down the road, it can do wonders for increasing team loyalty and morale. Even at the highest level, all staffers must put in time to be given the equity stock.

Every company should have a book on company pride and what is expected of the workforce. It is all part of building an enduring corporate culture.

Give employees a chance to improve themselves by offering inside training, attending conferences or matriculating at schools that will improve skill sets. At conferences, there is always a risk they will be noticed by competitors who may attempt to hire them away. If you have respectful employee practices and stock options, you will rarely lose anyone.

Conferences and seminars provide employees with not only an in depth education, but your attendees will announce to the industry that your company is a terrific place to work, making future hiring easier.

你的人力资源团队必须接受培训，要事先准备并且事后评估公司的申请表或调查表，如果应聘者填写的表格令人满意，就会进入面试环节，对于某些职位，我赞同用角色扮演的方式，来考察应聘者怎样处理假定的情况和问题。和有上进心的应聘者在一起的时间越长，就越有机会招到对的人，而且别忘了，有些有能力的人容易害羞，但是一个称职的面试官，应该可以让他们放松下来，并发掘出其真正品质。

利用所有的方法招募合格的候选人，包括引荐、猎头、网站、校园招聘或招聘大会，以及你公司开展业务的任何地方。

就像前面提到过的，在你的新雇员开始工作之间，要先与其签署劳动合同，这个做法既让每个人都与团队精神紧密相连，又制订出要遵循的基本指导方针。

即使是最底层的员工，也要让他们有股票期权，这样做是有意义的。如果你给一名员工股份（可赎回），并在未来几年里授予，会有提升团队的忠诚和士气的功效。就算在最高级别，也只有达到一定工作年限的雇员才能拿到权益股。

每个公司都应该有一本记载着公司引以为豪的事以及员工愿景的书，建立一个持久的企业文化必须要做到这一点。

通过提供内部培训，给员工一个提升自我的机会，参加会议或入校学习，可以提高综合技能。与会期间，总会有让竞争对手注意到他们并想挖走他们的风险。如果你一直敬重员工，又给他们股票期权，你便不会轻易失去他们。

会议和研讨会不仅能给员工提供深入的教育，还能让与会员工，在行业内部宣传你们公司的良好工作环境，使得以后招聘员工变得更容易。

I believe in soliciting employee input, either anonymously or with the employee's name attached. The key is to tender a way for workers to voice their insider opinions. By allowing a staffer to furnish suggestions, the company will benefit and the employee will feel like an integral part of the team. If his/her idea is implemented and sales increase, then a reward should be given. However, I do not believe such compensation should be presented in front of others, which can create jealousy and other issues.

As a financier, always be aware of the philosophy and hiring practices of each company you invest in. Does the company think of the employee as a widget or instead as part of a family? This type analysis is easier to perform on early and late stage enterprises than on larger, listed companies.

If your company is seeking financing, proudly talk up your team and the magnitude you place on hiring, training, and retaining capable employees. If you emphasize this in your presentation, investors will see you are a well organized and wise leader. Smart hiring, not firing, is the sign of a successful company.

我主张征求员工建议，无论是匿名的还是具名的，关键在于提供一种方式，让员工说出他们的内心想法。通过允许雇员提建议，公司会因此受益，员工也会觉得自己是团队中不可或缺的一部分。如果某人的想法被采用后，销售额得到提升，那么就应给予奖励。然而，我认为奖金不应该当众发放，因为容易引起嫉恨和其他问题。

作为一名金融行业者，一定要认识到，在你投资的每个公司中，他们的从业理念和雇佣政策，公司是把员工当做摆设，还是家中一员呢？这种分析在企业前期和末期时容易实施，对于较大的上市公司就不太容易了。

如果你的公司想要筹措资金，要自豪地赞扬你的团队，以及你对招聘、培训和保留得力员工的重视程度。如果你在融资演讲中强调这些，投资者会认为你是一个组织有序、精明强干的领导。聪明地雇人而不是解雇，是一个成功公司的标志。

Supply Chain

A supply chain is a system of organizations, people, activities, information, and resources involved in moving a product or service from supplier to customer. Activities entail the transformation of natural resources, raw materials, and other components into a finished product that is delivered to the end user "customer."

We fully dissect the supply chain to identify how to maximize the process before moving forward on all investments. Look for parts of the procession that can be replaced to save costs. This exploration also sheds light on where things can break down and potentially damage the reputation of the company, in addition to creating financial loss. There are many books on this comprehensive subject and worth the time to study further.

New companies often disregard possible supply chain pitfalls, ignorantly believing that everybody and every little thing along the route will operate to perfection. Before investing, make certain that the company principals completely understand their specific delivery progression. If an investment prospect lacks insight on the movement of his/her company provisions, then we become worried about coming onboard.

Take the time to plot an easily reviewable chart for your supply chain.

供应链

供应链是一个包含人员、活动、信息和资源的综合体系，是将产品或服务从供应商转移到消费者的过程。此活动包括将自然资源、原材料和其他部件转化为成品，并交付给最终用户“消费者”手中。

在进行所有投资之前，我们会充分剖析供应链，以确定如何将这一系列过程的利益最大化。寻找在此过程中可以被替换的环节，以便节约成本。这一探索会让你知道在哪个环节会出现问题，并可能损害公司的声誉，外加还会造成财务损失。有很多关于这一综合学科的书籍，值得花时间进一步研究。

新公司往往会忽视各种可能的供应链陷阱，无知地相信在前进的道路上，每个人和每一件小事都会完美运行。在投资之前，要确保公司的负责人完全了解他们的具体交付过程。如果该负责人对其公司供给的运作都不明晰的话，那么我们就会担心是否要投资。

花点时间去为你的供应链绘制一个简单清晰的图表。

Packaging

The packaging of a product can be the difference between consumers purchasing your merchandise over a competitor. Spend significant time and effort on creating package designs. For example, Apple is famous for the care it takes in the packaging of its smart phones.

Effective packaging gives a customer a good feeling about the product even before opening it.Which would you rather take home a product in a plain cardboard box or the same item in a beautiful sachet with colorful patterns or images that inspire you?

Some customers retain attractive packaging long after they use the product, such as bags from exclusive brands like Hermes, Channel, LV, Dior, Gucci, and Prada or empty designer perfume bottles. Most people assume that once a product is purchased, the sale is complete. To us, the sale is only the start. We see packaging as a mode to expand the brand and increase repeat purchases.

The extra costs associated with designing a lustrous package are generally worth the expense. It is not obligatory to cut every company cost for the business to grow. We want the buyer to enlighten others about our radiant product. The best way to achieve this marketing goal is in the packaging.

Proper packaging can also be an "up-sell" opportunity. Within the package, it might be cost-effective to include a discount coupon for a complementary product or for the purchase of a second unit.

Checkmate Investing considers packaging as essential as the product itself because it directly influences the lasting impression of the brand. Take the time to create innovative packaging, and the benefits to the company will be momentous.

包　装

产品的包装可以让顾客购买你的商品而不是对手的商品。请花费足够的时间和精力来做包装设计。例如，苹果公司（Apple）就以其智能手机精心的包装而闻名。

一个好的包装可以让顾客在打开之前就对产品拥有良好的感觉。同样的物品，一个装在普通的纸箱子里，另一个用漂亮的香囊包裹，上面还有让你眼前一亮的五颜六色的图案装饰，你愿意把哪一件商品买回家呢？

一些顾客在使用产品后很长时间，依然还保留着其精美的包装，比如爱马仕（Hermes）、香奈儿（Channel）、路易威登（LV）、迪奥（Dior）、古驰（Gucci）和普拉达（Prada）等高档品牌的袋子，或是著名品牌的空香水瓶。大多数人认为一旦产品卖出去了，销售就完成了。而对我们来说，销售只是开始。我们认为包装是推广品牌和增加重复购买的一种方式。

为设计一个光鲜亮丽的包装而支付额外费用通常是值得的。为了让企业营业额增长，并不是必须削减每项成本。我们希望顾客可以向其他人推广我们的好产品。而实现这个营销目标的最好方法就是包装。

适当的包装也可以成为“提升销售额”的机会。在包装内加入一种购买互补产品或第二单的折扣券会更划算。

“将军投资”认为包装与产品本身一样重要，因为它直接影响品牌的持久形象。花些时间打造创新的包装，将给公司带来巨大的利益。

Warranties and Representations

Most contracts for investments or acquisitions include a list of warranties and representations. In a proposed deal, a representation is a statement of details which a party is expected to rely upon. A warranty is a party's assurance that particular information is true and is combined with an indemnification obligation if those facts are false. The indemnity can include a responsibility to pay money damages or the return of funds, depending on the agreement. It can also include rights to terminate part or the entire contract.

Beware of contractual inaccuracies for several reasons. Sometimes innocent mistakes occur in the list of facts. In a large investment, there can be negligence in defining the details due to tired staff members making nonsensical blunders or transposing digits. It is easy to do, particularly if there is a time crunch and people are under duress.

Often people let their enthusiasm run wild and create overly optimistic estimates with inflated numbers. Truth is stretched to the breaking point; where the end result is divorced from anything close to reality.

Then there are shysters trying to cheat you from the start. They are consciously plotting to misrepresent and have no ethics whatsoever about deceiving you.

Plan ahead and have options to counteract inaccurate representations. The warranties and representations clause of the contract must be your basis for recourse. This legal document is complicated and must be reviewed thoroughly before investing, which is why we suggest an attorney be consulted on all transactions.

After college graduation and prior to entering the investment field, I started out as an auditor at a CPA firm. I observed scores of ways that numbers could be manipulated and misstated. It was amazing how companies buried items in their statements which taught me to never trust a financial statement, no matter who audited it. Always assume that whatever documentation is presented to you, it is not 100% accurate.

保证与陈述

大多数投资合同或者收购合同内都包括保证和陈述清单。在拟定交易中，陈述是对一方需要遵守的细节叙述。保证是一方担保特定信息是真实的，如果这些事实有错误，会有赔偿义务。这种赔偿可以包括，根据协议支付资金损失或返还资金的义务，还可以包括终止部分或全部合同的权利。

要谨防一些导致合同不准确的原因。有时，一些无心的错误会出现在实际的清单上。在一项大的投资中，当制订细节的时候，会出现因为员工的疲倦而导致荒谬的错误，或者数字颠倒顺序这种粗心大意的事情。尤其是在时间紧迫和压力重重之下，这样的事情更容易发生。

人们往往会让自己的热情失控，用夸大的数字来制造过于乐观的估计。事实离我们越来越远，终会造成与现实之间天差地别。

然后会有一些骗子试图从一开始就骗你。他们有意歪曲事实，千方百计欺骗于你，没有丝毫道德可言。

要提前计划，而且要有备选方案，以抵消不准确的陈述。合同的保证和陈述条款就是你追索的依据。这份法律文件很复杂，必须在投资前彻底审查，这就是为什么我们建议，在所有交易上都要征求律师的意见。

大学毕业后，进入投资领域前，我在一家会计师事务所（CPA）从审计员做起。我观察到许多数字被操纵和谎报的方法。公司在报表中隐藏一些条目的方式，着实令人吃惊，这教会了我永远不要相信财务报表，不管是谁审计的。无论摆在你面前的是什么文件，要始终假定它不是100% 准确。

When we encounter a prospect who will not sign an agreement that includes representations previously outlined in an oral or written manner, then we will either reduce our offer or not complete the investment. Due to our steadfast approach of assuming the worse, we have been very successful at not being duped.

Once we were considering funding an innovative invention and were told that no other device like this existed. In addition to facing zero competition, we were told the company had full patent protection. We sent a due diligence employee to the site, and he came back with a conflicting report, so we passed.

As is customary, we instantaneously notified them that we would not invest. Two days later, our same employee went to a store and found the same exact device produced by another company. The potential investment had been an audacious lie and illustrates how impossible it can be to verify every statement made by the other side.

For fun, I sent the fraudulent company a photo of the competitor's identical product. The charlatan acknowledged the product, saying he did not divulge it because that competitor had no money to expand. This is a true story and another exemplar of the credence of warranties and representations.

我们遇到一位不愿签署协议的潜在客户，协议中包括的陈述，之前已经通过口头或书面形式概述出来了，这种时候，我们要么就减少出资额，要么就终止投资。正因为我们坚持采取未雨绸缪的理念，使我们在免予受骗方面非常成功。

有一次，我们在考虑投资一项创新发明的时候，被告知市面并不存在其他相似设备。除了面临没有竞争对手之外，我们还被告知该公司拥有完整的专利保护。我们派了一个尽职调查人员到现场勘察，然而他带回了一份与之相矛盾的报告，所以我们放弃了该项投资。

按照惯例，我们立即将不会投资的消息通知对方。两天后，我们的那名做尽职调查的员工去了一家商店，发现了由另一家公司生产的同样设备。这个潜在的投资简直是个天大的谎言，并说明要想验证另一方的每一个陈述是多么的不可能。

为了好玩，我把别家公司那款相同产品的照片，发给了这家骗子公司。那个骗子承认了该产品，并表示他没有透露这件事的原因，是因为那家公司根本没有资金进行扩张。这是一个真实的故事，也是保证和陈述作为凭证的另一个范例。

Advisors and Committees

It is obvious that I am adamant about utilizing advisors and committees. Other voices add discipline and provide a range of insight to better comprehend potential investment opportunities.

There are several types of committees, each with a different purpose. One is an advisory group of famous names from the world of investing. A panel of experts who have "been there and done that" and can be called upon for guidance rather than a working and voting committee. Most large funds and investment houses maintain such committees to resolve problems with voices of reason and experience.

Usually an advisory committee of legendary names is only window dressing for raising capital. A strategy illustrating those experts believe in the proposed venture. If you can recruit such professionals to lend their names, then why not also reap their experience?

Members of an advisory committee should have the clout to connect you with the unreachable principal at the top of any organization. This kind of high profile introduction adds enough credibility to make that first meeting triumphant. It could take months to sit down with an executive at Apple or Samsung, but with such an influential group, maybe one phone call will procure a meeting. The individuals on your advisory committee should be powerful and travel in such circles. Even if they personally do not know who to contact, they probably have a colleague who does.

On the other hand, working committees plan sessions to unearth specific answers and solutions. There can be more than one such group, each focusing on different criteria. Set limits and rules to assure that these committees are actually functional. I have observed factions where egotistical members use the forum to showcase their wayward intelligence.

顾问及委员会

显然我坚持认为要利用顾问和委员会。他人的意见可以加强纪律、提供一系列的洞察力，使我们更好地理解潜在的投资机会。

有几种不同类型的委员会，各自的目的也不同。其中一种是由投资界的知名人士组成的顾问组，这些专家都是担任过“某个要职”或有过“某种成就”的人，他们不是工作委员会或选举委员会，而是给公司做指导的专家组。许多大的基金会或投资公司都设有这种委员会，用他们理性的、富有经验的想法，解决公司的问题。

通常这种包含传奇人物的顾问委员会，只是融资时的噱头。这一策略说明这些专家认可这一投资。如果你能请到如此专业的人士装点门面，为什么不借此得到他们的经验呢？

顾问委员会的成员，应该有能力让你接触到那些高不可攀的、任何组织的负责人，这种高调的引荐，给第一次的成功会见，增加了足够的可能性。你自己可能需要努力几个月，才能和苹果或三星的高管坐下来商谈，但是有这样一个有影响力的专家组，也许一个电话就能见面了。顾问委员会的成员应该有实力，并能出入这种圈子，即使他们自己不知道联系谁，他的同事也一定知道。

另外，工作委员会负责制订会议会期，发掘具体的答案和解决方法。可以同时有几个这样的委员会，每个专注不同的方面。要给这些委员会设置权限和规则，以确保他们能真正发挥作用。我见过这种委员会的内斗，以自我为中心的成员们，利用讨论会展现他们任性的心智。

Before each meeting, plan an agenda with topics for debate. First, review the listed subjects, then at the end, open the gathering for discussion. All such meetings should start on schedule and have a predetermined time period. You want committee affiliates to look forward to the constructive and inclusive weekly assemblies and never view them as squandering time. Besides these group meetings, encourage all employees to submit ideas and thoughts in an organized manner.

There should be the viability of calling an emergency meeting. But keep those assemblages to a minimum. Remember, emergency meetings are for real emergencies!

Chat rooms, supportive programs, software, and apps are options committee members can access to discover fresh ideas. I also recommend staffers participate in forums to ponder solutions before the actual committee meeting. Another concern, avoid embarrassing the boss at these gatherings. Your team must work as a unit and not blame others, but instead focus on solutions. This does not mean a little healthy conflict to resolving an issue cannot exist.

Committees are only supplemental tools and not meant to replace the management of the company. I have never observed an enterprise that runs efficiently being operated by a committee.

Even at the board level, their primary job should be hiring the best individual to achieve the company's goals and not interfering with daily activities. In most cases, a board trying to run a business has been a disaster.

First and foremost, every company must have a strong leader. The formation of various committees and advisors is only to enhance productivity, not to lead. Work groups are designed to make recommendations, not firm decisions.

I am also resolute about having the right to override a committee in making the final decision. I want to hear their opinions and reasoning, but my judgment must take precedence. It is rare that I will diverge from the verdict of a committee. However, when my intuition (coupled with external feedback) tells me group think is inaccurate, I will follow my gut instincts. And I've always been correct.

每次会议之前要规划好辩论话题的议程，首先，回顾所有列出的项目，最后，让大家集思广益讨论问题。这种会议一定要按时召开，并预先制定会期。你要让委员会成员对这种具有建设性和包容性的例会有所期待，而不认为是在浪费时间。除这样的小组会议以外，要以组织有序的方式，鼓励所有员工提出建议和想法。

要有召开紧急会议的机制，但要尽量减少召开次数。记住，紧急会议是十万火急的时候才需要召开的！

委员会成员可以通过聊天室、辅助程序、软件、应用，来发现新想法。我还建议在真正的委员会会议之前，先让员工在论坛中参与讨论，衡量对策。这样做的另一层含义，可以避免老板在这种集会中为难。你们的团队必须团结一心，不要相互责备，而是关注解决方法。这并不是说，为了解决问题而出现的、微小有益的冲突不能存在。

委员会只是补充工具，不能取代公司的管理层。我从未发现有一个企业是在委员会的操控下有效运转的。

即使是到了董事会的层面，他们的首要工作应该是雇用一个有能力的人，来完成公司目标，而不会干涉其日常活动。大部分情况下，如果董事会试图运营业务，会是一个灾难。

首要的是，每个公司都必须有一个强有力的领导，各种委员会和顾问的形成只是为了提高生产率，而不是去领导。工作组的目的是提出建议，而不是作决定。

我还坚信领导在作最后决定时，可以有权推翻委员会的建议，我想听到他们的观点和论证，但是我的判断必须优先考虑。我很少和委员会得出的结论背道而驰，然而，当我的直觉（配合外部的反馈）告诉我，委员会的想法是错误的时候，我会按照我的直觉办事，而且基本上每次都正确。

CHAPTER 4
Understanding Investment Principles

The investment process is complicated, and it is crucial for both investors and entrepreneurs to have the ability to pragmatically assess each specific situation. There are an abundance of theories and accepted formulas for success that may have been steadfast in the past, but may not be applicable or have become archaic in today's evolving global investment marketplace. From presentation to exit strategy, every investor and entrepreneur should have acute knowledge of investment structure, budgets and expenditures, financial balance, IPO particulars, realistic time frames, and many more investment principles.

第四章

了解投资原则

投资过程是复杂的，所以非常有必要让投资者和创业者双方都有能力，去实事求是地评估每一种特殊情况。为了确保投资成功，有许多现成的理论和认可的公式，在以前很可能行得通，但是对于今天这个不断变化的全球投资市场来讲，可能就不太适用或已经变得陈旧落伍了。从融资演讲到退出策略，每个投资者和创业者都应该对于：投资结构、经费预算、费用支出、账务平衡、上市细节、切实的时间规划等许多投资原则，拥有敏锐的认识。

Investing Rules

I have read umpteen books claiming to encompass "The Rules to Investing" ,but still don't believe there are unwavering parameters. Instead, there are rational guidelines for investors and entrepreneurs. The world advances with time which affects markets, trends, economics, governments, and even the meaning of words. These changes also affect investments and expected ratios from year to year.

For example, some authorities suggest using a percentage to determine your cash reserve amount. I disagree with a predetermined, fixed rate. The current economy and personal needs will resolve the ultimate proportion of capital you should maintain in reserve.

Simply put, be intelligent, flexible, and actively understand your potential investment. The evaluation process is convoluted enough without being bogged down with hard and fast rules.

In the back of this book, there is an appendix of reminder checklists. These are not rules, but helpful guidelines to investing wisely. Feel free to add to these compilations, as unique profit bearing opportunities and worldwide markets are constantly shifting.

投资规则

我曾读过很多声称其包含“投资规则”的书籍，但我始终认为没有不变的参数。那些只不过是对投资者和创业者的合理指导而已。世界随时间的推移而前进，它会影响：市场、趋势、经济、政府甚至词义，这种变化也在年复一年地影响投资及预期比率。

例如，某些权威人士建议用一个百分比来确定你的现金储备额，我不同意这种预先确定的固定比率。当前经济和个人需求会决定你应该最终保有资本中多少比例的现金储备。

简单来说，你要聪慧地、灵活地、积极地了解潜在的投资。因为即使没被固定规则困在其中，仅仅是评估过程就已经足够烦琐了。

本书最后，有一个提示清单的附录，这些不是投资规则，是让你可以明智投资的实用指导方针，你可以随意往这些汇编上增加内容，因为会有独特的获利机遇并且全球市场也在不断变化。

Investment Structure

From day one, protect all investments by structuring for the future, including strategizing for tax consequences and establishing a solid exit strategy.

I do not believe in investing to offset taxes with losses. We always factor in taxes and optimize the lowest rate possible based on current laws. To create, build, and implement this type of structuring, we always engage outside counsel.

Your exit strategy should assure that your fiscal goal will be achieved. If you plan on going public at some later date, make sure that the structure of the investment and company is in line with that objective.

If the investment structure does not protect your expenditures, dilution may result from future rounds of funding. Of course, you want to avoid being reduced, so the less mature the investment, the more dilution protection you require.

Never suffer dilution due to management not achieving their projections. To avoid this, create a scheme beforehand to shield losing investments. As an example, a convertible loan is a higher priority in the case the company should fail. A convertible loan will be paid back to investors before the common stockholder is considered. The common stock holder stands last in line and oftenreceives zero should a company fail.A common stock position offers the greatest return, but also the greatest risk. A convertible or preferred stock will have conversion features to the common stock.

Always have a legal strategy in place with each investment. If there is a grievance, there are policies to minimize the chance of a lawsuit and other tactics to diminish the financial impact.

In many cases, a startup company will not have sufficient capital to adequately structure for the future which will likely result in costly mistakes. Once the company is growing and has extra cash, revisit the initial constitution of the business.

投资结构

从第一天起，通过对未来进行规划，来保护你的所有投资，其中包括制定税务问题的战略和建立一个可靠的退出策略。

在计算投资成本时，我们总是把纳税这个因素考虑进去，我不主张通过投资损失来抵消纳税损失，而是根据现行法律，尽量优化至最低比率以减少纳税。为了创建、构建和实现这种结构，我们通常聘请外部顾问。

你的退出策略应该确保财政目标能够完成。如果你打算晚些时候上市，要确保投资结构和公司结构符合这一目标。

如果投资结构不能保护经费支出，这将可能会稀释未来几轮的融资。你当然想避免融资减少，所以如果投资越不成熟，你需要的稀释保护就越多。

永远不要因为管理层没有达到预期而忍受稀释。为了避免这种情况，预先制定一个计划以保护投资损失。举个例子，如果被投公司倒闭了，可转换贷款有更高的优先级，会在返还普通股持有者之前，优先返还可转换贷款投资者，普通股持有者排在最末位，通常在公司倒闭的情况下会颗粒无收。普通股持仓提供的回报率最大，但同时风险也最大。可转换股或者优先股具有转换成普通股的特性。

对于每项投资都应制定一个法律策略。一旦存在不满情绪，就要有相应的政策将诉讼的可能性降到最低，以及有其他策略帮助你减少财务影响。

在许多情况下，一家初创公司并没有足够的资金来让他们对未来的架构做出充足准备，这可能会导致他们走很多冤枉路。一旦公司开始增长并拥有额外的现金，请重新考虑公司的初始章程。

There are many economic arrangements that can reduce risk while still keeping the upside. Sometimes on a very attractive investment, you must accept what has been structured. Still, you should try to negotiate a more advantageous deal than what has been offered.

You only wield the power to demand structural changes before you invest. Never be shy insisting on modifications as it is your money. The composition of the company is absolute, so hire top professionals to optimize that structure in your favor.

有许多经济措施可以降低风险，同时可以保持上行。有时候对于一项非常吸引人的投资，你必须接受其现已形成的结构。尽管如此，仍然应该设法进行商谈，以期达成比提供的更有利的交易。

只有在投资之前，你才有要求结构变化的权力。不要胆怯，坚持修改，因为这是你投的钱。公司的结构已经组成了，然后聘请顶级专业人员，在符合你的利益基础上来优化结构。

Pertinent Questions

What questions should be posed when meeting with management of a targeted investment? It depends on the stage of the deal and previously researched intelligence from the due diligence process.

Like curious children, every answer to every question only creates another question. We like this inquisitive approach because each subsequent answer brings us closer to making a decision on whether to invest or walk. I refer to prepared lists and begin with the very basics.

Be aware of company executives who evade discussing the technicalities of their business and only concentrate on the end goal, but not how to get there. You need to know those answers along with other relevant information like: (1) "How did the company get where it is?" (2) "What is the track record of the CEO and other team leaders?" (3) "What about past projects, both successes and failures?" In advance, prep ten or twenty pertinent questions.

Every entrepreneur seeking funds must prepare for all queries that might impede their ambitions. If you do not have an appropriate solution to a question, you must at least provide an option to finding an answer. Maybe you can arrange to revisit the question in the near future or call a group meeting with your trusted team and find a solution. If you want a prosperous enterprise, anticipating problems is critical. Just as importantly, anticipate your success. Thorough preparation pays dividends.

Ask relevant questions and demand concise answers. Before long, you will get a Checkmate.

相关问题

当你与目标投资项目的管理层会面时，应该提出什么问题呢？这取决于交易的阶段，以及预先从尽职调查过程中研究的情报。

就像好奇的孩子，每个问题的回复只会引起另一个问题。我们喜欢这种爱问的方式，因为每个随后的回复，会让我们距离作出是否投资的决定更近一步。我指的这些问题是事先准备好的问题清单，而且要从最基本的问题开始。

要注意有些公司的高管，他们会避免讨论业务上的技术细节，只关注最终目标，不提怎么实现目标。你需要知道这些答案，以及其他相关信息，例如：（1）“公司是怎样发展至今的”？（2）“首席执行官和其他团队领导有过哪些业绩？”（3）“之前做的项目怎么样？成功或失败都要说明”。在之前，要准备 10 个到 20 个相关问题。

每个创业者在寻求资金的时候，都必须准备所有可能阻止他们志向的质询，如果针对一个问题，你没有恰当的解决方案，也必须至少提供一个让人能找到答案的选项。也许你可以安排在不久的将来重新讨论该问题，或者与你信任的团队召开一次小组会议，并找到解决方案。如果你想让自己的公司繁荣兴旺，预测各种问题至关重要，就像预期你的成功一样，充分的准备终会带来回报。

询问相关的问题，并要求简明的回答。很快，你就能在博弈中“将一军”了。

Double-Check Information

The axiom "garbage in, garbage out" means poor quality input will always produce poor quality output. This truism couldn't be more apt than when investing. If you are reviewing inaccurate reports, you will arrive at incorrect conclusions. It is impossible to make an intelligent decision with flawed information.

Meticulously search for signs of imprecise data. Do the financial statements look haphazard? Do the business operating statistics make logical sense? If not, then ask for the raw figures and compute the numbers yourself.

Maybe their bookkeeper does not possess the proper skills or software to prepare the records you are requesting. This is common, and we have assisted companies in hiring more qualified accountants to shore up the weaknesses.

When we make an acquisition or invest in a company, their financial and operational data must be precise. We expect our investments to grow, so the more organized the enterprise the more likely they can adroitly manage future growth. Without exception, double check all data to assure it is correct before investing.

仔细检查信息

有句名言:“废料进废料出”意思是指低质量的输入总会导致低质量的输出。这句名言在投资领域真是再恰当不过了。如果你正在审查不准确的报告，那么你将得出错误的结论。用有瑕疵的信息不可能作出明智决定。

仔细寻找不精确数据的迹象。财务报表是否看起来杂乱无章？企业经营统计是否合乎逻辑？如果没有，那就让他们提供原始数据并自己计算数字。

也许他们的会计并没有掌握适当的技能，或者不会使用特定的软件来准备你需要的记录。这种事情很普遍，我们帮助过一些公司，通过雇用更能胜任的会计师来弥补这些不足。

当我们对一家公司进行收购或投资时，他们的财务和运营数据必须是精确的。我们希望投资能够增长，因此一个企业越有组织性，就越有可能熟练地掌控企业未来发展。这件事没有例外，投资前仔细检查所有数据，确保其正确。

Divulging Acquaintances

If you've noticed, I do not drop individual's names and rarely list company names. It can be a consequential mistake when investing to disclose who you know.

Name-dropping makes you look like a minor leaguer who is unsure of yourself. The people you encounter only care about you, not your famous "friend."If you do mention a renowned person, first confer with that celebrity to reassure the nature of their recommendation.

Another potential problem of name-dropping is the reaction from the person you are endeavoring to impress. Maybe he/she does not respect or, worse yet, hates the person you are lauding. Boosting your ego is never prudent in a business meeting. Introducing unnecessary information will only turn people off.

Name-dropping is often used as bait for subordinates to arrange a meeting with the CEO. With patience and determination, I can reach the unreachable person with a cold call and attain a conference with anyone in the world. An old trick is to call during off hours. Most executives arrive early and work late, so if you call during those times, the targeted person will likely answer their phone.

Knowing famous people is wonderful, but will seldom facilitate the closing of a deal. If a well-known figure introduces you to an investment, that's one thing. Otherwise, there is no place for hero worship in the world of investing. Have confidence in yourself, have a first-class presentation, be prepared for all questions, and you will be on your way to prosperity.

提及熟人姓名

你应该注意到了，我不会提别人的真实姓名，而且很少列出各个公司的名称。当投资时，如果披露你认识的人，可能会是一个重大的错误。

通过提及名人来抬高自身身价，会让你看起来像一个不自信的小人物。你遇到的人只在乎你，而不是你那些著名的“朋友”。如果你就是想要提到某个名人，首先要和名人商量一下，告知推荐的性质以使对方安心。

提及别人姓名的另一个潜在问题，在于你努力使其加深印象的听者之反应。也许听者并不尊重你所赞美的人，或者更糟的是讨厌此人。在商务会议上，抬高自我从来都是不精明的。引入不必要的信息只会让人厌烦。

提及别人姓名通常是让下属安排与首席执行官会面的诱饵。只要有耐心和决心，通过一个无约电话，我就能联系到无法企及的人，并且跟世界上的任何人一同参加会议。一个惯用伎俩就是在下班时间打电话。大多数高管都是早来晚走，所以如果你在这段时间打电话，你要找的人很可能会接听电话。

认识名人固然很好，但很少能因此促成交易。如果一个知名人物向你介绍一项投资，那就另当别论了，否则，在投资领域里没有英雄崇拜可言。要对自己有信心，准备一个最佳的融资演讲，为所有的问题做好准备，你的事业就会走向繁荣兴旺。

Budgeting and Spending

When seeking capital, investors will obviously inquire how the money will be spent to benefit the company. Hence, you must provide a detailed and logical budget. If you can demonstrate that in the past you have spent money wisely,it will be much easier to raise new funds.

After a successful fundraising, the budget must be adhered to at all times. Many sophisticated companies have ended up in financial trouble because they ignored following the budget.

I always require a business to verify how previously raised funds were depleted. If they spent foolishly, that doesn't mean we won't invest, but it does mean we will add a layer of safeguards, including hiring an independent accountant to distribute the use of funds. We also require that our new venture appoint an internal auditor and new CFO or treasurer. If we have major concerns, we keep those instrumental personnel on our payroll to completely control all expenditures.

We realize that not all young entrepreneurs are experienced in adhering to a funding schedule, but are brilliant in other areas. Everyone has weaknesses, and in most cases it is only a matter of having qualified professionals oversee the flow of money.

To better understand the use of funds, consider these crucial questions:

- Did spending in the past fall in line with the budget?
- Is the budget now detailed with enough line items to avoid reckless spending?
- Does the company have internal controls to monitor spending once it receives an investment?
- Will this latest round of finance get the company to a profitable position?
- Does the use of funds budget follow the lines of logic?

All these questions and more must be asked and detailed answers must be obtained before you invest. If you don't, you will have a hard time containing the issue afterward, so be firm on this upfront.

预算和支出

当你寻求资本的时候，投资者显然会询问这笔钱将会如何使公司受益，因此，你必须提供一个详细而合理的预算。如果你能证明之前花钱很明智，那么之后筹集新资金的时候就会容易很多。

在成功地筹集资金之后，必须时刻遵循预算。许多高端的公司最终陷入财务困境，就是因为他们忽视了预算。

我始终要求企业核查以前筹集的资金是如何耗尽的，如果他们花钱很愚蠢，并不意味着我们因此就不投资了，而是会多加一层安全措施，包括雇用一名独立会计师来分配资金的用途。我们也要求该企业指派一名内部审计员和新的首席执行官或财务主管。如果有特别关注的人员，我们会把那些有用的人才列入我们的工资表，以完全控制所有开支。

我们认识到，并不是所有的年轻创业者都对遵守资金计划有经验，他们更擅长其他方面。每个人都有弱点，而大多情况下，只是需要有资格的专业人士来监督资金流动的问题。

为了更好地理解资金的用途，要考虑这些关键的问题：

- 公司以前的支出是否与预算相符？
- 现在的预算中是否有足够的条款可以避免胡乱花费呢？
- 公司一旦得到资金后，会有内部控制来监管支出吗？
- 最新一轮的融资会使公司有获利的可能吗？
- 资金预算的使用情况合理吗？

在你投资之前，所有这些问题，也许更多，都必须询问他们，并且要获得详细答案。如果不这样，以后就会很难控制这些问题，所以事先必须要坚持这样做。

Small or Large Deals

Fund managers often say a deal is too small for them and just as much work as a big deal, so why bother doing small deals? I disagree.

The current size of a transaction is immaterial. All that matters is the future. Does the product or service have all the earmarks of the next "big thing" or is expansion limited? Checkmate Investing never considers any opportunity too undersized. Instead, we concentrate on associated risk, scalability, and profit margins.

It is true that investing in smaller deals is as much work as the bigger ones. However, if you invest in an immature prospect early on that develops into a booming success, you will earn munificent returns. There is more risk in early stage investments, but the possibility of more handsome profits cannot be ignored.

What about mega-sized deals? I take the same approach; there is no deal too big. If we do not have enough capital to complete the investment, then we pursue co-investors or other pliable financial sources to conclude the pact. If we can't find matching funds, then we will reconsider the merits of the opportunity.

Sometimes our larger investments will coincide with our synergistic approach and benefit the growth of our smaller prospects. We always look at both vertical and horizontal fits with all our investments.

When reviewing any size deal, you must know and understand:

• What is the company's potential growth?

• The time frame required to attain an attractive profit margin and can it be maintained?

• How will costs be controlled?

• If it is a smaller company, can it be scaled enough to eventually be a large company?

• What is the plan for the next stage (whatever that may be)?

小型或大型的交易

基金经理们总是说，这笔买卖对他们来说太小了，而且要做的工作和大买卖一样多，所以为什么还要费心去做小买卖呢？我不同意这种说法。

一笔交易现在的大小并不重要，重要的是将来怎样。这一产品或服务有没有下一个“大热门”的特征，或者扩展会受限吗？“将军投资”从不认为任何生意太小，相反，我们专注于相关的风险、可扩展性和利润空间。

确实是这样，投资小型的交易和大型的交易，要做的事情一样多，然而，如果你在早期该业务尚不成熟之时去投资，等到繁荣发展以后，你会得到丰厚的回报。早期投资的风险很大，但是会有丰厚利润的可能性也不能忽视。

对大型交易怎么样呢？我采用同一种方法，生意也没有太大之说。如果我们没有足够的资金来完成投资，会寻求共同投资者或其他灵活的资金来源以达成协议。如果我们找不到相应的资金，就要重新考虑该投资的优点了。

有时，较大的投资正好与我们的协作方法相一致，这会有利于我们较小投资的增长。我们总是考虑不管垂直领域还是水平领域都要适合我们的投资。

当你审核任何规模的交易时：你必须知道并了解：

- 公司的潜在增长是什么？
- 为了获得有吸引力的利润率所需的时间规划是什么，是否有可持续性？
- 如何控制成本？
- 如果是一家小公司，是否能扩展到足够大并最终成为一家大公司？
- 下一阶段的计划是什么（任何可能）？

- How diligently have funds been spent to date (keeping in mind that growth investments may need another round of capital before they are fully self-sustaining)?
- What is the landscape of the competition?
- Are ratios in line with the industry? If not, why?

The size of a business deal is immaterial. Will its future ROI justify the investment?

• 迄今为止是怎样节省花费资金的（要记住，成长中的企业，在他们完全自立之前，很可能还需要另一轮资本注入）？

• 竞争环境怎样？

• 公司比率与行业总体是否一致？如果不一致，为什么？

交易的大小不重要，它未来的投资回报率会证明是否值得投资？

Financial Balance

Several times previously, I've advocated keeping balance in your life and investments as the universe is evolving at a record pace. Yesterday's vision is today's reality.

Regardless of how attractive you believe a particular sector might be, investing too heavily in one area is risky. Asset allocation and balance are imperative to reducing risk and maximizing return.

Some investors covet out of favor sectors which are discounted and often much undervalued.If you are in for the long term, this can be a winning strategy. If the sector is in trouble, and there is ample reason to believe that it will rebound at some point, consider an industry rollup as your stratagem.

A rollup is when you acquire multiple companies in the same industry to create holistic synergies, efficiencies, and more sales channels. When the sector recovers, you are positioned to reap the rewards and enjoy above average returns. The risk concerns can vary: the sector takes longer to recover than expected or, even worse, never recovers. A rollup is a method to take a distressed sector or fragmented industry and rebalance it by merging weak companies and making one strong enterprise.

财务平衡

我在之前曾经多次主张，你应该保持生活和投资之间的平衡，因为宇宙正在以前所未有的速度快速发展。昨天的愿景在今天已成为现实。

无论你觉得某一行业有多么吸引人，在一个领域中投资过多是很危险的。资产分配和平衡是必要的，这样才能降低风险并使收益最大化。

一些投资者看好那些不被重视和那些经常被低估的冷门行业。如果你打算长期投资，这可能是一个成功的策略。如果这个行业陷入困境，但有充足的理由相信它会在某个时候反弹，可以考虑行业整合作为你的策略。

行业整合，就是当你在同一行业中收购多家公司的时候，用来创造整体的协同效应、高效和更多销售渠道的方式。当该行业复苏时，你将获得回报，并且享受到高出平均水平的回报。风险方面的担忧可能会有多种情况：行业复苏的时间比预期的要长，甚至更糟永远不会复苏。行业整合是在一个陷入困境的行业或支离破碎的行业中，通过合并弱势企业来建立一个强大的企业，以实现再平衡的一种手段。

Being Fully Invested

I often hear the argument: "Only a fool sits on cash." I believe only a fool sometimes sits on cash. You cannot profit if you don't invest. But having ready cash allows you to take advantage of new and better prospects.

All our life we hear that patience is a virtue. This is absolutely true when investing, so carefully choose only fully vetted ventures. Do not invest just to be invested and avoid having cash "doing nothing." Maintaining cash reserves and not being fully invested is practical.

You can always realign a portfolio to accommodate a promising investment, but this could also result in unnecessary losses. Our investments are generally long-term in nature and demand our patience to pay out admirable dividends.

Ignore hype from aggressive entrepreneurs who warn, "We have another investor, so if you don't move today, you will miss the opportunity." Such strong arm sales techniques are usually nothing more than a desperate bluff and will only drive investors further away from the deal.

充分投资

我经常听到这样的说法："只有傻瓜才会坐拥现金。"而我相信只有傻瓜才会有时坐拥现金。如果你不投资，就不能获利。但是拥有现金可以让你在新的和更好的潜在投资中占尽优势。

我们在一生中都会听到耐心是一种美德。在投资的时候，这是完全正确的，所以要谨慎地选择那些充分审查过的投资。既不要为了投资而投资，也不要让现金"无所事事"。保持现金储备，并且不要完全投资是切实可行的。

你可以随时调整投资组合以适应一个有前景的投资，但这也可能导致不必要的损失。我们的投资在本质上是长期的，需要付出足够的耐心，才能得到极高的红利。

不要理会那些咄咄逼人企业家的炒作，他们警告道："我们还有一个投资者，所以如果你今天不行动，就会错失良机。"这种高压手段的销售技巧通常只是一种歇斯底里的虚张声势，而这只会让投资者更加远离这笔交易。

Non-Disclosure Agreements (NDA)

A non-disclosure agreement is a legal document that helps investment parties feel comfortable sharing information. An NDA is basically a promise not to reveal any confidential facts or ideas learned from the other party.

Sometimes a NDA is a one way street: "I promise not to reveal any confidential information that I learn from you." Other times, it is mutual: "We both promise not to reveal any confidential information that we learn from each other."

An NDA is requisite in developing a relationship of trust. You want people to feel at ease sharing facts and opinions in confidence, as opposed to worrying about you exposing any secrets that could damage their company. You should never be reluctant to sign an NDA because it is the first step in honesty.

If someone refuses to sign a NDA, do not share any info and move on to the next prospect.NDA's are a significant element of the investing process, and I advise utilizing these protective agreements.

保密协议

保密协议是一份法律文件，可以帮助投资双方在分享信息时感觉安心。保密协议从根本上说是一个承诺，不泄露从另一方获悉的任何机密事实或想法。

有时候保密协议是单方的：“我保证不泄露任何从你方获悉的机密信息。”其他时候，是双方的：“我们承诺不泄露从另一方获悉的任何机密信息。”

保密协议是建立信任关系的必要条件。你希望人们可以安心地与你分享机密的事实和观点，而不是让他们担心你会暴露任何可能损害其公司利益的秘密。你要甘心情愿地去签一个保密协议，因为这是诚实的第一步。

如果有人拒绝签署保密协议，那就不要与其分享任何信息，继续寻找下一个潜在投资机会。保密协议是投资过程的重要组成部分，我建议利用好这些保护性协议。

Pitch Deck

A pitch deck is similar to a business plan and fashioned to attract investors to your idea. It explicates the product or service overview, while also addressing use of funds, the target market, competitive landscape, sales strategy, stage of the opportunity, exit strategy and other particulars.

A strong pitch deck also points out negative aspects and provides pragmatic solutions. This shows financiers that you are well aware of all challenges associated with achieving your vision.

Overtaking the competition is not always the goal. Instead of becoming the dominant player, maybe you aspire to create a niche market to reap a much higher profit margin.

A pitch deck is not meant to sell the deal alone. It is the basis for a professional presentation, so include excellent visual appeal which accurately represents your vision. If you do not have such organizational and artistic skills, then hire a graphic artist to assist you in the aesthetics of the presentation.

Practice your presentation over and over in front of associates or friends. Also, use your phone to video yourself going through the routine. Think of questions that will be asked and practice answering them. Then carefully listen to your responses and make necessary revisions in vocabulary, tone of voice, enunciation, and likability. Even a seasoned pro can benefit from such an exercise. Plan on thirty minutes or less for your performance, leaving ample time to answer questions.

Also, never be annoyed with any question that a potential investor asks. You are seeking money, meaning there is never a stupid question and each one deserves an answer. If you aren't sure of the appropriate response, do the best you can, but never leave it unreciprocated. Later you can always contact the inquisitive person if you have a better answer.

融资演讲稿

融资演讲稿与商务计划相似，是为了吸引投资者对你的想法感兴趣而设计的。它说明了产品或服务的概况，同时也提到了资金用途、目标市场、竞争环境、销售策略、投资阶段、退出策略和其他细节。

一个有力的融资演讲稿也会指出消极的方面，并提供实际的解决方案。这让投资者感到，你很清楚自己为了实现愿景所要面临的挑战。

你的目标并非总是要超越竞争对手，也许你渴望创造一个利基市场，来获得更高的利润率，而不是成为主导者。

要融资并不意味着只靠一个融资演讲稿，它是专业演示的基础，所以你做的演示一定要有卓越的视觉吸引力，能精确地代表你的愿景，如果你不拥有这种编排和艺术技能，那就雇用一个图文艺术家来帮你制作一个优美的展示。

在同伴和朋友面前反复练习演讲，并且用手机给自己全程摄像，想想别人会问的问题并练习怎么回答他们，然后仔细聆听自己的回答，对词汇、声调、发音、亲和力方面，进行必要的修改。即使是经验丰富的专业人士也能从这样的练习中获益。计划在 30 分钟或更短的时间内做演讲，留出充足的时间来回答问题。

此外，千万不要对潜在投资者提出的任何问题感到恼火。你在寻求资金，说明不可能有愚蠢的问题，而且每个问题都值得回复。如果你不确定恰当的答案，那就尽量做到最好，总之不能置之不理。之后如果你有了更好的答案，总能联系到那个当初提问的人。

If the same question is asked over and over again, patiently answer it each time. Simply say, "I want to apologize, as you asked a similar question before, and it is obvious I did not answer adequately. I understand this is a very important topic, so I want to drill down on my answer until you are totally satisfied." That is an effective and respectful strategy to repetitious questions. In fact, after the presentation I send those unrelenting people an email addressing the same question again. This professional attitude shows that you value their input which may be influential in winning them over and securing their investment.

Additionally, make sure to obtain the contact information of everyone in attendance. When a question is asked, I always have my assistant write it down and identify the inquirer. This way, I can later contact the prospective investor by telephone or email to reassure their contentment and reconnect for a second time. To ensure that I heard a questioner precisely, I often reiterate their query before providing my answer which enhances accuracy for both parties.

The same is true of operating a business. All questions must be answered. Sometimes there are no immediate solutions, but an erudite response still must be forthcoming.

Realize that some people will never invest in you no matter how fabulous your project or pitch is. Nonetheless, these individuals are important because they can shed light on the way others think. And they provide a live audience for you to practice and improve your presentation. The more objections I hear, the better presentation I will make the next time.

And don't minimize body language. The art of reading a person's physical expressions is real, and you need to learn this skill. Read up on the powerful imagery and impact of body language. Learn how your subconscious movements translate to others and which actions to emphasis and avoid. Your pitch deck could be the finest in the world, but will still fail if you don't look and sound confident in your quest for success.

如果同一个问题被反复问到，每次都要耐心回答。可以简单地说：“我想向你道歉，因为你之前问过类似的问题，很明显我回答得不够充分。我明白这是一个非常重要的话题，所以我想就此问题进行深度探究，直到你完全满意为止。”这是对重复性问题有效而尊重的策略。事实上，会议结束以后，我会给那些反复提问的人发一封电子邮件，再说明一下该问题。这种专业的态度，展现出你重视他们的建议，这会影响到最终能争取到他们，并确保能得到他们的投资。

还有，要确保能够获得每个与会人员的联系方式。当有人提问的时候，我总是让助理记录下来，并确认提问者，通过这种方式，我就能在之后的时间里，通过电话或电子邮件，联系该潜在投资者，让他们安心，并能再次联系到他们。为了确保我能准确地理解提问者的问题，我经常在提供答案之前重申一遍他们的问题，这样就提高了双方的准确性。

经营企业也是如此，所有的问题都要回答，有时候没有快速的解决方案，但仍必须有一种博学的快速应答。

要认识到有些人永远不会给你投资，无论你的项目或演讲多么精彩。尽管如此，这些人很重要，因为他们可以提示我们，其他人的思考方式。而且他们还充当现场观众，帮你练习并能改善演讲。听到的反对意见越多，下次的演讲就会做得越好。

而且不要低估肢体语言。关于解读一个人的肢体语言的艺术是真实的，你需要学会这个技能。仔细研究肢体语言的强大意象和影响。要了解你下意识的动作是如何传递给他人的，以及哪些动作要加强或避免。你的融资演讲稿很可能是世界上最棒的，但是如果你在追求成功的过程中，看起来和听起来都不自信的话，你仍然会失败。

Presentation Experts

Hiring a third party expert for presentations is typically not done, but should be. An authority can add credibility to your pitch deck. In the courtroom, it is normal to bring in an independent and accredited witness, and often this specialist is the linchpin of all final decisions. During meetings with potential investors, an expert is a clever way to build your case.

Of course, you must be assured the paid authority will reinforce and enhance your vision. With some advanced role playing, you will better gauge the expert's replies when interrogated. Most specialists charge a substantial fee for both the preparation time and actual presentation. Deem whether such fees will fortify your venture or weaken your sincere effort.

Hired experts are not truly independent because everyone knows you are paying them to spew out superlatives on your behalf. But they are credible in their fields of expertise and can be very persuasive. True professionals want to preserve their standing in the industry and will not risk destroying their reputations by lying. Before writing a check, make sure they really believe in your product.

Some people make their living as hired experts and are easily located. Unusual circumstances might compel you to find someone less conspicuous to act as an authority. For example, a retired executive, professor, or industry consultant will suffice.

If your expert cannot physically attend the presentation, try a pre-recorded video screening or a slide show itemizing his/her related findings and biography. Although there is nothing like a live presentation, some enactment is better than nothing.

I once brought in my expert via a video conference call. He was a well known professor, who did not have time to travel to 19 cities to pitch various investors, but he was able to make himself available for one hour each day. This visual medium allowed the presentation group to see him live and ask questions. It was an immensely effective tool in closing the deal.

演讲专家

通常大家都不会雇用第三方专家来演讲，但是应该这样做。一个权威人士可以给你的融资演讲增加可信度。就像在法庭上，通常会带来一个中立而备受认可的证人，这个专业人士会是最终判决的关键。在与潜在投资者开融资会议时，请一个专家为你演讲，会是你创造成功机会的明智之举。

当然，你必须确认这个雇来的权威人士会加固和增强你的愿景。通过一些事先的演习，你可以更好地测评专家对问题的回答效果。大多数专业人士对于事先演习和实际演讲都会收取大量费用。看看这项花费的结果，是会强化你的企业，还是会削弱你真诚的努力。

雇来的专家不是真的中立，因为大家都知道他们是收了你的钱，才会以你的名义演说得那么好。但他们在专业领域上是可信的，而且会很有说服力。真正的专业人士希望保持自己在行业中的地位，不会冒着破坏自己声誉的风险而撒谎。在支付专家费用之前，确保他们真正地相信你的产品。

有些人以雇佣专家的身份谋生，而且干得不错。在某些特殊情况下，可能会迫使你去找一个不太有名的人作为权威人士。比如，退休的高管、教授或行业顾问都能胜任。

如果专家不能亲身参加演讲，那就事先录一段视频，或制作一个幻灯片，列出与其相关的研究结果和个人传记。虽然没有现场演说效果好，但有这些措施总比没有强。

我曾经有一次，通过一个视频电话把我的专家请到其中，他是一个知名教授，没有时间穿梭于 19 个城市来给各类投资者演讲，但他每天能抽出一个小时的时间，这种视觉媒介让与会人员能看到他的现场演说，并提出问题。这可以说是达成交易的制胜法宝。

As a side note, your expert is not to answer questions about your offering. You must make it clear that his/her only job is to respond to technical questions. If your specialist does start drifting away from the technology, then I advise stepping in immediately and redirecting the authority back to his/her field of expertise.

If the potential investors demand to ask your expert questions about the offering, calmly clarify that he/she is an independent consultant with no knowledge of the internal workings of the company or whether this is a good or bad investment. We want to maintain the credibility of both the expert and our company, so we separate the two and avoid any conflicts.

附注一点，你雇的专家不应负责回答关于你募资的问题，你必须清楚，专家唯一要做的就是回答技术问题。如果专家开始偏离技术话题，那我建议你马上介入，令其转回自己的专业领域。

如果潜在投资者要求你的专家回答关于募资的问题，要平静地向他们说明，专家只是一个中立的顾问，不了解公司内部的运作情况，也不清楚这是否是一个好的投资。我们想要保持专家和公司的信誉，所以我们要把两者分开，避免任何冲突。

Initial Public Offering (IPO)

An IPO is often the favored exit strategy for many enterprises. When a company goes public, it denotes registering shares of the company's stock with the United States of America Securities and Exchange Commission (SEC), listing the stock on an exchange, and offering shares to the public for the first time.

The drawback with going public is the listing process is expensive and time consuming. There are legal, filing, and accounting fees, plus ongoing expenses, retainers, and much more than you ever imagined. You will also have new responsibilities to shareholders and be under more scrutiny and regulations.

Going and being public is an outstanding structure to raise money and create liquidity without having to sell the company. However, you must think carefully before embarking on such an inclusive journey.

The process normally takes between six months to two years. Listing time can be shorter if you complete a reverse merger, or it can be longer if there are auditing issues or such complications. And where will you list (NASDAQ, NYSE)?

Once listed, you are required to be punctual with reports. Businesses that release late reports are perceived as troubled companies, and its stock will suffer. Perception is one of the biggest problems with taking a business public.

Advisors and an investment bank will be needed to guide you through the process which is also time consuming and expensive. Furthermore, you will want to hire an investors' relations representative along with a public relations firm. Assiduously choose the right team by interviewing multiple professionals for each position.

Going public will also take you away from your business, so hire in-house people to assist with daily operations.

首次公开发行

对于许多企业来说，首次公开发行往往是一种受欢迎的退出策略。当一家公司上市时，它是指在美国证券交易委员会注册该公司的股票，将股票在交易所挂牌上市，并首次向公众发行该股票。

上市的缺点是挂牌的过程既昂贵又费时。其中有法律、文档和会计费用，除此之外还有日常开销、预付费用，以及多得超乎你想象的各种费用。你还将对股东承担新的责任，并受到更多的审查和监管。

企业上市这种结构非常好，因为它可以在不出售公司的情况下筹集资金并且创造流动性。然而在开始这样一段包罗万象的行程之前，你必须仔细思考。

上市这一过程通常需要 6 个月到 2 年不等。如果你完成了反向兼并，那么上市时间可能会短一些，反之如果出现审计或类似复杂的问题，那么上市所需的时间会变得更长。还有你将在哪里上市呢(纳斯达克或纽约证券交易所)？

一旦上市，你就必须准时提交报告。晚提交报告的企业会被视为陷入困境的公司，其股价也将受到影响。当一个公司公开上市时，公众认知就是最大的问题之一。

在此过程中你将需要顾问和投资银行的指导，这是费时又费钱的过程。此外，你还需要聘用一名股东关系代表和一家公关公司。通过每遴选一个职位，都要面试多名专业人士，来努力选择合适的团队。

上市也会让你远离自己的业务，所以要雇用内部人员协助日常运营。

Aside from the above precautions, there are many benefits to going public. In addition to creating liquidity for investors, employees, and executives, stock options can be used to retain valuable employees. You can also use the stock for acquiring other businesses rather than spending cash or taking a loan.

This approach has certain tax advantages and gives the acquired company's owners the option of more upside or selling. On such a transaction, the seller receives stock that may have certain restrictions regarding its liquidation. Over time they will be able to sell the stock, maybe just not instantly.

Being public will perpetuate the longevity of an enterprise. A family owned private company often has trouble with succession. Some family businesses have an abundance of qualified family members who all want to be the new leader. Others have no competent family members to ascend to headship. Often at this point, the company must be sold or will fail. If that same company had been public, it likely would have proficient personnel in place to pass on the torch. No longer would the leader have to be a family member, but instead the most capable candidate for the job.

Public companies normally have a higher market value than private companies which have no liquidity. Once you are public, this penalty is eliminated.

Not all businesses are meant to be public. Some industry sectors are just not appealing to the general public and will not trade well enough to justify the listing. In fact, some commercial groups trade below the actual value of the company. Another problem is that once public, you must build out an entire compliance infrastructure. You will also need an Investors Relations structure (IR) which includes both internal and external functions supporting IR. Lastly, you may even be subject to a hostile takeover.

There are so many benefits and detriments to going public. Prior to making your decision, hire knowledgeable advisors and carefully understand their suggestions, and only then choose what is best for your company. There is a checklist in the back of this book to help you go public.

除上述注意事项以外，上市还有很多好处。除为投资者、员工和高管创造流动性之外，股票期权还可以用来留住那些有价值的员工。你也可以用股票来收购其他公司，而不是用现金或者贷款。

这种方法可以在纳税时有一定的优势，并且可以给予被收购公司所有者更多好处，或将其售出的选择权。在这样的交易中，卖方收到的可能是对清算有一定限制的股票。也许不是立即就能兑现的，但是随着时间的推移，他们就能卖出该股票。

上市可以使企业长久存在。私有家族企业常常会出现继承的问题。一些家族企业中有很多合格的家庭成员，他们都想成为新的领导者。而另一些家族企业没有一个称职的家庭成员堪当领导。通常这种情况，公司肯定要出售或倒闭。如果这家公司已经上市，很可能会有专业人员来接管大旗。领导人不再必须是家庭成员，而是那个最有能力的候选人。

上市公司通常比没有流动性的私人公司拥有更高的市场价值。一旦上市，不利即消除了。

并不是所有的公司都要上市。一些行业对普通大众没有吸引力，也不会有足够的交易来证明上市的合理性。事实上，一些商业团体的交易低于公司的实际价值。另一个问题是，一旦上市，你必须构建一个完整的合规基础结构。你还需要一个股东关系结构，包括内部和外部的职能来支持股东关系。最后，你甚至可能要服从恶意收购。

上市既有许多好处也有许多坏处。在作出决定之前，聘请有见识的顾问，仔细理解他们的建议，然后再选择最有利的方案。这本书的后面有一张清单，可以帮助你怎样上市。

Exit Strategies

An exit strategy is salient! From day one of every investment, Checkmate Investing plans the exit strategy. Paper profit, as defined by increase in value, must eventually be turned into cash. When and how are critical along the pathway to success. We consider an IPO (listing), selling to a third party, or selling a piece of the company to reimburse our initial investment. Our fund is structured to dividend cash or shares to our investors, which gives us the possibility of holding, while most funds must eventually sell to meet the liquidation life of the fund.

During the dot.com boom, Internet stocks were in a frenzy. In those early days, investors never assumed that future earnings were guaranteed and that income would eventually materialize. For some, this scenario turned out to be true and made them very rich. Others never developed a working revenue model and ultimately failed. Remember, you can only revisit the investment well so many times before the financiers dry up.

We often invest in Internet companies that have reasonable chances of being bought out by more established enterprises. Even when our primary exit strategy is to sell to a pre-targeted buyer, we still have to craft a self-sustaining revenue producing business.

A stupendous example is Snapchat. They turned down a three billion dollar offer from Facebook who sought to capitalize on Snapchat's gigantic user base to grow their (Facebook) company. Snapchat had achieved their exit strategy which was to sell to a third party. But Snapchat's metrics were so good they decided not to sell. The investment world was stunned, including me, but they were right. Three years later, Snapchat had a market cap of over twenty billion dollars and still growing.

Snapchat proved the importance of multiple exit strategies. I cannot predict Snapchat's future, but their judgment points out the dynamic nature of the investing world. We must be flexible and rethink all angles as circumstances change. Sadly, there are many other examples of Internet companies that renounced solid offers and later went out of business. A savvy investor will reach beyond the numbers and reevaluate the current economic climate when making exit strategy decisions.

退出策略

退出策略是最重要的！“将军投资”从第一天起就开始计划退出策略。按照价值增长的定义，账面利润最终必须转化为现金。何时以及如何实施退出策略，在通往成功的道路上至关重要。我们认为可以通过 IPO（上市）、出售给第三方或出售公司的一部分，以偿还我们的初始投资。我们的基金是基于向投资者派发股息或股份的结构，以使我们具备持有基金的可能性，而大多数基金最终必须按照清盘期限售出。

在互联网繁荣期间，网上证券处于疯狂状态。在早些时候，投资者从来没有设想到未来的收益是有保障的，而且收入最终会实现。对一些人来说，这个情景真的实现了，并且让他们变得非常富有。其他人则从未开发出成功的盈利模式，最终失败了。要记住，你能做的只是在投资者没干涸之前，多拜访几次投资之井。

我们经常投资那些极有可能被更成熟的企业收购的互联网公司。即使我们的主要退出策略是向预定目标的买家售出，但我们仍然需要打造一个能自给自足的生产企业。

色拉布（Snapchat）是一个另人惊叹的例子，脸书试图利用色拉布庞大的用户群来壮大自己，出资 30 亿美元意欲收购色拉布，但被其拒绝。色拉布通过卖予第三方完成了退出策略，但是色拉布的指标非常好，他们又决定不出售了。包括我在内的整个投资界都震惊了，但是他们是正确的，3 年后，色拉布的市值超过了 200 亿美元，并且还在增长。

色拉布证明了多种退出策略的重要性。我无法预测色拉布的未来，但他们的决断表明了投资领域的动态本质。当情况变化时，我们必须要灵活地、从各个角度重新思考问题。遗憾的是，还有许多其他关于互联网公司的例子，他们放弃了可观的报价并未售出，然而后来却倒闭了。精明的投资者不会只在意那些数字，在制定退出战略时会重新评估当前的经济形势。

Realistic Time Frames

All astute poker gamblers abide by the maxim, "Know when to hold and know when to fold." Knowing how long to hold an investment before reaching the exit point is always a gamble. Since there are so many unknown and volatile factors, we have rational time frames for maintaining each investment. These schedules are not fixed, but instead serve as guidelines.

By having timetables, we are better able to set milestones and reach our destination. If a new product is to be released, specify a date when its objective will be reached.

When you miss objectives or jump ahead of schedule, review and readjust accordingly to fully understand what happened. Throwing out dates, without realistic time frames, occurs frequently with inexperienced leaders. This irresponsible behavior chews up money without producing income and forces another round of fundraising which means your stock will suffer dilution. If your goal is to prosper, dilution is your enemy.

Conversely, rushing a product to market before it is ready spells disaster. It can create something worse than dilution, and that is called bankruptcy. Marketing flawed products will generate returns and a bad reputation. For a fledgling company, returns not only mean you have lost a sale, but the product you invested in may be worthless.

Many companies have became insolvent for bringing their product to market either too slowly or too quickly. A product does not have to be perfect to go to market. It just has to function properly. Look at the original Apple iPhone, which was not faultless, but good enough to satisfy most users. Apple could have spent more years perfecting it before launching, like their competitors did, and missed the market.

There is a school of thinking that cautions companies not to release their best version first, but to initially market their lesser product and obtain consumer approval. Later, after customers have accepted your product, release the next generation. This is called seeding the market.

切实的时间规划

所有精明的扑克赌徒都遵守这条格言："知道什么时候该坚持，什么时候该放弃。"知道在投资到达退出点之前要持有它多长时间就是一种赌博。由于有许多未知和不稳定的因素，我们要有合理的时间规划来维持每项投资。这些时间表不是固定的，只是作为指南。

因为有了时间表，我们能够更好地设置目标并完成。如果要发布新产品，那就要制定实现目标的日期。

当你没能完成任务或者提前完成任务的时候，回顾并重新调整时间表，以充分理解到底发生了什么事情。没有设定日期，也没有切实的时间规划，通常是没有经验的领导者会犯的错误。这种不负责任的行为，会在不产生收入的情况下把钱榨干，并迫使另一轮融资，这意味着你的股票将会稀释。如果你的目标是成功，那么稀释就是你的敌人。

相反，如果在产品还没有成熟的时候就将其推向市场，那么会招致灾难。它可以创造比稀释更糟糕的东西，那就是破产。营销有缺陷的产品会带来退货和差评。对于一个刚刚起步的公司来说，退货不仅意味着你失去了一笔销售额，而且说明你投资的产品可能毫无价值。

许多公司因为其产品过慢或是过快地进入市场，而导致最终破产。一款产品进入市场，没有必要一定是完美的。它只需要能正常工作。看看苹果最初的iPhone，它不是完美无瑕的，但它足以让大多用户满意。苹果本可以在进入市场前花更多的时间去完善它，就像他们的竞争对手那样，然而那些竞争对手却错过了市场。

有一种思维模式告诫企业不要一开始就发布最好的版本，而要先把他们低等级的产品推向市场，来获得消费者的认可。然后当客户已经接受你的产品的时候再发布下一代。这叫作"播种市场"。

If you follow this strategy, then a limited release of the first generation whets consumers' appetites. Make it special, a status symbol that is difficult to obtain. By the second or third generation, you can release more products for the now burgeoning demand.

I advise marketing your product as soon as feasible, even if it is not perfect. If the product is satisfactory, people will thirst for the next generation.

Respect time frames and learn to live by them, as this is paramount to success.

如果你使用这一策略，那么通过限量发行第一代产品来刺激消费者的胃口。让它变得特别，成为一个难以企及的身份象征。等到第二代或第三代，你可以为现在迅速增长的需求增加产品发行量。

我建议尽快将你的产品推向市场，即使它并不完美。如果产品令人满意，人们就会渴望下一代。

尊重时间规划并且学习依靠时间规划来生活，因为这对成功至关重要。

CHAPTER 5

Types of Investment Opportunities

There are all kinds of investments and each one has associated issues. Deciding which investments are best for you depends on your field(s) of expertise or your desire to enter a new industry or simply your interest in any opportunity that appears to be a winner. Real estate, entertainment, the stock market, manufacturing, and other sectors are affected by fluctuating valuations and consumers' fickle buying patterns. Deciding whether to rent, lease, or buy property or equipment will also affect the investment. Choosing any investment should be predicated on the same goal, making money.

第五章
投资机会类型

投资有许多种类，而且每种都有相关的问题。要决定哪种投资最适合你，取决于想要选择你自己的专业领域，还是希望进入一个全新的行业，或者你只对那些看起来容易成为赢家的机会感兴趣。房地产、娱乐业、股票市场、制造业和其他行业都受到估值波动和消费者变幻莫测的购买模式之影响。决定是要租赁，还是购买财产或设备也会影响投资。选择任何投资都应该以同样的目标为基础，就是赚钱。

Safe Investments

What does a safe investment actually mean? Is a secured investment even possible? The true answer is maybe, and only if you invest for the long term.

What seems safe today may not be safe tomorrow. In America during the forties, fifties, and sixties, there was almost no inflation, and it was considered "safe" to invest in long term bonds. But once the seventies hit, so did inflation. And by the eighties, this increase in prices and decrease in purchasing value drained the savings of those living on interest income from long term bonds and drastically changed their lives. Thus, the safe investment turned out to be anything but "safe."

I remember when it was deemed safe to invest in utility stocks due to a secure dividend. Again, times changed and many losses were taken from such investments. Some investors point to real estate, which seemingly always rises in value, so it must be a safe investment. In the long term, this choice might be the closest you'll get to a "safe" investment. However, real estate also has cycles, and money can easily be lost in a down market.

Learn to accept there is no "safe" investment and no true guarantees, except possibly the US government. Nevertheless, many cities and counties have had defaults. Even with government assurance, be sure to find out which sector of the government is backing the warranty. Is it a local USA administration or is it actually the main federal government issuing the guarantee?

Even when making "safe" investments, you must be prepared for anything, including failure. I become suspect when dealing with an "expert" investor who has never had a loss. If true, this person either has made very few investments or is not telling the truth. It's like someone saying he/she is an expert skier who has never fallen, which is beyond preposterous.

安全投资

安全投资的实际含义是什么呢？真的有可以担保的投资吗？正确的答案是：有可能，而且只有当你长期投资的时候才行。

今天看起来安全的东西，到了明天就未必安全。美国 20 世纪四五十年代及 60 年代几乎没有通货膨胀，投资长期债券被认为是“安全”的。但是 70 年代刚一来到，通货膨胀随即接踵而至，到了 80 年代，物价的上涨和购买力的下降，使那些靠长期债券利息收入为生的人，花光了储蓄，并彻底改变了他们的生活。因此，所谓的“安全”投资被证明是最不安全的。

我记得曾经认为投资公用事业股票是安全的，因为可以确保得到红利。再一次，由于时代的变迁，这项投资造成了很多损失。一些投资者指出，房地产似乎总是在升值，因此它肯定是一项安全的投资。从长远来看，这可能是最接近“安全”投资的选择。然而，房地产行业也有周期，而在市场低迷的时候，很可能会赔钱。

要学会接受没有“安全”的投资，除美国政府有可能以外，没有真正的保证。尽管这样，许多城市和小镇也都出现了违约。即使有政府担保，也要确定政府的哪个部门支持担保，是美国的地方政府还是主要的联邦政府实际上做担保？

即使在进行“安全”投资时，你也必须做好一切准备，包括失败。在与一位从未失败过的“专家”投资者打交道时，我表示怀疑，如果是真的，这个人要么很少投资，要么没有说实话。这就像有人说自己是滑雪高手，从来没有摔倒过一样，简直荒谬至极。

The key to success is obviously having more winners than losers. If your investment is not panning out, then cut your losses as soon as possible rather than hoping it will suddenly change. You can't change a bad situation, but you can find a better alternative as a replacement. I have opted out on the second and third rounds of an investment even when I had the right of first refusal.

Taking losses is just part of winning. Never be afraid to either suffer a failure or cash in a profit. I am never embarrassed to have a "loser" investment because I've had many more winners. And that is what the Checkmate Investing style is all about—making money!

成功的关键显然是赢多输少。如果你的投资没有成功，那就果断放弃以减少损失，不要指望它会突然变化。你不能改变不好的局面，但是你可以找到一个更好的替代方法。投资时我曾有过这种时候，尽管我在开始时就有拒绝的权利，但却在第二轮或第三轮的时候才退出。

承担损失只是成功的一部分。不要害怕失败，也不要害怕挣钱。我从来不会因为一次“失败”的投资而感到难堪，因为我赢的时候更多。而这正是“将军投资”的风格——赚钱！

Investment Valuation

One rudimentary tenet of investing is never overpay. The lower the price when purchasing a company, the greater the income when exiting.

Whether listed stocks or a private enterprise, how do you determine if you should invest? With listed companies, the value is already set and plenty of intelligence has gone into the current valuation. However, listed stocks are often over or under priced and very few are actually fairly priced.

There are many reasons for mispricing, but basically it is because no one knows the future. Consequently, analysts use terms like the predictability of earnings.

Last stage investments are a better bet because many sophisticated financiers are already onboard and much valuation vetting has already taken place. This is why when considering investments in private companies, it is wise to inquire who else has invested. While we are all prone to errors in valuation and judgment, the more committed institutional investors involved, the more reliable the current appraisal.

On private companies, you must know the number of rounds of investments and at what valuations. Does the company have intellectual property? Are there any lawsuits? What are the executives being paid? What potential dilution exists? What is the cash position of the company? Are they behind on payments? How much debt exists? All of these and more go into valuing the company.

Startups are the hardest to assess as they have no value, only future predictions, and those can fluctuate. Often, the management cannot be analyzed because they have no experience. Look at the passion and dedication of the leadership team and determine if the founder is 100% devoted to the venture.

For all investments, examine the company's five year future earnings projections. On last stage companies, I cut the projections by as much as 50%. On startups, I discount them as much as 90%, but certainly at least by half.

投资估值

投资的一个基本原则是永远不要超额支付。收购公司时的价格越低，退出时的收入就越高。

无论是上市公司还是私营企业，你如何决定是否应该投资呢？上市公司的价值已经确定，而且大量情报都已计入当前估值，然而上市股票的定价往往高于或低于实际价值，很少有公平的定价。

有很多原因会造成错误定价，但最主要的是没有人可以预测未来，因此分析师会使用收益的可预测性这样的术语。

最后阶段的投资是一个很好的选择，因为许多有经验的投资人都已加入其中，并且已经进行了大量的估值审查。这就是为什么在考虑投资私营企业的时候，最好询问一下还有谁也参加投资了。当我们都易于在估值和判断上出现失误时，涉及的机构投资者越多，当前的评估就越可靠。

对于私营公司，你必须要清楚一共有几轮投资，以及按照什么估值。他们有知识产权吗？有诉讼官司吗？高管的薪酬是多少？有什么潜在的稀释存在吗？公司的现金状况怎样？有拖欠款项吗？有多少债务呢？所有这些以及更多方面都应该加入公司的评估中。

新创业的公司是最难评估的，因为他们没有价值，只有对未来的预测，而这些都是会波动的。通常对管理人员也无法进行分析，因为他们没有经验。看看领导团队是否有激情和奉献精神，以决定创业者是否百分之百地投入企业中了。

对于所有的投资，都要检查公司未来 5 年的收益预期。对于最后阶段的公司，我将收益预期下调 50%，对于刚起步的公司，我会下调高达 90%，但至少要 50%。

The newer the company, the more inquisitions regarding predictability of earnings, competition, branding strategy, and so forth.If there is a product, who will manufacture it? Can profit margin be held? Is the product or service scalable? What about future employee requirements, sales projections, future management needs? How long will it take to realize initial sales? It is a laborious process that cannot and does not have any shortcuts.

There are actions to protect against being incorrect on valuation, such as applying penalties if goals are not reached or insisting on receiving more shares if the venture does not reach specific milestones. Holding the company responsible for their performance should be embedded in every deal. If the company does not believe in their projections and recoils at setting non-performance penalties, be suspicious. If the company believes in itself, they will always consent to such stipulations.

Earn-outs are another means to protect against erroneous valuation. Earn-outs are an alternative to pay less or more based on the results after the acquisition is completed. Maybe you can create an earn-out as part of the initial financing, thus reducing your risk and meeting middle ground with the seller. If the company reaches the agreed upon targets at a later date, you pay more. If the company falls short of the projections, you pay less. Earn-outs are a safer way to invest if you are unsure of the opportunity.

公司越新，关于收益可预测性、竞争、品牌战略等的调查就越多。如果有一个产品，谁来制造？利润率能维持吗？产品或服务可扩展吗？未来员工的需求、销售预期以及未来管理的需求都是什么？要多长时间才能实现初始销售？这是一个艰难的过程，没有也不会有任何捷径。

有一些措施可以防止在估值上的不准确，比如，如果目标没有实现就实行惩罚，或者在没有达到特定目标的情况下，坚持要求获得更多的股份。要让公司对业绩负责，这应该纳入每一笔交易中。如果公司不相信对他们的预测，并对设置违约惩罚措施感到畏缩，那就值得怀疑。如果公司对自身有信心，他们则会对这种规定表示赞同。

获利能力付款是防止错误估值的另一种手段。选择这种付款方式，多支付或少支付取决于完成收购之后的结果。也许你可以创造一种获利能力计划，作为最初融资的一部分，从而降低风险，并与卖家达成协议。如果公司在之后的时间里达成了商定的目标，你就会支付得多；如果公司没有达到预期的目标，你就会支付得少。当你对投资不确定的时候，获利能力付款是一个安全的方法。

Brand Building

Brand building is a lucid path to higher profits. Often, products from competing companies are manufactured in the same factory and have the same components, yet one is ultimately sold for a much higher price. The only difference is one has a well known brand name while the other is unknown.

Branding is essential if you want to maximize the profit margin of your product. When we review opportunities, whether a startup or mature company, we vigilantly review their brand promotion programs to ascertain the perception of their brand by the public.

Simply because a brand is well known does not always mean that's a good thing. For instance, some brands are thought of as cheap and hence cannot add profit margin to the product. Even the most admired brands must have ongoing campaigns to assure that their name remains valuable and popular. Sometimes we look at old brands for acquisition with the intent of re-launching that trade name.

Without doubt, the brand name can mean much to a company's bottom line. When we invest in a well known brand, it opens up many more distribution channels. For example, Internet searches direct the consumer to known brands. Shelf space, bank loans, and even new investments are easier to obtain if your brand is recognized.

If you have a great product, but no brand, then a strategy and campaign must be created. Here are some options:

• Develop a solid written plan for building your brand that coincides with the product launch.

• License a known brand name for your product.

• Acquire a known brand through an M&A effort with existing distribution channels for your new product.

With such branding strategies, sales can be ramped up quickly through existing distributors.

品牌建设

品牌建设是一条通向更高利润的清晰途径。通常，两个相互竞争公司的产品都是源于同一工厂生产，并且拥有相同的部件，但最终还是有一家能以更高的价格售出。唯一的区别就是，其中一家公司的品牌知名度高，而另一家不为人知。

如果你想让产品的利润率最大化，品牌是必不可少的。无论是新创业公司还是成熟公司，当我们调查投资机会时，都会特别留心地审视其品牌推广计划，以确定公众对其品牌的认知。

仅仅因为一个品牌是众所周知的，并不总是意味着这是一件好事。例如，一些品牌被认为是廉价的，因此不能增加产品的利润率。即使是最受欢迎的品牌，也必须经常进行宣传活动，以确保它们的品牌价值长盛不衰。有时我们会考虑收购旧品牌，意欲将其重新投放市场。

毫无疑问，品牌对公司的盈亏有很大的影响。当我们投资一个耳熟能详的品牌时，就会打开许多销售渠道。例如，互联网的搜索引擎会把消费者导向知名品牌。如果你的品牌被认可，陈列空间、银行贷款，甚至新的投资都更容易获得。

如果你有一个极好的产品，但没有品牌，那么就必须制定一个策略并开展宣传活动。这里有一些选项：

- 在产品发布的同时，制订一个可靠的书面计划，用以建立品牌。

- 为你的产品授权一个已知的品牌。

- 通过企业并购（M&A）获得一个知名品牌，使你的新产品可以利用其现有的销售渠道。

有了这样的品牌战略，销售额可以通过现有的经销商迅速增加。

Once the brand is built, you must keep it fresh and alive and take conscious steps to maintain the visibility and respect for that name, which is expensive and must be ongoing. When you stop advertising, that brand will fade out and soon be forgotten.

Many thriving brands from the past are only remembered by historians. Look at your favorite song, movie, television show, or a toy from your childhood, and you will agree that being popular in the past means nothing today. Unless the brand is constantly seen by the public, it will perish.

There is also the likelihood of being replaced by a new or revised product, eliminating the older model. The newest electronic gadget or recently premiered movie is the talk of the town today, but within a few months most consumers barely remember the movie or the device. When building a brand, reflect on this familiar adage, "Out of sight, out of mind." Initially, make your brand visible by using multiple promotional platforms, and then keep it visible with ongoing campaigns and garner the continuing benefits.

For years, television has advertised consumer products every day on every channel. The same companies keep repeating their commercials over and over. Most notable are Coca Cola, Ford, McDonald's, Budweiser, Geico, and others who spend colossal amounts of money to maintain sales. They understand the significance of incessantly promoting their brand. Only by staying in the forefront of the consumer's mind, can they obtain and retain success.

品牌一旦建立起来，你必须保持它的新鲜和活力，并有意识地采取措施以保持其知名度及对该品牌的尊重，这虽然很费钱，但是必须要坚持。当你停止广告时，这个品牌就会渐渐消失，很快就会被遗忘。

之前一度风光无限的品牌只有历史学家会记住。看看你最喜欢的歌曲、电影、电视节目或者你童年时代的玩具，你就会认同这一点，那些过去受欢迎的东西，对于今天来讲一文不值。除非这个品牌不断出现在公众面前，否则迟早会消亡。

还有可能就是该产品被一种新的或改良过的产品取代，从而淘汰了旧的型号。最新的电子产品或最近上映的电影，在今天是城镇里的话题，但几个月后，大多数消费者几乎不记得该电子产品或电影了。当建立一个品牌时，回想一下这句熟悉的格言："眼不见，心不念。"首先，通过多个推广平台让你的品牌随处可见，其次，在持续开展的活动中保持它的出现频率，并获得长久的利益。

多年来，电视台每天都在各个频道上宣传消费品。同一个公司的广告不断重复播放。最著名的就是可口可乐（Coca Cola）、福特（Ford）、麦当劳（McDonald's）、百威（Budweiser）、盖可保险（Geico）以及其他那些花费巨额资金来维持销售的公司。他们明白不断推广自己品牌的重要性。只有占据在消费者意识中的最前端，他们才能获得并保持成功。

Rent or Buy

Do you want to own the facility where you are located or is it better to rent or lease?

In some businesses, renting can come back to haunt you. Let's take a restaurant or store that opens in a new mall. Assume the space is not very desirable and rent is cheap. Before long that restaurant or store earns significant profits, and everyone is happy. Until the end of the lease when the landlord gets greedy and raises the rent, maybe even triples it! The landlord realizes how much you're earning and will justify higher rent as a result.

This happens all the time and can cause a business to go broke. Sometimes the problem cannot be avoided. However, there are usually solutions, including making the landlord a part of the business from the beginning and locking in a permanent rent provision.

Another solution is a long term lease that has automatic rollovers for the future with maximum rent bumps attached.Other alternatives may be to purchase the land and building or have an option to buy the real estate at a fixed price.

Aside from avaricious landlords, there are many variables when deciding to rent or buy:

• How about parking, does that building have adequate parking to service your customer base?

• Will you have to lease a second property just to meet parking needs? Businesses that do not offer parking, except in places like New York City, have a difficult time succeeding.

• How about signage? Believe it or not, there are landlords and smaller towns like Santa Barbara that will not allow you to erect a sign. A restaurant will suffer without a visual display revealing their type of food.

• What about hours of operation? Will you be allowed to remain open as many hours as you want? Often, restrictions from the landlord or city ordinances will limit your hours of operation.

租赁还是购买

你是想购买所在地的房产，还是觉得租赁更好呢？

在某些行业，租房可能会让你感到困扰，就以在一个新的购物中心里的一家餐厅或商店为例，假设空间不是很理想，但租金十分便宜，然而没过多久，餐厅或商店就赚到了可观的利润，每个人都很开心。直到租期结束时，房东变得贪婪，提高了租金，甚至还可能把租金提高三倍！房东要是得知你赚了多少钱，结果便是想办法让你的房租更高。

这种事情经常发生，并且会导致企业破产，有些时候这种问题不可避免。然而，通常还是有解决办法的，包括从一开始就让房东成为企业的一员，并签订永久的租金条款。

另一个解决方法是长期租赁，租约将来可以自动滚续，并后附最高租金限额。还可以选择购买土地和建筑，或者选择以固定价格购买房地产。

除了贪婪的房东，在决定租房或买房的时候还有很多变数：

• 停车方面怎样，大厦是否有充足的停车位来为你的顾客服务？

• 为了满足停车的需要，你还需要再租一套房子吗？除了纽约这种地方以外，那些不提供停车服务的企业，很难取得成功。

• 招牌方面呢？信不信由你，有一些房东和像圣塔芭芭拉这样的小城，不允许商户竖起标牌。餐厅将由于无法展示他们的菜品而饱受痛苦。

• 营业时间方面呢？你是否想营业到几点都行呢？通常房东或城市法令会限制你的营业时间。

• How about noise controls? Will you be told to limit the noise due to local residents?

• How about access? What may appear to be a fine location may be exigent for people to reach due to traffic congestion or deficient public transportation.

• At some point will your business require more or less space? Is there any adjacent land or buildings to accommodate expansion or down-sizing?

• Sometime buying the location will solve all problems, but where will you obtain the funds to complete the purchase?

As investors, always ask for the real estate plan. But don't be surprised if the enterprise has no such plan. In these cases, we insist they prepare one for our review.

• 噪声控制方面呢？由于周边居民的原因，会被要求限制噪声吗？

• 顾客如何光顾？看起来不错的地理位置，由于交通堵塞或公交不足，人们可能很难光顾。

• 在某种情况下，你的业务是否需要更大或更小的空间？是否有邻近的土地或建筑可以调节扩大或缩小营业面积？

• 有时购买房产会解决所有的问题，但是你要从哪里获得购买房子的资金呢？

作为投资者，你一定要询问房地产计划。但如果企业没有这样的计划，也不要感到惊讶。在这种情况下，我们会坚持要他们准备一份计划，以备我们审查。

Real Estate Investments

Over the years, we have closed numerous real estate investments. Regardless of the dimensions, property development requires many steps and many hurdles must be jumped.

As is our credo, an experienced team is required to implement property improvements. Real estate is unique as there are many profit centers along the way, but costs can easily spiral out of control. It is easy to over spend if the developer has little or no experience.

The purchasing of an existing building is less complicated than being a developer. To acquire a property or portfolio of properties necessitates a careful analysis of its condition and anticipated repairs, plus comps on similar properties, market analysis, rent rolls, etc.

Should the real estate market soften, and it often does, it must be considered illiquid. In a down market, no matter how much you lower the price, you might not attract a buyer.

Think of real estate as a long term investment, not a quick flip as many believe. If you keep buying and flipping, you will eventually be caught in a down market and go broke. Treat property as a lasting investment if you seek a practical venture.

It is always shrewd to employ local people, who are situated near your investment property, such as realtors, contractors, and legal authorities. Only people from that geographic region can truly understand the "lay of the land".

Often in real estate, you'll need to make zoning changes, which will require various permits and other municipality approvals. If you hire local people, they likely know the administrative personnel you will be encountering, and the process will be smoother and faster.

When purchasing property, engage well-informed agents. Even though you must pay a commission, the results will more than offset any fees paid.

Also recognize that every month a property remains vacant, money is lost and will never be recovered. A reliable agency will lease up or sell a property at a more expeditious rate than trying to do it yourself.

房地产投资

多年以来我们做成了无数个房地产投资，无论规模大小，房地产开发都需要许多步骤并且要跨越许多障碍。

正如我们的信条：一个经验丰富的团队需要实现财产增值，房地产投资很特别，到处都有可观的利润，但是成本很难控制，如果开发商没什么经验，很容易造成费用超支。

购买现有建筑不像开发新房产那样复杂。要想获得一项或多项房产，必须仔细分析其现状以及维修预期，外加与类似的物业相比较、做市场分析、查看租金账册等。

如果房地产市场疲软，而且这种情况经常会发生，那么就必须要考虑到会缺少流动资金。市场低迷的时候，无论你降多少价，都不会吸引买家。

要把房地产视为一项长期投资，而不是像许多人认为的那样可以快速转手。如果你不停地买进和卖出，总会有一天被困在低迷的市场，然后破产。如果你寻求一种实际的投资，就要把房地产当做长期投资。

雇用当地人是精明的举措，他们就在你投资的房产附近，比如房地产经纪人、承包商和法律部门。只有来自那个地理区域的人，才能真正了解“地况”。

通常在房地产行业中，可能需要改变分区，这就需要各种许可证和其他市政批准。如果你雇用当地人，他们很可能认识那些将来你要打交道的管理人员，整个过程将会更加顺畅和快速。

购买房产时，要与消息灵通的代理人接洽。尽管你必须支付佣金，但结果省出来的钱可以抵销那些花费。

同时也要认识到，每当房产空置一个月，失去的租金就永远无法收回。一个可靠的代理，会比你自己更快地出租或出售房产。

If you own a shopping center or building, consider a flexible rent structure. For example, a popular coffee shop, restaurant, gym or other admired tenant can add prestige to the building and make it more attractive to other occupants. And that translates directly into higher rents across the board for the property.

In some cases, consider offering free rent to a high profile tenant who can justify raising overall rental rates and thus creating more profits.Many landlords are myopic and refrain from imaginative incentives, even if it increases the overall yield of the property. Furthermore, a building with an auspicious blend of tenants will fill up quicker than one with no synergy.

A conducive mix of renters translates to fewer vacancies. A prestigious grocery store, like Trader Joe's or Whole Foods, will fill the parking lot with cars, creating more customers for other tenants. If an office building or strip mall has restaurants, a deli, and a coffee shop, the occupants do not have to go elsewhere for lunch or to entertain clients. This means less time spent on travel and more time being productive.

Busted real estate deals are often a hidden goldmine. Every once in a while, a recession or depression will occur and property development will become insolvent. Some aborted deals can be revisited. Maybe there is a latent project that was torpedoed because it took too long to execute a zoning change. Or a partially completed building that just needs completion funds. Bank owned foreclosures can be acquired at below market prices. Sometimes packages of real estate can be purchased from banks at very attractive levels.

I love busted real estate deals, as they can produce amazing returns. They also typically produce much faster returns than projects from scratch. The majority of the times, such abandoned deals offer risks that are far below other kinds of real estate opportunities. One shortcoming is the capacity to scale such derelict properties due to a scarcity of them.

Even in strong markets, aberrations will exist where you can purchase a defunct property and achieve robust returns. However, just like any investment, do not buy just because it is cheap. Have a strategy before investing in any property and ask yourself these crucial questions:

- What is the potential of the tainted property?
- How will the future liquidity fare when you want to later sell the property?

如果你拥有一个购物中心或大厦，考虑一个灵活的出租结构。例如，一间受欢迎的咖啡厅、餐馆、健身房或其他受人尊敬的租户，可以增加大厦的声望，也可以吸引其他租户。这样做的直接结果就是租金的全面提高。

在某些情况下，可以考虑免去知名租户的租金，因为他们的存在可以提高整体出租率，从而创造更多的利润。许多房东都目光短浅，即使有些办法可以增加房产的整体收益，他们也不愿开动脑筋采取这种激励措施。此外，一个大厦里面如果有福运旺盛的租户融入其中，将会比那些没有协同效应的更易出租。

各种租户的有益组合意味着低空房率，一家有名望的杂货店，像 Trader Joe's 或 Whole Foods，会让停车场停满汽车，为其他租户创造更多的顾客。如果一个写字楼或商业街有餐馆、熟食店和咖啡厅，租户就不必去别的地方吃午饭或招待客户。这意味着花在路上的时间更少，而有效工作的时间更多。

已经破产的房地产交易通常是隐藏的金矿。每隔一段时间，就会出现经济衰退或者大萧条，房地产开发商便会破产。这些中止的投资可以重新审视。也许有一个潜在的项目被扼杀了，只是因为进行分区变更花费了太长的时间或者尚未建成的建筑需要完工资金。银行拥有的止赎权可以按低于市场的价格获得。有时还可以从银行以极具吸引力的价格打包购买房地产。

我喜欢已经破产的房地产交易，因为可以带来惊人的回报。它们通常会比从零开始的项目更快地得到回报。大多数时候，这种被放弃的交易带来的风险，远远低于其他类型的房地产投资。不足之处在于，这种被弃房产可遇而不可求。

即使在市场兴旺的时候，你也有微小的概率买到一个废弃的房产，并获得丰厚的回报。然而，就像任何投资一样，不要仅仅因为它便宜就买。在投资任何房产之前都要有一个策略，问自己这些关键问题：

- 有问题的房产潜力何在？
- 如果你想晚些时候出售该房产，未来的流动性如何？

• If it is an empty building, how long will it take to lease out?

• What is the energy efficiency of the building you are purchasing?

• What are some impediments you might face in completing the building?

• Are there any environmental issues?

It is also easier to attain financing for real estate than other investment markets. And there are many ways to create a capital stack or layers to the financing of a project. Conversely, in bad times the capital markets will shrink, banks will stop lending, and other financing sources may run out of money. Unless you are a cash buyer, there may be intervals when it is implausible to finance the purchase of real estate.

In prosperous times, lenders can be found who foolishly buy into inflated, unrealistic real estate projects. Soon after construction, the imprudent property owner will be unable to make its debt payments and go bankrupt. Oddly, the more sophisticated and grander the project, the more chance this scenario will occur.This happens because of the large fees that come with large projects. Often the desire to earn excessive fees will warp the judgment of even the most urbane bankers and financial professionals.

In certain ways, this is acceptable. Without such incentives and gluttony, mega projects would never be built or completed. Sure there are bankruptcies, but many of the best projects in the world were constructed only because of the allure of the fees along the way. Due to these costs, a mammoth real estate project can take decades to complete.

Investing in older buildings is another strategy. Existing buildings can be bought inexpensively due to the lack of efficiencies, which can add much to operational expenses. Repairs and other updates can eat up profits. Retrofitting is a possibility, but sometimes not practical. For example, some older properties have pollution or environmental issues that must be cleaned up or face closure by government agencies. Such cleanup can cost more than constructing a new factory or building.

I caution the real estate world is not a part time job, and to prosper as a developer or speculator requires skill and experience. Think long term, assemble a professional team, and be patient.

- 如果大厦还没向外出租，要用多久可以租出去呢？
- 你购买的大厦能源效率是多少？
- 要想盖完这座大厦，你可能会面临哪些障碍？
- 有关于环境的问题吗？

与其他投资市场相比，获得房地产融资会更容易一些。有很多方法可以为项目的融资创建一个资本堆栈或层。相反，在经济不景气的时候，资本市场会萎缩，银行会停止放贷，而其他融资渠道可能会资金不足。除非你是一个现金买家，否则在购买不动产时，要想融资，可能会有一些不合理的时间间隔。

在繁荣时期，会有一些贷款者愚蠢地购买那些膨胀的、不切实际的房地产项目。施工后不久，轻率的业主将无法偿还债务并破产。奇怪的是，一个项目越复杂、规模越大，这种情况发生的可能性就越大。这是因为大型项目会产生高额费用。即使是最温文尔雅的银行家和金融专业人士，也常常因为渴望赚取超高的费用，而扭曲其判断。

在某些方面，这是可以接受的。如果没有这种激励的手段和贪婪的想法，大型项目将永远不会建造或完成。当然会有破产的情况，但是世界上许多最好的项目，都是因为其过程中产生费用的诱惑而建造的。正是因为这些花费，一个庞大的房地产项目可能需要几十年才能完成。

投资旧建筑是另一个策略。由于现有的建筑效率低下，我们可以廉价购买下来，但会增加运营费用。修理和其他更新可能会消耗利润。还可以对已有建筑进行改造，但有时不太实际。例如，一些老旧的房产有污染或环境问题，必须进行清理，否则会被政府机构强行关闭。这样的清理比建造一个新的工厂或建筑物花费的还要多。

我在此警告，不能把投资房地产当成一份兼职工作，作为一名开发商或投机者，要想获得成功，就需要技巧和经验。要长远考虑，组建一支专业团队，并且要耐心等待。

Movie Investments

A business that offers no barriers to entry is show biz, the television and motion picture industries. Today, anyone can produce a TV program on an iPhone and obtain editing software for free. Once completed, there are platform after platform to place a show.

However, earning money in the movie and television industry can be very complicated if you don't surround yourself with experienced talent, crew, and distribution outlets. Producing movies or TV shows can be feast or famine, but one box office hit or top ten TV program can easily outweigh the losses.

Understanding the various paths to entertainment revenue is not as clear cut as many might posit. Part of the equation is that most exhibition avenues offer little returns. Every day, the platforms for displaying visual presentations expand and multiply.

The dollars available to spend on entertainment have an inelastic band width. The amount of moviegoers is a finite number and will not increase as platforms to watch movies grow. Also, more movie platforms do not translate into more dollars from consumers.

Producing a low budget movie means little. A film completed for one hundred thousand dollars that looks like a one hundred million dollar movie is admirable, but it does not guarantee a bonanza of revenue. No matter how spectacular a particular movie is, without a large advertising and promotional campaign, people will not be aware of it and rush to the theaters.

The contemporary movie business is all about distribution and advertising. Actually, distribution is straightforward if you have capital to market the picture. A movie with no ad campaign, even with distribution in place, will return little or no money. A movie with a big advertising budget can always find distribution and has a very realistic chance to earn money.

Movie theaters are a separate entity, and the owners may be apathetic about a film's content, more preoccupied with selling seats and profiting from concession sales.

电影投资

娱乐圈、电视和电影，是一个没有进入壁垒的行业。如今任何人都可以在iPhone上制作一个电视节目，还可以免费下载编辑软件。制作完成后，就可以在很多播放平台上推送这一节目。

然而，如果你周围缺乏有经验的人才、工作人员和发行渠道，那么要想在影视行业上赚钱就会非常艰难。制作电影或电视节目可能是一场盛宴，也可能是大饥荒，但是如果电影票房大卖或电视节目收视前十的话，会很容易扭亏为盈。

要了解娱乐收入的各种途径，并不像许多人想象的那样清晰。部分原因是大多数的播放途径都没有什么回报。这种视频播放平台每天都在扩大和繁殖。

可用于花费在娱乐上的钱是有限的。观影人数是有限的，不会随着观影平台的增长而增加。而且增多的观影平台不会从消费者那里挣到更多的美元。

制作一部低成本的电影意义不大。一部耗资10万美元的电影，看起来像一部1亿美元的电影，是令人钦佩的，但它却不能保证财源滚滚。无论一部电影多么壮观，如果没有大型广告和推广活动，人们就不会意识到它的存在，也不会冲入电影院。

当代电影行业主要依靠发行和广告。事实上只要你有大量资金推广影片，发行是很容易的。一部电影如果没有广告宣传，即使发行到位，也收不到多少回报。一部拥有巨额广告预算的电影总是能够顺利发行，并且会有很现实的赚钱机会。

电影院是一个独立的实体，其所有者可能并不关心电影的实际内容，而更专注于影片是否卖座以及能否从特许销售中获利。

I recommend against investing in movies unless the advertising budget is already in place or you will most likely lose your investment.

In the film industry, the advertising budget is normally paid back before any other contributor. Obtaining distribution is almost impossible if based solely on the merits of the movie without ad money attached. For example, a film produced for ten million dollars might require another thirty million dollars for advertising, and whoever ponies up those promotional funds will be reimbursed in full before any other investor.

In addition to recouping his/her initial investment, the advertising financier will earn a return on that investment. Let's assume the advertising angel contracted to earn a twenty percent profit for investing. This means that the movie must earn at least thirty-six million (the $30M plus the 20% interest owed) before any and all other investors earn their money. Assuming the movie does not generate any other earnings, the actual production investors will lose their entire ten million dollar investment.

Young, inexperienced producers often pitch me to invest and typically make claims like, "We can easily get distribution." The truth is: obtaining distribution is only easy if you have the capital to promote the movie.

By and large, the public has no conception of the mechanics of the film business and envisions lucrative returns from such investments. Money can be earned from movies, but it all starts with a vigorous advertising campaign.

Box office gold like Star Wars, Jurassic Park, Titanic, and Spider Man have returned billions and made their investors incredibly wealthy. Actually, the best ROI in Hollywood is from investing in horror movies because they don't require major stars, can be produced comparatively cheaply, and have a very loyal, global following. There is no question movies have the potential to create bountiful revenue if all the essentials are in place.

As for investments in the TV sector, that dynamic is slightly different. It is always a challenge to produce a quality show. It is even more daunting to secure a network or cable distributor to air original entertainment. Akin to movies requiring advertising and promotion investors, TV programs need sponsors to foot the bill. Without a major corporate sponsor, like Chevrolet or General Electric, most TV executives won't even look at a TV Pilot, never mind contracting for an entire season of episodes.

我不建议去投资电影，除非广告预算已经到位，否则你很可能会赔钱。

在电影行业，广告预算通常是先于其他出资者，最先偿付的。如果仅仅基于电影的价值而没有广告费的支持，获得发行几乎是不可能的。例如，一部花费 1000 万美元制作成本的电影，可能需要另外 3000 万美元的广告费，而这笔宣传费用的出资人，会早于任何其他投资者，优先得到全部偿还。

除了收回初始投资外，广告出资者还将获得这项投资的回报。让我们假设这个广告出资者所签订的合同是想赚取 20% 的利润。这意味着，在所有其他投资者赚到钱之前，该电影必须至少赚到 3600 万美元（3000 万美元，外加 20% 的利息）。假设这部电影不会再产生任何其他收益，那么实际的制作投资者，将会失去他们全部的 1000 万美元投资。

年轻而毫无经验的制作人总是劝我投资，而且通常会说："我们可以很容易获得电影发行。"事实是：只要你有宣传这部电影的资金，获得发行是很容易的。

总地来说，公众对电影行业的机制并无概念，却期望从这些投资中获得丰厚的回报。电影确实可以赚钱，但这一切都始于一个得力的广告宣传活动。

像《星球大战》《侏罗纪公园》《泰坦尼克号》和《蜘蛛侠》这样的票房冠军，已经赚了数 10 亿美元，让他们的投资者非常富有。实际上，在好莱坞投资电影，投资回报率最高的是恐怖片，因为他们不需要大明星，制作成本相对低廉，而且拥有非常忠诚的全球追随者。毫无疑问，如果所有的关键因素都到位，电影就会有潜力创造丰厚的收益。

至于对电视行业的投资，情况则略有不同。制作高质量的节目总是一个挑战。更有挑战性的是让一个网络或有线电视发行者来播放原创的娱乐节目。类似于电影需要广告和宣传的投资者，电视节目需要赞助商来埋单。如果没有像雪佛兰（Chevrolet）和通用电气（General Electric）这种大的企业赞助商，大多数电视台的高管甚至不会观看电视试播节目，更别提承接一整季的电视剧了。

Like movies, excessive amounts of money can be returned if all the elements of a TV show fall into place. The Sopranos, the N.C.I.S. franchise (New York, L.A., Chicago, etc.), Law & Order, and The Simpsons (on air for 30 years) are a few examples attesting to the viability of becoming tremendously wealthy from TV investments.

Speaking of The Simpsons, let's analyze the popularity of animated entertainment. Often a movie or television show is nothing more than a billboard for products. People adore and identify with these cuddly screen characters to such a degree that licensing and merchandising opportunities arise, ranging from games to toys to clothes. When you couple the influence of the TV program or movie with social media, you have the potential to create an ongoing demand for products. Displaying these unique characters' images on fast food cups, in slot machines, at theme parks, and many other commercial arenas will have an even greater impact and result in more income. This innovative investment philosophy impels us to pursue all revenue avenues and not just one road to generate higher profits.

The key to investing in movies and TV and expecting to profit goes beyond the traditional return of merely the box office receipts or sponsorship fees. It's the ancillary markets that will bring the greatest ROI, so before making an investment assure the elements are in place to promote the project and create massive audience recognition which will drive the supplementary markets.

如同电影一样，如果电视节目中的所有元素都到位，就可以得到丰厚的回报。《黑道家族》、《海军罪案调查处》（纽约、洛杉矶、芝加哥等）、《法律与秩序》、《辛普森一家》（上映了 30 年）是其中一些例子，证明了从电视投资中获利丰厚的可行性。

说到《辛普森一家》，让我们来分析一下动画片的流行程度。通常，电影或电视节目只不过是产品的广告牌而已。人们对这些可爱的屏幕角色特别喜爱和认同，以至于在游戏、玩具和服装等领域出现了授权许可和销售机会。当你把电视节目或电影与社交媒体的影响结合在一起时，你就有可能创造出对产品的持续需求。在快餐杯、老虎机、主题公园以及其他许多商业领域中，展示这些独特的人物形象，会造成更大的影响，以致得到更多的收入。这种创新的投资理念促使我们追求所有的收入途径，而不只是通过一条路谋求更高利润。

投资影视，并期望除了传统的票房收入或赞助费以外，还能获得利润，关键在于影视的辅助市场，它将带来最大的投资回报率，因此在进行投资前，确保这些能够促进项目的要素全部到位，并创造大量的观众认知，从而推动辅助市场的发展。

The Stock Market

Learning to be a proficient investor in the stock market is arduous, and some say impossible. No matter how many books you read on the intricacies of the stock market, it is unlikely you will grasp enough knowledge to jump right in and be a thriving trader. There are many theories to investing in stocks, yet no one has found the crystal ball that guarantees enduring success. You only learn by actually doing.

To begin with, the stock market is liquid. Most stocks can be sold immediately when you desire your money back. Of course, you will not know what amount you will actually receive as it always fluctuates.

Unknown factors constantly arise that will influence stocks. Once shares are purchased, the subsequent valuations are out of your control. Sometimes a stock will move higher or lower because of the company fundamentals, but market movements, which are known as market risk, can also cause stocks to oscillate. I have observed situations where a stock will drop in price after what should have been good news. On the other hand, what some experts call bad news can cause a rise in price.

Presumptions on buying and selling stock may have no reliance at all on the fundamentals of the company. Many investors make their decisions solely on studying charts or by watching and interpreting sector rotation. Others prefer the balanced approach, but then some believe in concentration as the secret to success, meaning buy only one or two stocks that they deem to have a huge upside. Similar to the stock market itself, theories and strategies are always changing.

The stock market is a passive investment, and normally you cannot affect the movement of the shares you are buying. Stocks are very important to the capital markets, so you take time to understand the basics.

Another caution is that the stock market can be addicting. Do not allow it to distract you from current business at hand unless you are committed to trading as a full time job.

股 市

在股市中要想学成一个精通的投资者是很困难的，有人说根本不可能。不管你读了多少有关错综复杂股市的书，你都不可能掌握足够的知识，让自己直接投入其中，并成为一个长胜的交易者。投资股票有很多理论，但没人可以找到能保证持久成功的水晶球。你只能通过实践来学习。

首先，股票市场是流动的。当你想要收回资金的时候，大多数股票都可以立即卖出。当然你不可能知道实际能收回的金额，因为股价总是波动。

不断出现的未知因素会影响股票。股票一旦买进，随后的估价就超出了你的控制范围。有时由于公司的基本面，股票将会上涨或下跌，但市场波动，又称为市场风险，也会导致股票振荡。我曾经观察到过这种情况，在应该有好消息之后，股票价格会下跌。而另外，一些专家所说的坏消息却会导致股价上涨。

推断是要买进或者卖出股票，可能与公司的基本面毫无关系。许多投资者仅仅是通过研究图表，或观察及理解板块轮动来作出的决定。其他人倾向于采用平衡的方式，但有些人则认为专心是成功的秘诀，这意味着只买一两种他们认为可能会大幅上扬的股票。与股市本身类似，理论和策略也在不断变化。

股票市场是一种被动投资，通常你影响不了自己买进股票的走势。股票对资本市场非常重要，所以你需要花些时间去了解基础知识。

另一个警告是，股市可能会让人上瘾。不要让它分散你对现有业务的注意力，除非你将其视为全职工作。

Onetime Events

When assessing a company, be careful of a onetime event, and how it may affect earnings. A onetime event means a company will have a portion of its earnings attributed to an occurrence that will never be repeated again. In other words, an investor should not calculate onetime events into future earnings.

Onetime events may also emerge when a loss is involved, such as a onetime write-off that will not happen again. Such news is often viewed as bad news, when maybe it might be good news. This is why you must always take the time to break down the earnings report to see exactly how it is composed.

A onetime loss or gain must be fully investigated because it could morph into a multiple time event. For instance, the windfall of a big sales quarter due to a competitor going out of business may bring new customers to you. If manipulated correctly, some of these onetime customers will be retained.

As another example, a company's thermal blanket sales increased by 600% during the coldest winter in one hundred years. This is a classic onetime event as it may be another one hundred years before that happens again. In such a case, we would call a strategy session and analyze what else can be sold to these newfound "onetime" customers, who now know your brand, and if satisfied, may buy your other products.

Maybe this onetime event has been so successful that it elevated your brand to a higher level. If you can develop a proper strategy, then you can ride this onetime event into something larger and longer lasting. Momentum, regardless of how it is created, must be exploited to propel success.

The point is a onetime event should not be overlooked and presumed to never happen again. When sales occur for whatever reason, learn how to repeat those sales. Instead of feeling you got lucky, examine what can be done to retain those new customers.

一次性事件

在评估一个公司时，要注意一次性事件，以及它会如何影响收益。一次性事件意味着公司会有一部分收益来自一个事件，而这一事件以后不会再发生。换句话说，投资者在预测未来收益时，不应该将一次性事件所得的收益计算进来。

当涉及损失时，也可能会出现一次性事件，例如，一次性报废，这种情况不会再次发生。这类消息常常被看做坏消息，但很可能是好消息。这就是为什么你必须花时间来剖析收益报告，看看它到底是如何组成的。

必须充分地调查一次性的损失或收益，因为它可以转变成多次性事件。例如，季度大甩卖时，由于竞争对手破产而得到意外收益，可能会给你带来新的客户。如果处理正确，将会留住其中一部分客户。

另一个例子是，在百年一遇的最冷冬天，一家公司的保暖毛毯销售额增长了6倍。这是一个经典的一次性事件，因为很可能要再过一百年才会再次发生。在这种情况下，我们会召集一个战略会议，分析还有哪些产品可以卖给这些新得到的“一次性”客户，他们现在熟悉了你的品牌，如果满意的话，就很有可能购买你的其他产品。

或许这个一次性事件特别成功，将你的品牌提升到一个更高的水平。如果你能制订出一个合适的策略，那么你就可以使这个一次性事件变得更大并且更持久。不管这个强劲势头是怎样创造出来的，都必须加以利用来推动成功。

关键是我们不应该忽视一次性事件，并且认为它不会再发生。一旦出现销售额增长，不管出于何种原因，要学会如何重复这种增长。不要觉得你很幸运，而是要检查你能做些什么来留住这些新客户。

Mergers and Acquisitions

A rapid way to growth is by acquiring another company. Maybe the purchased company is a spinoff of a larger private or public enterprise that can bring immediate credibility and financial rewards. Mergers and acquisitions (M&A) can at times be an excellent expansion strategy.

However, consider why the company is for sale and whether you are acquiring a winner that you can cultivate or a loser that is in serious trouble and beyond repair.

I know of two very large department stores, with outdated methodology, that were experiencing difficulties appealing to consumers. The two companies decided to merge together to create efficiencies and trim overlapping departments. The strategy was not to dilute each other by fighting for the same customer base and thus become one successful entity.

This merger had the smartest bankers in the world involved, yet I did not comprehend the logic behind combining two unsuccessful companies and assuming that together they would become healthy. The real problem of an outdated approach to retailing was not addressed and the confluence didn't resolve their troubles. It did reduce costs, which is always a good idea, but did not devise solutions to increase earnings and profit margin, which is always a bad idea.

To identify concrete M&A targets, notify as many influential people as you can, including lawyers, brokerage firms, accounting firms, industry associations, publications and more.

Sometimes a company is for sale, but too embarrassed to let the public know. They worry if their customer base were aware of a pending sale, then those consumers would be lost.

The best way to find such distressed companies is to call upon them privately. Sometimes when you ask, they will say no at first. By inquiring, you have now planted a seed in their mind. Simply be patient and before long they may contact you back. If they do not, then maybe contact them again six months later.

企业并购

收购另一家公司是一个快速增长的方法。也许被收购的公司是一个更大的私营或公立企业的子公司，它可以带来直接的信誉和财务回报。企业并购(M&A)有时是一种极好的扩张策略。

但是还要考虑一下为什么这家公司要出售，你即将获得的是一个可以栽培的摇钱树，还是一个处于严重困境和无法修复的赔钱货。

我知道有两家非常大的百货公司，由于使用过时的方法，在吸引消费者方面遇到了困难。这两家公司决定合并，以创造效率并精简重叠的部门。这一策略是想避免他们通过争夺相同的客户群而削弱对方，从而成为一个成功的实体。

这次合并有世界上最聪明的银行家参与其中，但我不理解这种，将两家不成功的公司合并起来，并期望在一起后情况就能好转的逻辑。这种过时的零售方式，其真正的问题没有得到处理，而融合并没有解决他们的困境。它确实降低了成本，这是个好主意，但并没有设计出解决方案以提高收入和利润率，这就绝对不是好主意。

为了确定具体的并购目标，要竭尽所能更多地通知那些有影响力的人，包括律师、经纪公司、会计师事务所、行业协会、出版物等。

有时一家公司想要出售，但却羞于让公众知道。他们担心，如果自己的客户知道公司行将出售，那么他们将会失去这些客户。

要找到这些陷入困境的公司，最好的办法就是私下拜访他们。有时当你询问他们的时候，他们会首先否认。但是通过这次询问，你已经在他们心中播下了种子。只要有耐心，不久他们就会联系你。如果他们一直没联系，那就6个月之后再联系他们。

Family based companies can be ideal acquisition targets. Often there is no one in the family who is qualified to take over the reins of the company, so they welcome an interested buyer.

There are a myriad of avenues to find M&A opportunities, including speaking at seminars and writing articles for industry publications. In the back of this book, a checklist will be helpful in your quest to acquire enterprises.

家族企业是理想的收购目标。通常都是家族中没有可以胜任的人来接管公司，所以他们欢迎有兴趣的买家。

有无数的途径可以找到并购机会，包括在研讨会上发言的时候，以及为行业出版物撰写文章的时候。在这本书的后面，有一份清单，当你想要兼并企业时，会对你有所帮助。

Local Partner Strategy

Previously, we touched upon hiring locals when investing outside of your region, but this strategy is worthy of more discussion. Collaboration is imperative before moving ahead on any investment in uncharted territories, particularly in international business. To understand a new community or country is a learning curve, and a knowledgeable partner will provide years of neighborhood experience, plus a network of competent affiliations that increase efficiency and reduce costs.

If you are investing in the international markets, having a native collaborator can be the difference between prosperity and adversity. In some countries, their laws will demand you to follow such a joint strategy. Even when there is no mandate, realize you are uninformed about navigating in a foreign land. Also, finding a reliable local partner is not an easy chore and will take time to get acquainted. Never be rushed to enter a foreign market.

Make sure all communications with your collaborators are written to avoid misunderstandings. I strongly believe in preparing notes that can be shared after each meeting to assure you are both on the same page. Also, begin the relationship with a written and agreed upon method to dissolve the partnership should it not work out.

The agreement must be fair to all parties and contain apposite motivating factors. Contracts that are one sided never produce long-term results. Local partners must receive enough in return to keep them motivated throughout the term.

If it is merely a sales territory and you are giving an exclusive, make sure to have performance clauses as part of the contract to assure that your new associate takes the relationship seriously. You must have a way to exit if your partner is not creating sales.

On the other side of the equation, make sure the agreement has a long enough term to encourage the resident partner to invest money into marketing and brand building. If the contractual term is too short, the local collaborator may not be willing to properly promote the products. You want to structure the agreement so that the native connection is motivated to build the brand.

当地合作伙伴策略

在此之前，谈到在其他区域投资的时候，曾提到过要雇用当地人，但这种策略值得更多的讨论。推进在未知领域的任何投资之前，尤其是在国际业务领域，合作是势在必行的。了解一个新的地区或国家需要一段时间，一个知识渊博的合作伙伴会提供多年的本地经验，外加一个能够提高效率和降低成本的有能力的关系网络。

如果你在国际市场上投资，能有一个本地的合作伙伴，是决定胜负的关键。在一些国家，他们的法律会要求你遵循这样的联合策略。即使没有这样的规定，也要意识到你对于外国如何操作一无所知。而且要找一个可靠的当地伙伴并不是一件容易的事，需要时间来了解。千万不要急于进入外国市场。

要确保将你和合作伙伴的所有沟通都记录下来，以避免误解。我强烈主张准备好笔记，可以在每次会后分享，以确保双方达成共识。同样，合作初始写下并认可一个解除合作的办法，以防合作不成功。

签署的协议必须公平对待所有各方，并包含适当的激励因素。单方面的合同永远不会长久。本地合作伙伴必须获得足够的回报，以使他们在整个合作期中都保持动力。

如果仅仅是一个销售领域，并且你是独家销售，务必将绩效条款作为合同的一部分，以确保你的新同事认真对待合作关系。如果该伙伴没有销售业绩，你必须有相应的退出办法。

重要的是，要确保签署长期合作协议，来鼓励本地伙伴将资金投入营销和品牌建设。如果合同期限过短，本地伙伴可能不愿意真正地推销产品。你应该拟订一份协议，以激发本地伙伴建设品牌的积极性。

The same rules apply to local partners in domestic markets. For example, if your business is based in California, you may find it helpful to hire a local inhabitant on the West Coast to cover that specific region of the United States. Depending on the product, local market partners can be instrumental to growing your earnings. Of course, be familiar with the collaborator before entering into any agreement.

这种合作伙伴规则也适用于美国国内市场。例如，如果你的公司位于加州，你会发现雇用西海岸当地居民来处理这一美国特定区域的业务，是很有帮助的。视产品而定，当地伙伴可以帮助你增加收入。当然在达成任何协议之前，要熟悉合作伙伴。

Crowdfunding

Crowdfunding is an existent alternative for obtaining funds. At first, crowdfunding was only for new and smaller budgeted ideas, but now is a source for just about any capital needs.As crowdfunding has matured, so have the unlimited amounts that can be raised by this method.

A big advantage of crowdfunding is that it does not demand the type of due diligence of an institutional fund. That is not to infer crowdfunding is as simple as posting an idea. The campaign must be well organized and well planned out.

A slick and informative crowdfunding video is one of the many components you should integrate into your campaign presentation. Media coverage and any other innovative exposure can help potential investors notice your idea and increase the chances for a successful offering.

Crowdfunding is analogous to Angel Investing. In most crowdfunding campaigns, you must promise to deliver something to each person who contributes a certain amount. This is often an early version of your product or service. However, whatever you offer in your crowdfunding campaign, you must deliver.

I have observed several large crowdfunding campaigns that never delivered what was promised. This can create an enormous amount of bad publicity, particularly in social media. That is one of the downside risks of crowdfunding. If you fail to deliver what you promised, you can ruin your reputation and make thousands or even tens of thousands of people very angry.

Another potential downside of crowdfunding is the danger of losing some of your patent rights. A presentation video of an early version of your product, including a detailed description, and the aforementioned offer that a contributor to the campaign will receive the product could amount to a public disclosure of the product and make it difficult to obtain a patent. This is a particular concern if you are using crowdfunding to finance the development of high-tech products.

众　筹

众筹是获得资金的一种可行性选择。起初，众筹只适用于新的和小的预算方案，但现在是任何资本需求的来源。由于众筹已经成熟，因此可以通过这种方法筹集到没有金额限制的资金。

众筹的一大优势在于，它不需要机构基金那类的尽职调查。这并不是说众筹就像发布一个想法那样简单，而是整个运作过程都必须组织有序、计划周密。

一个流畅并且信息丰富的众筹视频，是你应该组合到活动发布中的众多要素之一。媒体报道和任何其他新颖的曝光手段，都可以帮助潜在的投资者注意到你的想法，并增加筹集资金的成功概率。

众筹与天使投资类似。在大多数的众筹活动中，你必须承诺向每个投入了一定资金的支持者提供一些东西，通常是你的产品或服务的早期版本。然而，无论你在众筹活动中提供什么，你都必须有所提供。

我观察过几次大规模的众筹活动，他们一直没有兑现提供交付的承诺。这会造成大量的负面影响，尤其是在社交媒体上。这是众筹的下行风险之一。如果你没有兑现承诺提供的东西，就会毁掉你的声誉，惹得成千上万的人都不高兴。

众筹的另一个潜在下行风险是失去一些专利权的危险。产品早期版本的演示视频，包括详细的描述，以及前面提到的为该活动的支持者所提供的产品，就相当于将产品公开披露，致使其难以获得专利。如果你用众筹来资助高科技产品的开发，这就是一个特别需要关注的问题。

If you are unfamiliar with crowdfunding, be prudent and hire consultants to help organize a campaign. Of course, there will be fees to pay, but I advise that you bring on a team that has the experience to make your campaign a success. There are also conferences on crowdfunding where you will meet people who have run flourishing crowdfunding campaigns and will share their knowledge. I also suggest educating yourself by reading books on crowdfunding.

We broach crowdfunding because money is money, and no matter where you acquire it, the cost of capital is eventually the deciding factor.

如果你不熟悉众筹，一定要谨慎，要聘请顾问来组织这一活动。当然要付出一些费用，但我建议你聘请一个有经验的团队以使活动成功。也有一些关于众筹的会议，你会在那里遇到一些人，他们的众筹活动办得有声有色，会分享其中的知识。我还建议你通过阅读关于众筹的书籍来进行自我学习。

我们之所以谈起众筹，因为钱就是钱，无论你在哪里获得资金，资本成本最终都是决定因素。

Reinventing Industries

Investment opportunities do not have to be entirely original ideas. They can stem from an old initiative revisited. Take a simple pizza. For many years in America, if you wanted a pizza, you either went to a pizza parlor or it was delivered to you. Most pizza shops had to incur additional costs by owning and insuring delivery vehicles. The CEO of the Pizza company indeed a very clever person devised the novel idea of hiring drivers with their own cars and paying for their own insurance. Thereby, avoiding the company have to use up capital buying cars and paying for expensive insurance. Before long, this one company changed the entire pizza industry, often using 20 vehicles instead of one or two for each location. The scheme was scalable, and the company quickly became a multibillion dollar enterprise.

An industry that has struggled since the early days of the Internet is the music industry. Prior to 2000, a successful musician could earn a good living selling their recordings. After file sharing was introduced on the Internet, the music business went sideways due to free song downloads. For years, there were legal battles as the industry tried to stop the illegal downloading.

While the music business won many battles, they lost the war. What could the recording artist do to make a decent living? The first solution was to continue to record, offer the music for free, and use the downloads as an advertising tool which could make the artist popular enough to earn a living by touring.

As time went on, merchandise and licensing could also be a viable revenue source for the musician. Writing and recording songs that created themes and sold t-shirts and other consumer products became part of the reinvention of the industry.

重塑行业

投资机会并不一定是完全原创的想法。可以是对源自旧想法的重新审视。以吃一个简单的比萨为例，在美国多年以来，如果你想吃比萨，要么去比萨店，要么就预订外卖。大多数的比萨店都必须为拥有和投保送货车辆而承担额外的费用。一家比萨店的首席执行官确实是个聪明人，想出一个新奇的主意，雇用司机并用他们自己的汽车，自上保险。因此，使公司免予耗费资本购买汽车及支付高昂的保险费，不久之后，这家公司改变了整个比萨行业，他们在同一个店铺经常使用二十辆车，而不止是之前的一两辆。这一方案是可扩展的，该公司迅速成为一个价值数 10 亿美元的企业。

音乐产业是自互联网诞生之初就一直苦苦挣扎的一个行业。在 2000 年之前，一个成功的音乐家可以靠卖唱片为生。当互联网引入文件共享之后，由于可以下载免费的歌曲，传统音乐行业便靠边站了。多年来，在业界试图阻止非法下载的过程中，出现了许多法律纠纷。

虽然音乐行业打赢了许多官司，但他们输掉了大的战场。靠卖唱片为生的艺术家该怎样做才能过上体面的生活？第一个解决办法是继续录音，提供免费的音乐，让下载音乐作为一个广告工具，可以使艺术家备受欢迎并依靠巡回演出来谋生。

随着时间的推移，对于音乐家来说，商品和许可也可以当做一个可行的收入来源。写歌和录制歌曲用以创建主题、出售 T 恤和其他消费产品，成为重塑行业的一部分。

Other options have surfaced, like placing those characters created in songs and merchandise into an amusement park or feature movie. Building a web series or television show with a song as the foundation looms as another possibility. A new app or game could also be created from the song. The music industry is still a work in progress and constantly needs to reinvent itself to create fresh revenue channels, but it is a prime example of reinventing and winning.

Examine old brands and ideas from your past experiences, and you may discover the seed for the next big thing. How can contemporary technologies pump new life into a creation from long ago? Is the next billion dollar company built on a product overhauled from your childhood? I believe in the concept of reinventing. The idea worked in the past, has merit, and is something you may wish to explore.

其他的选择也已显露出来，比如，将歌曲和商品中所创造的角色，放到游乐园或故事片里。以一首歌作为基础来打造一个网络系列或电视节目，是另一种可能性。还可以从一首歌中开发一个新的应用程序或游戏。音乐产业是仍在发展的产业，需要不断重塑自身以创造新的收入渠道，但这是重塑和成功的最好例子。

审视老品牌和你过去的想法，你可能会发现下一个大热门的种子。如何利用当代技术，将很久以前的创作注入新的生命？下一个价值数十亿美元的公司，是源自对你童年产品加以修补的吗？我赞同重塑的概念。一个想法在过去行得通，定有其可取之处，而这正是你可能想要去探索的东西。

CHAPTER 6

Modern World Investing

Modern technology has become the primary investment tool for investors and entrepreneurs worldwide. The advent of the Internet propagated countless communication platforms, including websites, chat rooms, social media, news outlets, virtual offices, and other electronically based alternatives to easily access and pursue a plethora of investments. While technology has made communicating simpler, it has also bred unseen criminals who lurk behind your computer screen and can wreak havoc on your business and personal life.

第六章

当代世界投资

现代科技已成为全球投资者和创业者的主要投资工具。由于互联网的出现而孕育出无数的交流平台，包括网站、聊天室、社交媒体、新闻媒体、虚拟办公室以及其他基于电子的方式，便于轻松使用和从事大量的投资。虽然科技让沟通变得更加简单，但也滋生出潜伏在电脑屏幕后面、看不见的罪犯，他们会严重破坏你的事业和个人生活。

Using Modern Technology

Being a consistently proficient investor requires having an edge. Anything you can learn or use to improve yourself and your company will give you an advantage over your competitors.

Technology is one such tool to gaining the upper hand by replacing many of the slower, more tedious options of the past. The comparing of ratios and other analysis can now be done by computers and software. Work that used to take weeks to complete can be done in seconds and with more accuracy. Graphs, charts and other helpful visuals can be configured immediately for macro and micro reviews. Video conferencing will never replace in person contact, but is very helpful in creating efficiency. Phone apps are helpful in just about everything you do on a daily basis including unlimited research. Technology is not the sole solution for analysis and decision making, but it surely will boost competence.

Take the time to learn which technology is preeminent for your specific needs. How to best use it is another challenge. I suggest joining groups and clubs along with reading journals from your industry. Most conferences offer breakout sessions on the applications of pioneering technology. Scientific knowledge can be outmoded quickly, so stay on top of innovative revisions. New inventions are marketed every month and year that create more efficiency in the investment process.

Some people become so immersed in technology that they forget the human ingredient and may miss changes in management, changes in laws, etc. While software and other technologies can make investing less complicated, the world is dynamic, not static. As such, the human touch is always going to be salient to the process. Even artificial intelligence (AI) has its limitations.

Technology is your friend, so embrace it, but realize investing is not purely mechanical and must be combined with human instinct to maximize your goal of consistently producing winning investment results.

使用现代科技

作为一贯熟练的投资者需要拥有优势。你可以学习或使用任何方法来提升自己及公司，以优于竞争对手。

科技是这样一种工具，它通过替换许多以前缓慢而冗长的方法来占得先机。现在可以通过计算机和软件，来完成比率及其他分析的比较。过去花几周时间才能完成的工作，如今可以在几秒钟内完成，而且具有更高的准确度。还可以立即配置出图形、图表和其他有用的视觉效果用于宏观或微观检阅。视频会议永远不会取代面对面的交流，但有助于创造效率。手机应用程序对你每天要做的几乎每件事都很有帮助，包括可以进行无限制的研究。科技不是进行分析和作出决策的唯一方法，但它肯定能够提高能力。

花些时间去了解哪种科技最适合你的具体需求。如何更好地利用它则是另一挑战。我建议你加入团体和俱乐部，并且阅读所在行业的学术期刊。大多数会议都会有关于创新技术应用的分组会议。科学知识可能很快就会过时，所以要走在创新最前沿。每个月和每年都有新的发明进入市场，并在投资过程中创造出更高的效率。

有些人沉迷于科技，以至于忘记了人为因素，就会忽略管理的变化、法律的变化等。虽然软件和其他科技可以使投资变得不那么复杂，但世界是动态的而非静态的。因此人为因素总是在这个过程中占主导。即使是人工智能（AI）也有其局限性。

科技是你的朋友，所以要热情接纳，但要意识到投资不是纯机械的，必须与人的本能相结合，才能使你不断创造成功投资成果的目标最大化。

Industry Organizations and Journals

As mentioned several times earlier, just about every business has an industry organization. Joining such an association generally requires an annual fee, but some are free. These affiliations allow you to meet the top people in that industry, which is crucial if you are investing. It gives you the chance to ask questions and prepare for the future.

These groups can be instrumental in finding executives with track records and hands-on experience to run a company that you are invested in. You'll also meet top consultants and potential employees while imparting current trends and novel ideas. Industry organizations have at least one annual meeting, so plan ahead to attend.

A simple Internet search will guide you to trade associations and their contact information. Also, joining such groups often leads to a chance to speak at their conferences, which is an excellent way to uncover fresh opportunities.

Industry groups typically have journals and websites that are a rich source of insider information and extremely helpful in developing resources for research. The larger organizations will even have libraries of books that you can access to complement your other investment analysts.

At Checkmate Investing, we write many instructive articles that are published on the Internet and in trade magazines. If you want the editorial to be noticed, then it is best to be short and sweet. When we write such an expose, we position it as a call for action. For added emphasis, we recommend taking out an advertisement in such magazines and websites.

As companies mature, they often start divisions to complement their core business. Later, they will sell or spin off that sector for various reasons. At some point, they may find that this new division is not complementary to their core business. These are referred to as "orphan companies." One of the best ways to find such an opportunity is by conversing with an industry organization.

行业组织与学术期刊

正如前面几次提到的，几乎每个企业都有一个行业组织。加入这样的协会通常需要交纳年费，但有些是免费的。这些组织能让你遇到这一行业中的顶尖人才，这对你的投资至关重要。你会有机会提问，为未来做准备。

这些团体可以帮助你找到那些有业绩记录和实际经验的管理人员，来管理你投资的公司。当你传授当前趋势和新奇想法时，会是遇到顶级顾问和潜在员工的好时机。行业组织每年至少有一次年会，所以要想参加就得提前计划。

上网简单搜索一下，就会获知加入行业协会的途径以及他们的联系方式。此外，加入这样的团体，通常会有机会在会议上发言，这是发现新机遇的绝佳方式。

行业组织通常有期刊和网站，这些是丰富的内部信息来源，并且有助于开发研究资源。大型组织甚至有图书馆，其中书籍你可以利用，并与其他的投资分析师进行互补。

在“将军投资”，我们撰写许多有指导意义的文章，发表在互联网和行业杂志上。如果你想让一篇社论受到关注，那么最好简明扼要。当我们写这样的公开文章时，把它定位为行动倡议。为了突出重点，我们建议要在这一杂志和网站上刊登一则广告。

随着公司的成熟，通常会开始分化部门，以补充其核心业务。之后，出于各种原因，他们将出售或剥离该部门，因为在某种情况下，他们可能会发现这个新的部门并不能补充他们的核心业务。这些被称为“孤儿公司”。与行业组织对话，就是可以找到这样机会的最好方法之一。

Understand that most Wall Street analysts have never worked in the industry that they cover, and therefore only know the "numbers" involved, which is only half the equation. An industry person knows the other half of the story with applied insights that the Wall Street analyst can never know. Combined, the analyst and industry person can help create a winning formula.

Once again, a balanced approach to decision making will produce favorable results for investors. So join an industry group if you want to become a better investor.

要知道，大多数华尔街分析师从未在他们所涉及的行业中工作过，因此只知道其中有关“数字”的部分，这只是等式的一边，而一个行业中人会知道等式的另一边，他有华尔街分析师永远不会知道的应用洞察力。综合起来，分析师和行业人士可以共同创造一个成功的公式。

再说一次，运用平衡的方法去做决策，将为投资者带来有利的结果。所以，如果你想成为一个更好的投资者，加入一个行业组织吧。

Chat Rooms and Blogs

Chat rooms afford you a chance to openly discuss various topics with previously unknown people. It can be helpful hearing what others are thinking, and how they arrive at their decisions. Chat rooms can become problematic when some people in the conversation attempt to sway the other participants to their individual way of thinking, often without logic or merit.

Both sophisticated and unsophisticated views will be voiced.Sometimes the unsophisticated vision, the uneducated angle is the most relevant because it will be based purely on common sense.At times the sophisticated analyst's observations are so technical that the real picture is cloudy.

Another chat room participant may have insider knowledge of a technology on the horizon that might negatively impact a company before the sophisticated analysts discover it. Such preliminary information might reveal unknown strengths or weaknesses in a company or product. The more education absorbed from any source, the more prudent decision will ultimately be made.

There are numerous and various chat rooms, so utilize these easily accessible forums by spending an hour a week reading appropriate comments.

Present your own comments on a chat site to hear constructive opinions from others. The results may facilitate a plan to spawn more money. Insights from kindred spirits might also realign your thinking so you don't lose money.

Blogs are similar to chat rooms, where an individual opines on some subject or idea. Blog writers are a mixed group. Some are outright wacky and completely off base while others are legitimate sources of intelligence. Blogs are normally free, so anyone can read them. Often a blog writer will have a space for people to comment which will balance and temper the views of the writer.

Again, we are urging modern technology to enhance your ability to gather information that can elicit intelligent decisions. Take full advantage of chat rooms and blogs as an additional resource for updated news and data.

聊天室和博客

聊天室可以让你有机会和以前不相识的人公开讨论各种话题。倾听别人在想什么，以及他们是如何作出决定的，对你很有帮助。聊天室可能也会出现问题，因为有些人通常毫无逻辑或优点，却在聊天中试图动摇其他参与者的个人思维方式。

无论是成熟的还是不成熟的观点都可以表达出来。有时候不成熟的看法、无知的角度是最切题的，因为完全出于基本常识。有时富有经验的分析师，其观察角度过于技术性，反倒看不清真实的情况。

聊天室的另一个参与者，可能会先于专业分析师，了解某项新科技会对一个公司产生负面影响的内部消息。这些提前信息可能会暴露出公司或产品中未知的优势或劣势。从各种渠道吸收的知识越多，最终作出的决定就越明智。

有许多不同的聊天室，所以要利用这些容易参与的论坛，每周花一小时阅读适当的评论。

在一个聊天网站上发表你自己的评论，并听取别人的建设性意见，结果可能会促成一项计划，而赢得更多的资金。这些来自同道中人的见解也会重新调整你的想法，这样你就不会赔钱。

博客类似于聊天室，个人可以对一些主题或想法发表看法。撰写博客的博主是一个混合群体。有些人极其古怪，完全荒谬，而另一些人则是情报的合法来源。博客通常是免费的，所以任何人都可以阅读。通常博主会有一个空间让人们发表评论，从而平衡和调和作者的观点。

再次，我们提倡利用现代科技提高你收集信息的能力，通过这些信息可以作出明智的决定。充分利用聊天室和博客作为更新消息和数据的额外资源。

Trusting the Media

Part of being a superior investor is learning to be inquisitive. Many investment ideas are derived from breaking news stories and then followed up by digging deeper to discover where to invest and capitalize. But be cautious when interpreting the media's version of events and learn to perform your own independent research.

The media is not really an independent news source. "Fake news" has become a reality, so categorize the media as a business that must sell advertising. News editors release information that is often either redacted or not fully clarified. Sometimes the story you read is pure fantasy. It is vital to stay in touch with current events, but realize the news you are being fed is just a scratch on the surface and can be misleading.

Some authors of investment books want us to believe that there is perfect dissemination of news. Others want us to believe that all the news is forged and put out to fallaciously influence the masses so only a select few can earn huge profits. The truth is that all these prognosticators are right at various times. Regardless of which way you think, when you hear news that may affect you, dig deep and find the real story.

Fake news can affect buying opportunities. The volatile stock market can drastically and instantly rise or dive on news reports. It may take hours or days to revise erroneous statements, enough time to purchase shares below value and then sell off when corrections are made and increased profits return.

To benefit from the news, absorb what interests you, then do your own independent research. At Checkmate Investing, we constantly review the daily news as a means to keep in touch with the common man's way of thinking and see where unanticipated investment opportunities materialize.

For example, there was a news story about a yet to be launched smart phone that boasted a two month battery life. That was a revolutionary story that aroused our team's curiosity because it could lead to future investment profits.

信任媒体

一名卓越投资者的一个特质，就是学会好奇。许多投资创意来自突发新闻报道，然后通过深入研究，去发现哪些地方可以进行投资和利用。但是，在理解媒体对事件的说法时要小心谨慎，要学会自己进行独立研究。

媒体并不是真正的独立新闻来源。“假新闻”已经屡见不鲜，所以要将媒体归类为必须兜售广告的行业。新闻编辑发布的往往是经过加工编辑的或者没有充分阐明的信息。有时你读到的报道纯粹是凭空想象的。时时关注新闻时事是至关重要的，但要意识到灌输给你的新闻只是冰山一角，而且可能会令人误入歧途。

一些关于投资方面书籍的作者想要我们相信存在完美的新闻传播，另一些作者想让我们相信所有的消息都是编造的，只会误导大众，所以只有少数人可以赚取巨额利润。事实是在不同时期这些预言者的观点是正确的。不管你怎么想，当你听到会对你有影响的消息时，要深入钻研，找出真相。

假新闻会影响买入机会。动荡的股市会因为新闻报道而大幅、迅速地上升或下跌。可能需要几小时或几天的时间才能改正错误的报道，这就可以有足够的时间购买低于价值的股票，然后在更正报道后卖出，以增加利润回报。

为了从新闻中获益，要注意你感兴趣的东西，然后做你自己的独立研究。在“将军投资”，我们经常查看每日新闻，以此作为一种与普通人思维相一致的方式，去发现在哪里可以找到不曾预料的投资机会。

例如，有一则新闻报道，鼓吹一款尚未推出的智能手机，其电池续航可以达到两个月。这是一则革命性的报道，激发了我们团队的好奇心，因为它可能会带来未来的投资利润。

And so we began our autonomous investigation with pertinent questions that must be bluntly answered. Why does the phone have a two month battery life? Is it because the phone has some new nano electronic configuration that makes it much more efficient? If this is the case, does the phone company own the IP on this technology or is it instead licensed from a third party? Can other phone companies gain access to this technology? Maybe the new technology is not new at all and is really public domain.

After reading or hearing such a news report and diligently performing your own independent research, it is time to make a decision on where to invest. Do you invest in the phone company or the technology company? Maybe the company that manufactures the battery has purchased some unique raw material and that supplier in the chain should be the investment. If you follow the path to all of these possibilities, you will reach a checkmate and make the best investment to gain the most wealth.

The news media is only a starting point to find bona fide money-making opportunities. At Checkmate Investing, our team is trained to let their curiosity lead them to exceptional investment ideas. We keep digging until we are thoroughly convinced that a breaking media story has economic merit. Otherwise, we patiently wait to explore the next "Big News Story."

因此，我们开始了自主调查，并提出了一些必须坦率回答的相关问题。为什么手机的电池可以续航两个月？是因为手机有了新的纳米电子配置，使它更有效率吗？如果是这种情况，手机公司是否拥有该技术的知识产权，还是从第三方获得的许可？其他的手机公司能获得这种技术吗？也许新技术根本不是新的，而实际上属于公有领域。

在阅读或听到这样的新闻报道，并努力进行独立研究之后，就是作出决定要从哪里开始投资的时候了。你是要投资手机公司还是科技公司？也许制造电池的公司已经购买了一些独特的原材料，而供应链中的供应商应该是投资对象。如果你沿着这条路找到所有这些可能性，你会找到制胜的关键一步，并开始最好的投资以获得最大的财富。

新闻媒体只是寻找真正赚钱机会的起点。在“将军投资”，我们的团队接受了培训，在好奇心引导下，他们获得卓越的投资理念。我们会不断钻研，直到完全相信一个突破性的媒体报道具有经济价值，否则，我们就耐心地等着去探索下一个“大新闻”。

Websites and Apps

Websites are essential when used properly. But if you are not directly selling a product or service, keep them very simple. Today, a web presence is mandatory, and often a landing page is enough to develop the credibility you are seeking.

Also, if you want people to contact you directly, make navigating your site easy. At a minimum list both an email address and info@someplace.com. If you are seeking complete accessibility, add a phone number.

Many websites require consumers to fill out a form, but provide no real information on how to contact key personnel in the company. I understand some enterprises choose to keep their contact information private, mostly to avoid unwanted solicitation, but such a clandestine approach will result in lost business.

It is the same with payment platforms; make it easy and convenient for consumers to transfer funds. Customers generally like to have choices on how to make payments. A website that forces consumers to use only one payment system, like PayPal, may lose potential business from those who would rather use credit or debit cards. When a buyer is ready to pay, make it easy!

Apps have become more prominent and can match websites in terms of functionality and purpose. Utilize every platform that is available to increase visibility. Whatever we talk about today, may be obsolete next year. However, some traditionalists are reluctant to change and will always use the older platforms, so don't dismiss them in your strategy.

Today's most successful companies maximize their digital space exposure with a full blown social media solution that uses both old and new platforms. Create as much visibility and credibility to capture as much business as possible.

网站和应用软件

如果你使用得当，网站是十分有用的。但如果你不是直接销售产品或服务，那就没必要那么复杂。如今，网络互动是必不可少的，而且通常一个登录页面就足以展现你所寻求的可信度。

此外，如果你想让人们直接联系到你，就要让网站导航更易于使用。至少要列出一个电子邮件地址和 info@someplace.com。如果你想让自己的联系方式更全面，请添加一个电话号码。

许多网站都要求消费者填写一份表格，但没有提供关于如何联系公司主要人员的真实信息。我理解一些企业选择不公开联络信息，主要是为了避免不必要的骚扰，但是这种秘密方式的结果会导致失去业务。

支付平台也是如此，要让消费者可以简单和方便地转账。客户通常喜欢选择如何付款。如果网站迫使消费者只能使用一种支付系统，如 PayPal，可能就会失去那些宁愿使用信用卡或借记卡的潜在客户。当买家准备付款时，一定要简单！

应用程序已经变得更加好用，并且可以在功能和用途方面与网站相匹配。利用所有可用的平台来增加知名度。无论我们今天谈论什么，明年都可能过时。然而，一些因循守旧的人不愿意改变，他们总是使用旧的平台，所以不要在你的策略中忽略他们。

当今最成功的公司，通过各种社交媒体，利用旧平台和新平台，最大限度地扩大了他们的数字空间曝光率。创建尽可能多的知名度和可信度来取得尽可能多的业务。

Data Losses and Breaches

The digital world is infested with hackers, viruses, and crashing computers, so you must take steps to avoid the loss of data. The global proliferation of computers has increased the chances of losing indispensable records. Taking the time to backup all files is critical and must be completed on a regular and methodical basis.

A single backup source is not enough. I believe in multiple backups or you risk losing all your data and years of hard work. Procrastinating backups is a recipe for disaster as computers seem to crash only when they have accumulated a profusion of valuable information.

When backing up sensitive statistics, have a fastidious plan that guarantees a safe and secure environment for storage. For larger organizations, you may decide to hire an industry expert to develop a solution for your company. For a smaller enterprise, it is easy to complete the backup system in house. Protecting the security of the customer base is also a moral obligation.

Unfortunately, other data breaches are prevalent. I do not understand the malicious behavior of hackers, who hack for fun, while others are espionage hackers. You must protect your business against such disruptive intruders. In the investment business, all the information we review is confidential. I dread how embarrassing it would be to admit to an investor that we lost their confidential information and must ask them for it again.

Luckily, we practice what we preach on such security issues and have never experienced a breach, but I know of others who have experienced those catastrophes. Regardless of the reason why it happened, a secure redundancy program will protect your company's crucial information.

数据丢失和泄露

数字世界充斥着黑客、病毒和崩溃的计算机，所以你必须采取措施避免数据丢失。计算机的全球普及增加了失去重要记录的可能性。花些时间备份所有文件是非常重要的，而且必须定期备份并有条不紊地完成。

单独的备份源是不够的。我信赖于多个备份，否则你可能会面临失去所有数据和多年辛苦工作成果的危险。拖延备份是造成灾难的一大因素，因为计算机似乎只有在积累了大量有价值的信息时才会崩溃。

当备份敏感的统计数据时，要设计一个精心的计划，以保证安全可靠的存储环境。对于较大的企业，你可能会决定聘请行业专家为公司开发一个解决方案。规模较小的企业，在内部完成备份系统是很容易的。保护所有客户的安全也是一个道德上的义务。

遗憾的是，另一方面数据泄露也很普遍。我不理解黑客的恶意行为，有些人只是为了好玩，而其他人则是黑客间谍。你必须保护企业避免这些破坏性入侵者的恶意行为。在投资行业中，我们查阅的所有信息都是机密的。我真害怕向投资者承认我们丢失了他们的机密信息，并且必须再次向他们索取，这将会多么令人尴尬。

幸运的是，我们在这种安全问题上实践了我们所倡导的东西，从来没有发生过泄露，但我知道有其他人经历过这些灾难。不管它发生的原因，一个安全的冗余程序将保护你公司的关键信息。

Creating Ongoing Sales

A company that produces ongoing sales is the hope of all investors.Many products only engender one quick sale like white goods. A refrigerator and washing machine, which have average life spans of 15 years, are onetime sales with no additional residual income.

Conversely, a utility company charges you predictable income every month, but they are a controlled industry and profits are regulated.

Pharmaceuticals are the quintessential ongoing sales product as drugs must be taken regularly and hold very high profit margins. But once drugs come off patents, then generics will flood the market and destroy the profit margin.

Checkmate Investing seeks investments in this area due to the recurring income. The dilemma is that it could take many years for the product of a biotech company to be FDA approved. Besides the prolonged time period, the costs to reach approval are astronomical. If you are not approved after years of testing, then the entire investment can go down the drain. Currently, the space has taken on a new strategy. If you can get your product to a certain point, even before it's approved, you can often find a buyer and keep a royalty.

There are a plethora of products that have been designed to create ongoing sales. For example, each razor company designs their shaver handle to accept only their blades. Once you buy the handle, you come back again and again to buy new blades from the same company.

The printer is another example, as ink must be replaced on a regular basis. The printer companies have designed the cartridges to have specific shapes to fit particular models. One protective aspect of the printer industry is that it depends heavily on patents to block generic ink cartridges from inundating the market.

Sometimes there are earnings to be made on electronic devices with ongoing sales for additional products. For example, some children's electronic toys are designed so that parents can order new games or a variety of learning software. The toy company makes an initial sale of the base unit and then profits further from add-on products.

创造可持续销售

一家可以持续销售的公司是所有投资者所期望的。许多产品只会像白色家电一样一次性快速销售。一台冰箱和洗衣机，平均寿命为 15 年，是一次性销售，没有额外的剩余收入。

相反，公用事业公司每月按你可预期的收入收取费用，但它们是受控制的行业，利润受到监管。

药品是最典型的可持续销售产品，因为人们必须定期服用药品，而且其利润率非常高。但一旦药品专利过期，仿制药品将充斥市场，并破坏利润率。

“将军投资”在这一领域寻求投资是因为经常性收入。目前的难点在于，一家生物科技公司的产品，可能需要很多年才能获得食品及药物管理局的批准。除了时间比较长外，要想获得批准，其成本也是天文数字。如果你在经过多年的测试后仍然没有得到批准，那么整个投资就会付诸东流。目前，该领域已经采取了新的策略。如果你能让产品达到某个程度，即使在它被批准之前，你也可以找到买家，并保有特许权使用费。

有大量的产品被设计用来创造可持续销售。例如，每个剃须刀公司都将他们的剃须刀手柄，设计成只能更换他们自己的刀片。你一旦买了剃须刀，就会一次又一次地从同一家公司购买新刀片。

打印机是另一个例子，因为墨盒必须定期更换。打印机公司设计了具有特定形状的墨盒以适合特定机型。打印机行业的保护措施之一，就是高度依赖专利来阻止仿制类墨盒大量涌入市场。

有时可以在电子设备上，通过附加产品的持续销售而盈利。例如，一些儿童的电子玩具，设计成需要家长购入新的游戏或各种学习软件。玩具公司通过初始销售，售出基本设备，然后再从附加产品中获得更多利润。

Needless to say, we want recurring income investments that can hold high profit margins. Identifying and improving on these types of investments will test your creativity as exemplified by the printer industry which was smart to sell the printer cheaply and then keep selling ink to the consumer. Take a look at your business and see if you can formulate a method to produce recurring revenue to assure the longevity of the company and your future.

毋庸置疑，我们需要的是能够保持高利润率的经常性收入投资。识别和改进这类投资将考验你的创造力，正如打印机行业所证明的那样，可以聪明地廉价出售打印机，然后不断向消费者销售墨盒。看看你自己的业务，是否也能规划出一种方法来产生经常性收入，以确保你的未来和公司的长盛不衰。

Virtual Offices

Virtual offices are a reality. Even the largest of funds and most powerful investors do most of their work on a virtual basis.

Many techies work out of their homes or even coffee shops. Virtual offices allow you to hire qualified employees who might not fit in a traditional office environment. It has become commonplace to find competent people who can work independently from their homes. For instance, a new mother, who can't venture far from her house, is a perfect virtual employee candidate. For others, operating alone in the comfort of their homes generates their most focused work. The majority of people want to live and work in a particular location for family reasons, cost concerns, or other auxiliary grounds, such as residing in remote regions to be closer to nature as opposed to a bustling city life.

Homebound employees are more flexible and able to think outside the box. This can be invaluable with creative analysis and uncovering original opportunities. Such people can be hired full-time or on a when-needed schedule.

Often investment opportunities can be discombobulating and perhaps a traditional consultant cannot fully understand the circumstances or is too expensive. In this case, we hire virtual consultants who can fill the need and requirements necessary to finalize our decision at an affordable price.

As time goes on, you will see more and more virtual employees as they have proven to be an effective alternative for people to operate efficiently. How much time is wasted on long commutes not to mention the frustration of the daily grind of traveling?

You might wonder how I can support the concept of virtual offices when I place so much significance on in-person relationships. Simple, we always take the time to meet all of our virtual employees before adding them to the payroll. A video call is a nice opener, but hardly allows you to adequately know someone's true character. Except in rare logistical or time constraints, always interview every prospective employee in person.

虚拟办公室

虚拟办公室已成为现实。即使是规模最大的基金和最有实力的投资者，其大部分工作都是在虚拟基础上完成的。

许多技术人员在家里甚至咖啡厅里工作。虚拟办公室可以让你雇用那些不适合传统办公环境的合格员工。找到可以在家中独立工作的称职雇员，现在已经变得司空见惯。例如，一个刚生完小孩的妈妈，不敢远离家门，是一个完美的虚拟雇员候选人。对另一些人来说，独自在舒适的家中工作会让他们更专注。大多数人希望在一个特定的地方居住和工作，可能出于家庭原因，成本问题，或其他辅助理由，比如居住在偏远地区可以更接近大自然，而不是繁忙的城市生活。

在家工作的员工更灵活，能够跳出固有思维模式。这对于创造性的分析和发现原始的机会是非常难能可贵的。这样的人可以全职工作，也可以在需要的时间工作。

经常有一些投资机会让人不知所措，也许一个传统的顾问不能完全理解混乱的情况，或者需要花昂贵的聘请费。在这种情况下，我们可以用能承受的价格雇用虚拟顾问，满足我们制定决策所必要的需要和需求。

随着时间的推移，你将会看到越来越多的虚拟员工，因为他们已经证明这是能够有效工作的一种方式。在漫长的通勤路上浪费了多少时间？更不用提每天一路奔波所带来的挫败感了。

你可能奇怪，当我认为人际关系如此重要时，为何支持虚拟办公室的概念。简单来说，我们在把所有虚拟员工加入工资名单之前，总是会花时间与他们见面。视频电话是一个很好的开始，但很难让你充分了解一个人的真实性格。除非是后勤不足或时间限制，否则一定要亲自面试每一位未来的员工。

Once hired, we have our virtual employees occasionally come into the office or have a meet up event to monitor their frame of mind. While it is important to know who works with you, it is not imperative to see them every day or even very often.

Virtual offices also allow us to hire capable people who we would normally never be able to employ. For example, we have a brilliant analyst who lives in Colorado and has done amazing work for us. He loves the mountains and would never live full-time in a congested city. If I did not embrace virtual employees, I would never have met this person, never mind hiring him. We have made two very successful investments based on that person's input.

I adamantly recommend including the virtual world as part of the process of being a consistent winner. This does not imply forgoing the formal structure. Instead, it is a fruitful add-on to a more traditional way of doing business. Structure is always evolving.

一旦雇用虚拟员工，要让他们不定期地进入办公室，或者组织一个见面会以监控其心理状态。虽然知道谁和你一起工作很重要，但也没必要每天或经常会面。

虚拟办公室也能让我们雇用那些通常无法雇到的有能力的人。例如，我们有一位杰出的分析师，他住在科罗拉多州，为我们做的工作很棒。他喜欢高山，绝不会在拥挤的城市里全职工作。如果我不接受虚拟员工，就不会遇到这个人，也不会想到雇用他。基于此人的意见和建议，我们做了两笔非常成功的投资。

我强烈建议将虚拟世界当做成为常胜赢家过程的一部分。这并不意味着要放弃正式结构。相反，这是对更为传统经商方式的有益补充。结构总是在不断进化中。

Paper or Electronic Presentations

When listening to a presentation, I always become more engaged by the use of multiple pitching elements. As such, an effective presentation requires both electronic and paper formats to fully capture your target's attention. Paper handouts are useful for note taking and as reminders for your prospects to review after the meeting.

If you have a product, a short demonstration of its purpose is protocol. Sometimes an embedded video with clean audio is acceptable, but always keep it less than a minute.

Later, deliver an electronic form of the presentation to further remind attendees of the concept. Another excellent policy is to send your presentation to a prospect before the meeting so more intelligent questions can be asked at the actual gathering.

Though old-fashioned, the use of a chalk or marker board can be very powerful. Visual content tends to leave a longer lasting impression.

For all earnings projections, illustrate expected sales plus profit margins and how they will be affected as you ramp up. An organized comparison of competition numbers along with sources and uses of funds must also be clearly presented as investors are eternally suspicious of how the company will spend the capital.

You may want to consider adding a SWOT analysis to your presentation. SWOT is an acronym for strengths, weaknesses, opportunities, and threats. A SWOT analysis can be carried out for a company, product, place, industry, or person. It involves specifying the objective of the business, venture, or project, and then identifying the internal and external factors that are favorable and unfavorable to achieve that objective.

- Strengths: characteristics of the business or project that are advantageous over others.
- Weaknesses: characteristics that are disadvantageous relative to others.
- Opportunities: elements in the environment that can be exploited to its advantage.
- Threats: elements in the environment that can cause future trouble for the business or project.

纸质版还是电子版介绍

在参加推介会的时候，我总是会被使用的多种演示元素所吸引。因此，一个有效的介绍既需要电子版，也需要纸质版，这样才能完全吸引目标人的注意力。纸质文稿很有用，可以方便记笔记，也便于提醒潜在投资者在会议结束后查阅。

如果你有一个产品，约定俗成要有一个关于其用途的简短演示。有时一个带有清晰音频讲解的内嵌视频是可接受的，但是千万不要超过一分钟。

稍后，可以发放一份电子版的介绍，以进一步提醒与会者这一概念。另一个绝佳的策略是在会议之前，把你的介绍发给一个潜在投资者，使其在真正开会时能够提出更睿智的问题。

虽然很老派，但使用粉笔或记事板可以非常有效。视觉内容往往会给人留下更持久的印象。

可以列出所有的收益预测，图解说明预期的销售额加利润率，以及当你发展壮大以后它们会受到怎样的影响。与竞争对手的数字比较要组织有序，资金来源和用途也必须清楚地显示出来，因为投资者对于公司将如何使用资金，会永远持怀疑态度。

你也可以考虑在你的演示中加入一个 SWOT 分析。SWOT 是优势、劣势、机会和威胁的缩写。对公司可以进行这四点分析：产品、地点、行业或个人。它涉及确定业务、风险、项目的目标，然后鉴别可以实现该目标的有利或不利的内部和外部因素。

- 优势：业务或项目的特点，与其他相较具有优势。
- 缺点：业务或项目的特点，与其他相较具有劣势。
- 机会：可以开发利用环境中的元素使其达到优势。
- 威胁：环境中的元素，会在将来给业务或项目带来麻烦。

The more elements used in your presentation, the more powerful the effect. The formal part of the presentation must have a time limit of 20 to 30 minutes. I usually schedule 60 to 90 minutes to allow plenty of time for follow up questions and answers. A typical meeting might include 15 minutes for social chatter, a 30 minute presentation, and 45 minutes to answer questions.

Before the presentation, control your expectations by asking the potential financiers what process and time frame they adhere to when making an investment. Your goal is to secure funding, so don't be shy. Congenially push the prospect to buy or invest; they expect you to be aggressive and enthused about your product or service.

The more the prospects think you are interested in them, the better chance they will be receptive during your presentation. Human nature is overriding in any demonstration, so always maintain direct eye contact with the audience and listen, don't just natter. Often by the time you give the presentation, it is only a formality because the prospect has already decided to invest due to previous meetings.

Every top salesperson knows not to talk yourself out of the deal by continuing to rattle on once the deal is done. When someone agrees to do what you ask, then it is time to stop presenting and take the order.

Most investors do not like being the first person in. So if you have others already committed to invest, let this be known. Also, it is best not to name drop as this can strain credibility.

It is normal for the prospect to rethink their decision before and after making an investment, so always follow up meetings with emails and calls in order to reinforce your presentation and product's value.

演示中使用的元素越多，效果就越强。演讲的正式部分必须限制在 20 分钟至 30 分钟之间。我通常会安排 60 分钟至 90 分钟进行后续环节，以便有足够的时间提问和回答。一个典型的推介会可能会包括 15 分钟的社交闲聊、30 分钟的演讲和 45 分钟的问答时间。

在演讲之前，通过询问潜在投资者，在做投资的时候，他们遵循什么程序和时间规划，来控制你的预期。你的目标是获得资金，所以不要胆怯。友好地推动潜在投资者购买或投资，他们希望你有进取心，并对自己的产品或服务充满热情。

潜在投资者越是认为你对他们感兴趣，就越有可能接受你的演讲。在任何情况下，人的天性都是压倒一切的，所以要始终保持与听众的目光直接接触，要倾听而不要只是唠叨。通常在你演讲的时候，只是一种形式而已，因为潜在投资者在之前的会议中已经决定投资了。

每一位顶尖的销售人员都知道，一旦交易完成，就不要继续喋喋不休地谈论你自己了。当有人同意按你的要求去做时，就是该停止演说并接受指令的时候了。

大多数投资者不喜欢成为第一个投资的人。因此，如果你已经有其他人选承诺投资时，要让他们知道。而且最好不要点名，因为这可能会影响可信度。

对于潜在投资者来说，在进行投资之前和之后，重新考虑他们的决定是很正常的，所以始终都要通过发邮件和打电话来跟进之后的会面，以加强演讲和产品的价值。

Environmental Issues and Opportunities

The world has ongoing waste and pollution problems. How do we deal with garbage, human waste, the burning of fossil fuels, and on and on?

We always look at what types of toxic waste will be produced as the result of an investment. We strive to be responsible human beings who take the time to understand contamination issues and the risks and costs of future smog related fines. These same issues also represent profitable investment prospects if concerned and creative minds can offer environmental solutions.

Ideally, it is honorable to be a green investor involved in the cleanup of these ecological predicaments. Sadly, new resolutions can occasionally create worse environmental hazards, so while green investing can be an attractive proposition, it can also be very risky. Like all investments, the green endeavors must be able to ultimately produce a profit. I have been pitched many waste solutions that initially appear auspicious, but later discover the profit side is precarious.

One of my recurring dreams is to earn money while solving some of the world's dire problems. We have had a fair amount of success investing in solar, wind, and renewable energy, and I would encourage others to follow our lead. At the very least, review such environmental opportunities because we only have one planet and must unite to protect it.

环境问题与投资机会

世界上不断存在垃圾和污染问题。我们如何处理垃圾、人类排泄物、燃烧的化石燃料等？

我们总会考虑一项投资的结果会产生何种类型的有毒废物。我们努力成为负责任的人，会花时间去了解污染问题，以及关于未来雾霾相关罚款的风险和成本。如果加以重视，并拥有可以提供环境解决方案的创意，这些问题也代表着有利的投资机会。

理想的是，成为一名绿色投资者，参与清理这些生态困境是无上荣光的。不幸的是，新的决议有时会造成更严重的环境危害，所以尽管绿色投资可能是一个有吸引力的提议，但它也可能是非常危险的。像所有的投资一样，绿色事业最终必须能够产生利润。我曾被劝说过做这类投资，那些垃圾解决方案最初看起来很不错，但后来发现利润方面很不稳定。

我经常做的一个梦是在赚钱的同时，解决世界上一些可怕的问题。我们在太阳能、风能和再生能源方面的投资取得了很大的成功，我会鼓励其他人追随我们的脚步。至少去查阅这样的环境机会，因为我们只有一个星球，必须联合起来保护它。

CHAPTER 7
Investing Internationally

When investing abroad, there are a multitude of complicated issues to contend with before and after the transaction. Foreign market trends and needs may be considerably different than domestic counterparts. Also currency fluctuations, cultural disparities, outsourcing challenges, changes in laws and politics, and barriers to entry are a sampling of obstacles that must be constantly dealt with to prosper. There is money to be made from the fertile global market if you remain focused on the following principles.

第七章
国际投资

在海外投资时，交易前后都会有许多复杂的问题需要处理。国外市场的趋势和需求，可能与国内的市场大不相同。此外，汇率波动、文化差异、外包挑战、法律和政治的变化，以及进入壁垒，这些只是部分障碍，必须不断克服这些障碍才能得到繁荣发展。如果你始终专注于以下原则，便可以从富饶的全球市场中盈利。

Market Trends

Market trends are effective indicators when judging which emerging ventures to pursue. There are short term, midterm and long term trends. All must be examined and understood to determine the most prudent investment.

There are local and national market trends. But you must also take into account overseas market trends to predict what impact they may have on your local and national trends.

Due to social media platforms, the dissemination of news, buying patterns, and styles move at a rapid pace. As previously mentioned, news is delivered over many platforms, so the media has more influence than ever before. Even in small isolated markets, world trends can impact the local thinking due to the Internet.

Today, a new product enters the market at a much faster velocity than previously. It used to take several years for merchandise to catch on, but now it can happen in less than a year. As such, you must be prepared to handle the demand for faster growth than anticipated.

When we do forecasts, we consider multiple scenarios. Normal circumstances breakdown to expected case, worst case, and best case. We will not invest in any enterprise that does not have a strategic action plan for all three scenarios and a disaster recovery plan to get back on track if business digresses. If the market performs as anticipated, plans must be in place to ascend to the next level. If the demand for your product or service far exceeds all expectations, you must be primed to promptly deliver the goods while maintaining quality control.

Trends are precursors of both admonition and opportunity. Analyzing reports is imperative, but also open your eyes and ears and observe what trends are around you. If you have children, examine what attracts them and what they are doing with their free time. If trend analysis is not part of your investment process, it should be.

市场趋势

市场趋势是判断应该从事哪些新兴行业的有效指标。有短期、中期和长期趋势。必须要调查和了解所有方面，以确定最明智的投资。

有本地和国内市场趋势。但也必须考虑到海外市场趋势，来预测其可能对本地和国内市场趋势有什么影响。

由于社交媒体平台的出现，新闻传播、购买模式及风格的变化异常迅速。正如前面提到的，新闻是在许多平台上传播的，因此媒体比以往任何时候都更有影响力。即使是在小而独立的市场，也会因互联网而使世界趋势影响到本地思维。

如今一种新产品会比原来更快地进入市场。以前商品要花几年的时间才能流行起来，但现在可以在一年之内发生。因此，你必须准备好去应对比预期更快的增长需求。

当我们进行预测时，会考虑多种情况。正常情况下会分为：预期的情况、最坏的情况、最好的情况。任何企业如果没有针对这三种情况制订战略行动计划，也没有当业务发生偏离能够引入正轨的灾难恢复计划，我们就不会进行投资。如果市场按预期进行，计划就必须到位，以提升到下一个层次。如果对你的产品或服务的需求远远超过了所有的预期，你必须准备好在保持质量的同时及时交付货物。

趋势既是警告也是机会的前兆。分析报告是十分必要的，但你也要睁开眼睛和打开耳朵，观察周围的趋势是什么。如果你有小孩，那就观察一下吸引他们的是什么，以及他们在空闲时间都做什么。如果趋势分析还不是你投资过程的一部分，那它应该是。

Investments have always been trend sensitive as embodied by the idiom: "Jumping on the bandwagon." When a trend is in fashion, it is always easier to raise money, go public, and build market share for sectors that are trending in the right direction.

Keep in mind that trends are yet another forecasting tool that can enhance a sustainable business model and increase the chances of producing winning results.

投资业一直都对趋势很敏感，就像“跟风”这个俗语所表达的。当一种趋势流行时，筹集资金、上市和为趋向正确的行业创造市场份额都是比较容易的。

请记住，趋势是另一种预测工具，可以增强可持续的商业模式，并增加获得成功的机会。

Global Sales

We live in a worldwide economy and will continue this prototype no matter what politicians, who are trying to garner votes, want you to believe.

International sales represent attractive opportunities and serious threats. Access to more consumers might equate to more sales. But a competitor from a far might also invade your territory with a similar product or service at a lower cost than you can provide.

In technology, app development in foreign countries is done at pennies on the dollar compared to USA expenses. If you are a domestic app developer, weigh your options to maintain a profitable business. If you are a premium developer, you have an advantage because unique architecture is hard to duplicate. You can offer the customer a product or service that is cutting edge and stands apart from others.

For the formula made app, perhaps you can modify your business and become a middle man. You outsource the manufacturing to these foreign suppliers, then manage the domestic sales process. With this approach, you guarantee better communications and quality control which the foreign supplier cannot execute.

Another solution is building a factory in an international market to reduce taxes, tariffs, and transportation costs. In China, there are many foreign cars on the road, but almost all vehicles are manufactured on their soil. For example, a BMW made in China can be bought at a very reasonable price and is comparable to other domestic choices. If you want to buy a BMW not manufactured in China, the cost will be almost double due to taxes and tariffs.

Maybe your product is a gadget that can be sold on the Internet. You can either ship it from your home country or you can open a foreign warehouse to be closer to that specific market and reduce logistics costs. In addition to the shipping expenses, the time frame for delivering the product will also influence the buyer. Sometimes it makes sense to collaborate with a third party, who is independent from your company, to handle overseas warehouse operations for a fee.

全球销售

我们生活在一个全球经济中，而且会继续这一模式，这与那些为了选票而想让民众相信他们的政客无关。

国际销售代表着诱人的机会和严重的威胁。接触更多的消费者可能意味着会有更多的销售额。但来自远方的竞争对手，会以类似的产品或服务侵入你的领地，而且比你所能提供的价格更低。

在技术方面，外国的应用程序开发费用要比美国低很多。如果你是一名美国国内应用程序开发人员，你可以权衡一下，以维持赢利的生意。如果你是高级开发人员，就会有优势，因为独特的程序架构很难复制。你可以向客户提供一种尖端产品或服务，并且与众不同。

对于模式化的应用程序，也许你可以改变自身业务，成为一个中间人，把制作外包给国外的供应商，然后管理国内的销售流程。用这种方法，你就可以保证良好的沟通及质量，外国供应商却做不到。

另一个解决方案是在国际市场上建造一个工厂，以减少税收、关税和运输成本。在中国，路上行驶着很多外国品牌车，但是几乎所有的车辆都是在它们本土生产的。例如，能够以非常合理的价格买到中国生产的宝马（BMW）汽车，并且与国内其他的品牌相比，完全有可比性。如果你想买一辆不是在中国本土生产的宝马，由于税收和关税，成本将几乎翻倍。

也许你的产品是一款可以在网上销售的小器具。你可以把它从本土运来，或者你可以建一个国外仓库来进入这一特定市场，以降低物流成本。除了运输费用外，交付产品的时间也会影响买方。有时候与独立的第三方合作，花些钱来处理海外仓库业务，也有一定的道理。

There are many global sales investments, but you must understand all calculations. For example, how do you manage refunds and returns in the international market? Refunds can involve fluctuating monetary exchange rates while returns are hard enough to process in a domestic market never mind relying on imprecise postal service around the world.

As noted previously, for each foreign market you enter, develop a dynamic strategy that is tailor made for that exclusive region. Learn the buying patterns and payment platforms as well as prognosticating realistic earnings to properly stock the local warehouse.

Sometimes a product may not sell very well in your domestic market, but demand will be high abroad. Determine what is driving international sales before expanding to such markets. I always recommend a test study as part of developing the business model to ascertain if the demand is indisputable and sustainable before setting a stratagem that will ultimately lead to ongoing success in any foreign market.

有许多全球销售的投资，但是你必须明白所有的计算方法。例如，你如何在国际市场上管理退款和退货？退款可能会涉及汇率波动，而退货即使是国内市场都难以处理，更不用提需要依赖于不精确邮政服务的全球业务了。

正如前面所提到的，对于想要进入的每个外国市场，都要制定一个针对该专属地区的动态策略。了解购买模式和支付平台，并预测实际收益，以便正确地储存本地仓库。

有时一种产品在国内市场上卖得不太好，但国外的需求却很高。在扩展到国外市场之前，要判断是什么推动了国际销售。在制定战略之前，我总是建议进行一项测试研究，作为发展商业模式的一部分，以确定这一需求是否具有无可争议和可持续性，从而最终在任何外国市场都能取得持续的成功。

Outsourcing Advantages

Outsourcing can at times be an excellent solution for your company's oscillating needs. Bringing in an expert may be required to troubleshoot or educate employees to move in the desired direction, but only for a short period of time. Such outsourcing could be a third party scientist who can carefully research a hypothesis or maybe a manufacturing consultant to assure that the product is constructed properly. Outsourcing, even for the mega companies, is a sound way to double check quality control, especially overseas.

Outsourcing on all levels should be measured as part of the equation. Take payroll, where a third party can complete all the proper filings to verify that there are never issues with employees' wages and salaries. Another intermittent outsourcing gig can be in the graphic arts department if you are a small to midsize company. It is fairly easy to locate talented freelance artists with fresh ideas and interpretations.

Legally, we hire an in house attorney for our investments, but we also employ outside counsel. On bigger investments, we may recruit multiple law firms to work in unison to achieve our goals. Specialty firms may possess an expertise we need, such as a particular component of IP law.

In some cases, the law firm may be conflicted out and not want to represent both parties involved. You can circumvent this divergence by signing a conflict waiver, but usually it is best to engage another legal concern to ensure integrity for all.

When using multiple attorneys, the internal counsel can better orchestrate the use of external leadership. Internal counsel will, in most cases, pay for itself by controlling runaway legal costs. Remember, the main purpose of a sharp lawyer is to protect you. Most attorneys are expensive and work by the hour which can and will add up fast. If you have an internal counsel, that person can monitor dubious third party expenditures and save lots of money.

外包优势

有时对于公司的需求波动来说，外包是一个很好的解决方案。有时可能需要引进专家来排除故障或教导员工朝着预期的方向前进，但只需要很短的时间。这样的外包可能是一个第三方科学家，可以仔细研究一个方案，或者可能是一个制造顾问，以确保产品正确的构造。外包，即使是对大型公司来说，也是一种双重检查质量控制的好方法，尤其是在海外。

所有级别的外包都应该作为等式的一部分来衡量。以工资单为例，第三方负责完成所有适当文件的提交，以确保不会出现任何有关员工工资薪金的问题。如果你是一家中小型公司，另一个间歇的外包工作可能是平面艺术部门。有才华的自由设计师很容易找到，他们会有新的想法和理解。

在法律方面，我们聘请一位内部律师为我们投资，但我们也聘请外部律师。在更大的投资上，我们可以聘请多家律师事务所共同协作，以达到我们的目标。专业律所可能拥有我们需要的专业知识，比如知识产权法的一个特定部分。

在某些情况下，律师事务所可能会发生对外冲突，不愿代表双方当事人。你可以通过签署一项冲突豁免来规避这种分歧，但通常最好是雇用另一律师事务所来确保所有方面的公正。

当雇用多个律师时，内部律师可以更好地协调外部律师的工作。在大多数情况下，内部律师会通过控制流失的法律成本来为自己埋单。请记住，一个精明律师的主要目的是保护你。大多数律师都很昂贵，工作按小时计算，时间可能而且必然快速增加。如果你有一个内部律师，此人就可以监控可疑的第三方费用，节省大量资金。

Sometimes in manufacturing, in an effort to protect the product, you may outsource different elements of the item to other manufacturers. Then you send the various pieces to one central factory to assemble the finished product. If the final assembly plant is company owned, this assures that no one manufacturer can make ersatz products and sell them in the marketplace. Only your company will have full knowledge of the end product. When manufacturing overseas, this is a common practice to protect the integrity of your product and brand.

I call this intelligent outsourcing as it shelters your merchandise from counterfeits. The biggest problem with outsourcing is quality control and timing. Be aware of outsourcing personnel who take on more work than they can manage, which leads to delivery times being delayed.

Obviously, the delivery time of a product or service is critical to making and sustaining sales. For this reason, I advise visiting your prospective factories before placing an order to reassure that they are absolutely capable. Often a foreign plant will take on any job just to contract business. This same company may not have the production capacity to manufacture your product, so they outsource themselves and consign the order elsewhere. In such cases, you will most likely end up with an end product that is not consistent.

Quality control also requires constant attention when using outsourced manufacturers who will occasionally cut corners. They may replace a superior component with a cheaper alternative to increase their profit margin, but reduce the quality of the end product. Don't forget the classic saying, "A chain is only as strong as its weakest link." That is why you must visit the factory to give surety that each product is built to your unerring specifications.

To some degree, most companies use "contract manufacturing" as a form of outsourcing simply because it is a prudent way to grow and control costs. When outsourcing, use common sense and watch out for red flags.

有时在制造业中为了保护产品，可能会将不同部件外包给其他制造商。然后再把各种零件送到一个中央工厂组装成品。如果最终的装配厂是本公司所有，这就保证了没有一个制造商可以生产仿制品并在市场上销售，只有你的公司完全掌握最终成品。在海外开办制造业时，这是一种常见的做法，以保护产品和品牌的完整性。

我称之为智能外包，因为它可以保护商品不受伪造品的影响。外包最大的问题是质量控制和时间安排。要意识到外包人员承担的工作量比他们能承受的要多，这会导致延迟交付时间。

产品或服务的交付时间显然对于创造和维持销售至关重要。为此我建议你在下订单之前，先参观一下这家工厂，以确保他们完全有能力。通常外国工厂为了签署合同愿意接收任何订单。而厂家可能没有能力生产你所需要的产品，因此他们会外包出去，把订单委托到别处。在这种情况下，你很可能最终得到前后不一致的产品。

当使用外包制造商时，需要持续关注质量控制，因为他们有时会偷工减料。为了增加利润率，他们会用便宜的组件来替代高级组件，这会降低最终产品的质量。不要忘记经典的名言：“链条的坚固程度取决于它最薄弱的环节。”这就是为什么你必须要视察工厂以保证每个产品都符合你的要求。

在某种程度上，大多数公司将“合同制造”作为一种外包形式，因为这是一种精明的方式，既能发展壮大又能控制成本。当外包时，要使用常识并注意危险信号。

Demographics

Demographics comprise statistical data about the characteristics of a population group, such as the age, religion, education level, gender, and income of those residents. Business wise, a demographic study will tell you the size of the audience for your product or service. Demographics can be broken down on a large scale, like a country, or a very small scale, like a region of a city.

Demographic studies can delineate noteworthy patterns of previous purchases. For an election, you can determine the thought tendencies of the inhabitants of that area. For a full-size store, it can help verify what to stock in various sections of the country beyond the obvious, like products affected by seasonal weather conditions, i.e., snow shovels, air conditioners, umbrellas.

With the latest products, you can learn the traditional adoption levels for fresh goods. Demographics can also estimate if a better educated person is more or less likely to purchase your product. Statistical data can even determine the expectations of how often people will replace goods. The reality is that buying patterns vary across the board.

Understanding and utilizing demographics will augment your sales matrix. Thanks to computers, population studies are more readily available and can be quickly composed on just about every subject.

However, a person's way of thinking can and does change over time. Relying solely on the latest demographic study can be a monumental mistake and should be used with caution. Each demographic is a supportive tool for investment analysis, but only when combined with other intelligence.

Industry focus groups can be helpful in determining how consumers will receive your product. Giving away samples is another technique to test your merchandise's appeal. The more you understand the potential buyer, the better your chances of selling them.

人口统计资料

人口统计资料包括人口群体特征的统计数据，如年龄、宗教、教育程度、性别和居民收入。商业智慧蕴含其中，人口统计研究能够告知你的产品或服务的受众规模。人口统计资料按规模可以分解，大到一个国家，或者小到一个城市的某个区域。

人口统计研究可以描绘出以前购物的显著模式。对于选举，你可以判断出该地区居民的思想倾向。对于一个大型商店，可以帮你核实一个国家的不同地区分别要存储哪些货物，除了那些显而易见的，比如受季节性天气条件影响的产品，像雪铲、空调、雨伞。

对于最新的产品，你可以了解到传统上接受新产品的情况。人口统计资料也可以估计出一个受过良好教育的人，会否购买你的产品。统计数据甚至可以判断出人们预期更换商品的频率。现实情况是购买模式各不相同。

了解和利用人口统计资料会让你的销售矩阵更为有效。要感谢计算机的存在，使人口研究更容易获得，而且可以迅速地应用于几乎每一门学科上。

然而一个人的思维方式可能而且确实随着时间而改变。仅仅依靠最新的人口统计研究可能是一个巨大的错误，应该谨慎使用。每个人口统计数据都是投资分析的有力工具，前提是要与其他情报相结合。

行业焦点小组可以帮助判断消费者会否接纳你的产品。赠送样品是检验商品吸引力的另一种方法。你越是了解潜在的买家，你就越有机会卖掉商品。

Currency Risks

In the international market, currency is an ever-present risk. How much you pay for something can change dramatically due to exchange fluctuations. Sometimes it can be advantageous, but other such cash swings can wipe out profits.

The best procedure to reducing this risk is to write contracts in the currency you believe will be the strongest. For example, if you are doing business in China, and you believe the dollar will strengthen against the RMB, then you would write all contracts in USD. If you believe that the Chinese currency will be the strong one, you write all contracts in RMB. The point being, no matter where you are doing business, the local currency is a real concern as it can affect the ultimate profits (or losses) of your company.

It's more complicated if you take loans. Some banks will allow you to bench that loan against a particular currency. When seeking a loan in a foreign country, take a look at this option if possible.

Hedging against currency risk is also a solution. Here, I caution against getting carried away and using the hedging in a speculative manner. When you are hedging with derivatives, be careful as it can cause you to lose too much money if not fully understood.

If hedging or currency trading is not your core business, then proceed in a very conservative manner. Often, the hedge group reacts immoderately, becomes too aggressive, and then ends up suffering huge losses. Infrequently, they will actually realize immense unexpected gains, but that connotes too much risk was initially assumed.

Keep in mind, the hedge protects against currency fluctuations and is not merely a tool to earn more money by creating trading profits. I enjoy the trading industry, but it should not be undertaken by a naive company unless such trading is the enterprise's core business. This type of trading is very speculative and has no place in normal business operations. In summary, currency hedging should be used in a conservative manner as a form of insurance to protect profits and nothing more.

货币风险

在国际市场上，货币是始终存在的风险。由于汇率波动，你为某件东西支付的费用会有很大的变化。有时这种现金波动可能是有利的，但其他时候可能把利润消耗掉了。

减少这种风险的最佳方法是按你认为最坚挺的货币来写合同。例如，如果你在中国做生意，你相信美元会比人民币坚挺，那么你就用美元来写所有的合同。如果你认为人民币会坚挺，你就可以用人民币来写所有的合同。关键是无论你在哪里做生意，当地货币都是一个真正需要关注的问题，因为它会影响到你们公司最终利润（或损失）。

如果你想贷款的话就会更复杂。一些银行会允许你针对某一特定货币贷款。在国外寻求贷款时，如果可能的话，考虑一下这个选择。

用对冲应对汇率风险也是一种解决办法。在这里我提醒大家不要被冲昏头脑，而用投机的方式使用对冲。当你用衍生工具进行对冲时，要格外小心，因为如果你不完全了解的话，可能会导致损失大量资金。

如果对冲或外汇交易不是你的核心业务，那就要以非常保守的方式进行。对冲集团通常会反应过度，变得过于激进，最终蒙受巨大损失。很少会有人真正实现巨大的意外收获，而这意味他们从最开始就预想到会有巨大的风险。

要记住，对冲可以防止汇率波动，而不仅仅是通过创造交易利润来赚钱的工具。我喜欢对冲交易行业，但毫无经验的公司不应该从事该行业，除非这种交易是企业的核心业务。这种类型的交易是非常投机的，在正常的商业操作中没有任何地位。总之，货币对冲交易应该以保守的方式来进行，作为一种保护利润的保险形式，仅此而已。

Currency issues take on greater magnitude when you build factories or buy real estate in foreign markets because they are not liquid assets. In a down market, it is almost impossible to sell such assets. If the currency has moved too much, it may not be practical and cost effective to continue manufacturing in a previously discounted region. The problem becomes the now non-liquid factory and what to do with the property. In other words, do not construct a factory in a foreign country if you do not intend to be there for the long haul. Think years ahead and compare all situations before building overseas.

当你在外国市场建造工厂或购买房地产时，货币问题会变得更大，因为房产不是流动资产。在一个下跌的市场，出售这些资产几乎是不可能的。如果汇率变动太大，在之前的打折地区继续制造可能不现实，也不划算。如今非流动资产的工厂以及如何处理这些财产成了问题。换句话说，如果你不打算长期待在国外，就不要在国外建工厂。在海外建造工厂之前，要提前数年综合考虑所有的情况。

Laws and Politics

I prefer not to mix politics and business, but at times it cannot be avoided. As such, I always take the time to evaluate the political landscape as it affects investments.

It is especially vital to scrutinize changes in laws as they can discourage or encourage investment opportunities. As an example, a law was passed that made it illegal to talk on a mobile phone which was held to the ear while driving. Inventors jumped in and quickly developed various solutions that returned colossal profits.

When you identify a change in law that could lead to a creative investment, you must examine all elements before rushing in with cash. Consider these important aspects:

- Maybe the opportunity has such a low barrier to entry that there will be too many competitors and the profit margin will be too low.
- Maybe the new law cannot effectively be enforced and nothing will really change.
- Maybe it is time sensitive and profits will only be realized for a short term.

You must also be aware of changes in politics, particularly when it comes to real estate. Political campaigns are funded by special interest groups who will, in turn, expect favors after their politician is voted into office. This can alter the way different branches of government spend money on infrastructure. It can also result in administrative agencies being more flexible when issuing building permits, enforcing zoning laws, etc. All of these changes can impact real estate investments.

It is also undeniable that corruption lurks within the political process. There are many cases where special interest groups donated money to local politicians who benefited from not only favors, but inside information that lead to steep profits in real estate.

The most lucrative insider trading in the world is not in the stock market, but the real estate market. Property values will skyrocket due to political favors like:

- A new exit off a freeway.

法律和政治

我不喜欢把政治和商业混为一谈，但有时是无法避免的。这种时候，我总是花时间评估政治形势，因为它会影响投资。

仔细留意法律的变化至关重要，因为它们可以阻挠或鼓励投资机会。例如，通过了一项法律，规定在开车时把手机放在耳边通话是违法的。发明家们便跃跃欲试，迅速开发出各种各样的会带来暴利的解决方案。

当你断定法律上的变化会导致创造性的投资时，你必须在匆忙投资之前，先检查所有的因素。考虑这些重要的方面：

- 也许这个投资机会的进入壁垒很低，因此会有很多竞争对手，利润率也会很低。

- 也许新的法律不能有效实施，并不会改变现状。

- 也许是有时效性的，利润只会在短期内实现。

你也必须意识到政治上的变化，尤其是在房地产方面。政治运动是由特殊利益集团资助的，这些团体反过来会在他们支持的政治家当选后得到利益。这可以改变政府不同部门在基础设施上的花费方式，也会导致行政机构在发放建筑许可证、执行分区法规等方面更加灵活，这些变化都会影响房地产投资。

腐败隐藏于政治进程中，也是不可否认的。在许多情况下，特殊利益集团会向当地政客捐款，不仅能从中得到好处，而且还能得到内部信息，以此获得房地产的高额利润。

世界上最赚钱的内幕交易不是在股票市场，而是在房地产市场。房地产价值会由于这些政治倾向而飙升：

- 一条高速公路的新出口。

• A new train stop where you can build a factory and bring in cheaper labor than previously feasible.

• A new port opening.

• A change in zoning.

• Special financial aid for a particular area.

Frequently, investors benefit from inside information on future government projects which allows them to snap up real estate that is almost certain to escalate in value. However, think twice as changes can take years before they become reality. For example, a new train route may take a decade to be implemented. For the long term investor, this is a plausible road to becoming wealthy. You don't necessarily have to be corrupt to benefit from such insider information, as in many instances the information is already public. An innovative train route will normally be debated in public meetings for years before it is built.

Politics can affect other construction projects which are normally open to competitive bidding and usually above board. The government will not make any decision solely based on budget estimates and accompanying paperwork for major projects. For a building contractor to procure such a deal involves earning trust from the government or, more precisely, knowing influential government employees, including politicians! Having more political connections is obviously desirable and can be the clout needed to legally obtain a government construction contract.

All attractive opportunities seem to revolve around who you know. Always maintain the same diligent manner when seeking a governmental or non-governmental transaction. Understand each prospect and the best approach to securing your intentions. When you finally break through and acquire a government contract, strive to exceed expectations and create a pipeline for many more chances at earning money.

While it is essential to be sentient of politics, it is more relevant to keep your focus on building all relationships. You shouldn't let any strong political opinions destroy friendships or business liaisons. It is wise to respectfully listen to other people's political views, but usually best to be reserved about your own political beliefs.

- 一座新的列车停靠站，你可以在那里建造工厂，并带来比以前更廉价的劳动力。

- 一个新的港口。

- 分区的变化。

- 为特定地区提供特殊的经济援助。

投资者通常会从未来政府项目的内部信息中获益，可以让他们抢购几乎肯定会升值的房地产。然而要再三考虑，因为一项变化可能需要数年才能成为现实。例如，一条新的铁路线可能需要10年才能实施。对于长期投资者来说，这是一条致富的可行之路。你不必为了从这些内幕信息中获益而腐败，因为在很多情况下，信息已经公开。创新的列车路线通常在真正建造的数年前，会在公开会议上讨论。

政治可以影响其他的建设项目，这些项目通常会光明正大地公开竞标。政府不会只根据预算和主要项目的文书而作出任何决定。对于一个建筑承包商来说，要获得这样一笔交易，需要得到政府的信任，或者更准确地说，要认识有影响力的政府雇员，包括政客！拥有更多的政治关系显然是可取的，而且可以成为合法获得政府建筑合同所需的影响力。

所有具有吸引力的机会似乎都围绕着你认识什么人。在寻求政府或非政府的交易时，要始终保持同样的勤奋态度。了解每一个机会和确保你达到目标的最佳方法。当你最终打开突破口，并获得一份政府合同时，要努力超越预期，开创更多赚钱机会的途径。

虽然有政治意识很重要，但更重要的是要把注意力集中在建立所有的关系上。你不应该让任何强烈的政治观点破坏友谊或业务联系。尊重他人的政治观点是明智的，但通常最好保留自己的政治信仰。

When you are in a foreign country, learn ahead of time what subjects are sensitive and which topics to avoid in discussions. It is always sagacious to respect your host's views, local residents' feelings, political issues, and the culture of that country.

If you encounter a business situation with political ramifications that you cannot grasp, you can hire law firms and lobbyists with existing relationships that can navigate you along the road to achievement. Such interconnected affiliations take years to develop, so I always outsource when in need of political help to reach my targeted audience.

A word of advice, do not seek political assistance from a politician's relative. At first, this appears to be a very effective entry point, but my experience tells a different story. Relatives are seldom taken seriously, and any meeting they set up is often a waste of everyone's time. If your meeting is instigated by a person that the politician actually respects, you have a much better chance of a positive outcome.

当你在国外的时候，提前学习哪些属于敏感话题，哪些话题要避免讨论。尊重当地主人的观点、当地居民的感受、政治问题以及这个国家的文化，总是明智之举。

如果你遇到了一种无法掌控政治后果的经营状况，你可以雇用律师事务所和说客，让他们利用现有的关系，指引你走向成功的道路。这种相互关联的关系需要经营多年才能发展起来，所以我在需要政治帮助的时候，总是外包出去，以接触我的目标人。

一句忠告，不要从政客的亲戚那里寻求政治帮助。刚开始这似乎是一个非常有效的切入点，但经验告诉我不是那么回事。那些亲戚很少被认真对待，他们发起的会晤通常都是浪费时间。如果这一会晤是由政客真正尊重的人发起的，那么你就有更大的机会取得积极的结果。

Barriers to Entry

When investigating a potential investment at home or abroad, it is compulsory to examine barriers to entry. One of the reasons I like Intellectual Property (IP) is because it is a natural barrier for others, which means less competition.

Regardless how formidable the barrier to entry might be, the fundamentals of a business deal trump the barrier. The combination of a solid business with a strong barrier to entry has a decided advantage over others.

There are lots of barriers to entry, such as branding, which is a type of IP. If you can establish a prestigious trademark that will have unambiguous meaning to the consumer, you will be in a superior position. For instance, at one time Xerox owned the universe of copy machines. When I was growing up, no one ever said, "Make a copy of the document." Instead, they said, "Make a Xerox." That is unequivocal brand domination, even if that advantage eventually faded.

No matter what benefit you currently have, there are always competitors waiting in the wings. If you have an advantage, preserve it for as long as possible. If you are a new company dominated by the established old guard, then uncover a weakness and exploit it.

There may be a fastidious law that creates the barrier to entry. Be careful and don't rely too heavily on some regulation for your business, as laws can and do change. Take an embargo where a foreign product cannot enter the American market, which in turn gives the local domestic product a price advantage. The foreign product is much cheaper and of the same quality, but due to a high import tax or tariff it cannot be competitive.

Investors must understand if this barrier is short or long term. Embargo's can suddenly be revoked, causing the advantage to evaporate. The medical equipment and electronics industries have seen this happen time and again. Prospects that are shielded by laws or regulations can change rapidly and bankrupt your investment.

进入壁垒

在调查国内外潜在投资时，必须要调查进入壁垒。我喜欢知识产权（IP）的一个原因，是它对其他人来说是一个天然的屏障，这就意味着很少有竞争。

无论进入壁垒有多么强大，商业交易的基本原则可以跨越障碍。稳固的企业与强大的进入壁垒相结合，会比其他企业更有优势。

有很多种进入壁垒，例如品牌，这是一种知识产权。如果你能建立一个对消费者有明确意义的知名商标，就会处于优势地位。例如，施乐（Xerox）公司曾一度占领复印机领域。在我成长的过程中，没有人会说："复印一份文件。"相反，他们说，"做一份施乐。"这是明确的品牌主导，即使这种优势最终消失了。

无论你现在有什么优点，总会有竞争者在旁虎视眈眈。如果你有优势，尽可能保持长久。如果你是一家新公司，被老牌保守派所主导，那就去发现弱点并加以利用。

可能因为一项严格的法律造成了进入壁垒。要当心，不要过于依赖对你企业的一些规定，因为法律可以而且必然会改变。对外国产品进入美国市场实行禁运，这反过来又会给当地的国内产品带来价格优势。相同质量外国产品的价格要便宜得多，但由于进口税高或关税高，所以不具有竞争力。

投资者必须明白，这种障碍是短期的还是长期的。禁运令会突然撤销，从而使其失去优势。医疗设备和电子行业已经多次出现过这种情况。受到法律或法规保护的投资机会可能会迅速改变，并使你的投资破产。

IP provides a barrier, but you still have to be careful. You must examine a company's patent to determine what it actually covers. Often a patent offers little or no protection except for some small slice of the pie. Also, patents have a limited lifetime. This is flagrant in the pharmaceutical industry where the patent creates a barrier to other companies selling the same drug until the patent expires. At that time, generic drug companies flood the market with low cost versions of the same drug.

Despite the strength of your competitive advantage, success centers on the execution and continued maintenance of a concrete business plan. For example, two cellular phone companies, Motorola and Nokia, pioneered and dominated that market. However, once those two companies slacked off and their market share eroded, it wasn't long before they became non-competitors.

Today, Amazon and eBay are first-class examples of very strong barriers to entry by the creation of their trademarked brands which dominate the industry. Both are in business areas that previously offered almost no barrier to entry.

These two companies grew so rapidly that their brand names created barriers to others. While anyone can sell books or open an auction website, most people consider these two the go-to sites. Both have expanded over the years by using their competitive advantage to enter other business sectors. Amazon and eBay are phenomenal case studies on the power of a brand dominating traditionally low entry barrier industries.

A recognizable and respected brand can also be the protection that enables you to hold profit margin. Studies confirm that a brand name captures significantly higher profit margins than identical products without a brand attached.

Furthermore, brands are instrumental in opening up new channels of distribution which are more likely to sell known brands as opposed to unknown generics. Famous products not only set up a protection against others entering the space, they also allow you to grow at an accelerated pace due to channel acceptance.

Barriers to entry are one element of every potential investment that we review closely. I must know all the obstacles associated with entering a particular space and what the effort and cost will be to overcome these barriers to entry. Then I can create an applicable strategy to make it more strenuous for others to compete or enter the space.

知识产权提供了一个障碍，但你仍然要小心。你必须审查一家公司的专利，以确定其实际上涵盖的内容。通常除了一小部分以外，专利几乎不提供任何保护。而且专利有使用期限。在制药行业当中，会有人明目张胆地这样做，在专利期内，为其他销售同一种药物的公司制造障碍。一旦到期，仿制药公司会将低成本的同一种药物大量投放市场。

尽管你的竞争优势很强大，但成功的关键在于执行和持续维护一个具体的商业计划。例如，两家手机公司，摩托罗拉（Motorola）和诺基亚（Nokia），开拓并主导了这一市场。然而，一旦这两家公司有所松懈，市场份额便受到侵蚀，不久他们就成为了非竞争对手。

现在亚马逊（Amazon）和易趣（eBay）都是最好的例子，通过在行业中占据主导地位的商标品牌建设，有着非常强大的进入壁垒。这两家公司都是在商业领域，以前几乎没有进入壁垒。

这两家公司发展如此之快，以至于他们的品牌给其他公司造成了障碍。虽然任何人都可以卖书或开一个拍卖网站，但大多数人都认为这两个网站是首选。两家公司都是多年来不断拓展，通过利用竞争优势进入其他业务领域。亚马逊和易趣，在品牌对于传统上低进入壁垒行业影响力方面，是现象级的个案研究。

一个辨识度高、受人尊敬的品牌，也可以在保持利润率方面起到防护作用。研究证实，同一个产品，著名品牌的利润率要比杂牌的高得多。

此外，品牌有助于开辟新的分销渠道，知名品牌产品要比没名气的杂牌产品更有销路。著名的产品不仅能设置保护措施禁止其他产品进入该领域，还能让你的企业因为有接收渠道而加速成长。

进入壁垒是我们密切关注于每一项潜在投资的一个要素。我必须知道进入一个特定领域会遇到的所有相关障碍，以及克服这些进入壁垒所需付出的努力和代价。然后我就可以制定一个适用的策略，让其他人对于竞争或进入该领域都会更加费力。

Consumer Perception

As stated above, Motorola and Nokia submerged due to the introduction of smartphones, but early on both companies possessed the smartphone technology. Still, they chose not to develop the innovation further, perceiving that it would never sell due to a short battery life.

Apple also recognized this smartphone weakness, but forged ahead with the belief that the variety of features would overcome objections to the low battery life. They even designed their iPhone so users couldn't change the batteries, which was risky because all cell phones up to that time enabled users to replace batteries. Who would ever buy an iPhone with one tenth the battery life and a source of power that couldn't be replaced, but could be recharged? Apple's precarious vision certainly paid off.

This attests that investors should never ignorantly accept the current perception of a product, but realize intellectual acuity can be changed with the right strategy. Nevertheless, the risk is considerable, so carefully deliberate before going down this road.One certainty remains constant; some of the absolutes you believe in now will change over time due to the natural dynamics of the world, so studying perceptions is a must when investing.

消费者认知

如上所述，摩托罗拉和诺基亚由于智能手机的引入而被淹没，但两家公司在早期都拥有智能手机技术。尽管如此，他们还是选择放弃进一步发展创新，因为他们认为，由于电池续航时间短，智能手机永远不会销售出去。

苹果也意识到这种智能手机的弱点，但他们继续前行，因为坚信各种各样的功能将胜过对电池续航时间短的反对。他们甚至设计出让用户无法更换电池的 iPhone 手机，这是有风险的，因为直到那个时候，所有的手机都能让用户更换电池。谁会去买一个只有 1/10 电池续航能力，并且无法更换电池，只能充电的 iPhone 呢？苹果公司这一有风险的愿景当然得到了回报。

这证明了投资者不应该盲目接受对产品的当前认知，而应该认识到可以用正确的策略来改变认知度。然而风险是相当大的，所以在走这条路之前，要经过深思熟虑。有一点会保持不变：你现在相信的一些绝对的东西，都会随着时间的推移而改变，因为世界永远处于变化之中，所以在投资时，必须研究认知。

Foreign Markets are Unique

The method to earning profits varies in each geographical region. Even though there may be high demand for your product or service, buying patterns and social structures can impact your sales area by area.

Understanding local culture is ultra important to prosperity. Let us take China, where if you are given a gift, you must immediately appreciate it. If you don't, you will lose future prospects with that person or company. In America, if you are given a gift, it is common not to accept the present by merely responding it is not necessary. There are thousands of social differences, but this example affirms that each market is unique and must be fully comprehended to succeed.

During my world travels, I noticed that McDonald's understands cultural differences by modifying its menu with regional fare to win over local consumers. With a food outlet, it is easier to make such alterations, but traveling sales personnel must also adapt to that region's cultural markets.

Oftentimes, I observe Americans who do not acclimate when conducting business outside the United States. They don't modify their social behavior or adjust to local customs even though it would behoove them. Although the individual approach differs, there is the common denominator of the monetary gain. So, if you want to invest internationally, prepare to adapt to the local environment.

Before arriving on foreign soil, research and read as much as possible about the targeted country. Try to locate a former resident who can convey knowledge of the local customs and business protocol. Many Americans have written books, blogs, and articles about their experiences in China, Europe, South America, and so on.

Any newfound awareness of an unfamiliar territory is vital and can help adjust your behavior to coincide with the basics of this new culture. Educating yourself always pays dividends.

独一无二的国外市场

在不同的地理区域，获取利润的方法也各不相同。即使你的产品或服务有很高的需求，购买模式和社会结构也会影响不同区域的销售。

了解当地文化对于成功非常重要。让我们来看看中国，如果你得到了一份礼物，你必须立刻表示感谢，如果你不这样做，你将失去与那个人或公司的未来发展机会。在美国，如果你得到了一份礼物，通常不接受很正常，只回复说没这个必要就行。虽然存在成千上万的社会差异，但这个例子证明了每个市场都是独一无二的，必须完全理解才能成功。

当我在世界旅行期间，注意到麦当劳餐厅就懂得文化差异，会通过用本地食品调整菜单的方式，来赢得当地消费者的青睐。食品有了销路，改变起来就更加容易，但出差旅行的销售人员也必须适应该地区的文化市场。

我经常观察到，有些在美国本土以外做生意的美国人，他们不能适应新环境，不会改变自己的社会行为，也不会适应当地的风俗习惯，即使他们理应去适应。尽管个人的方法不同，但能够营利的共同之处就在于此。所以，如果你想在国际上进行投资，就要准备适应当地的环境。

在出国前，要尽量多加研究和阅读有关目标国家的信息。设法找到一位曾经在当地生活过，能够传达当地风俗和商业礼仪知识的人。许多美国人写过书、博客和文章，讲述他们在中国、欧洲、南美等地的旅住经历。

任何对陌生地域的新认识都是至关重要的，可以帮助你调整自己的行为，以适应这种新文化的基本要求。自我教育总是能带来回报。

Integrating Investment Cultures

In America, we are taught to make quick, but intelligent decisions. We analyze data without always interacting with the people involved in the opportunity. We might mingle with the principals for a few minutes at a meet and greet, but not much more.

In China, it is much different as they generally think long term with investments. It is paradoxical because in their personal lives many Chinese love Las Vegas and gambling which is fraught with risk and super short term thrills.

To complete a deal in China entails a long process, including developing trust, friendship, and respect. We incorporate a similar approach in the Checkmate Investing style by being better acquainted with all people involved and assessing their character and instincts.

Nonetheless, embrace the American way of demanding a thorough analysis of all the components of a prospect. Identify where there is a latent weakness or multiple weaknesses in an investment. If a single ratio is off, it could be a warning sign. But it could still be a worthwhile endeavor if measures are taken to shore up the flaws and minimize risks.

Getting to know people does not mean spending time with their family and friends, but with them personally. And not only in business situations, but socially as well, like going out to dinner, a ballgame, concert, traveling, and other non-business activities.

It is also essential to personally know the individuals on your team. For a business to flow smoothly, your colleagues must share a constructive interrelationship which makes it painless to resolve differences of opinion and maintain a harmonious working environment. As a fund, we cannot let personal disparities influence our thinking and lead to unproductive arguments. I place a high priority on being familiar with my team en route to achieving our foremost objective: making money for our investors.

New friendships, at home or abroad, unearth new opportunities. Everyone knows someone else and sometimes those introductions can lead to unexpected and profitable ideas.

整合投资文化

在美国，我们被教导要作出快速而明智的决定。我们分析数据，而不总是和参与投资机会的人互动。我们可能会在见面时和当事人交流几分钟，但仅此而已。

在中国，情况就大不一样了，因为他们通常会考虑长期投资。与之相矛盾的是，许多中国人在个人生活中，喜欢拉斯维加斯和充满了风险及超短期刺激的赌博。

在中国要完成交易需要一个漫长的过程，包括加深信任、友谊和尊重。我们在“将军投资”的风格中采用了类似的方法，通过更好地了解所有相关人员，并评估他们的性格和直觉。

尽管如此，还是要采用美国式方法，要求对潜在机会的所有要素进行彻底的分析。确定投资中存在一个弱点或多个弱点。如果单独一个比率下降，很可能是一个警告信号。但是，如果采取措施来补救这些缺陷并将风险降到最低，还是值得努力去做的。

了解别人并不意味着要花时间与他的家人和朋友在一起，而是要和他们本人在一起，不仅在商务场合，也要在社交场合相聚，比如一起外出吃饭、打棒球、听音乐会、去旅行和其他非商务活动。

亲自去了解团队中的每个成员也是必要的。为了让企业顺利发展，同事之间必须分享一种建设性的相互关系，这会使得解决意见分歧和维持和谐的工作环境变得毫无痛苦。作为一个基金，我们不能让个人差异影响我们的思维，导致无谓的争论。我非常重视熟悉我的团队，以实现我们的首要目标：为我们的投资者赚钱。

无论在国内还是国外，新的友谊都能挖掘出新的机会。每个人又都与他人相识，有时候这些相互介绍会带来意想不到、有利可图的想法。

In China, friendships are the foundation of life, and people work relentlessly to build groups of amity which often go back to elementary school. Americans rarely stay in touch with old companions or co-workers which inhibits the volume of possible opportunities. Social media has somewhat altered this complacency and now many individuals are benefiting by rekindling long lost relationships.

Activate all resources to better acquaint yourself with potential business partners. In addition to making more prudent investments, you will also be rewarded by having cultivated a power group of friends for life.

友谊在中国是生活的基础，人们为了建立和睦的关系而不懈努力，这些友谊往往可以追溯到小学时代。美国人很少与昔日同伴或同事保持联系，这就抑制了许多潜在机会。社交媒体已经在某种程度上改变了这种自满情绪，现在许多人都因重拾旧谊而获益。

激活所有资源，以便更好地熟识潜在的业务伙伴。除了可以作出更明智的投资外，你还会因为培养了一群得力的终生朋友而获得回报。

CHAPTER 8
Maintaining Success

Okay, you've achieved your business and personal life goals; you've acquired wealth and happiness. Everything is running as smoothly as a new Rolls Royce. But guess what, even the most expensive car can and will break down if not sufficiently and routinely maintained. The same reality applies to successful individuals who do not maintain and grow their empire. Needless to say, there are many variables that can destroy or enhance your world. I've compiled some basic directives to help you stay ahead of the evolving game.

第八章
保持成功

很好，你已经实现了事业及个人生活目标；已经获得了财富和幸福。一切都像一辆新的劳斯莱斯一样运转顺利。但你猜怎么着，即使是最昂贵的汽车，如果没有足够及常规的维护保养，它也会抛锚。同样的情况也适用于那些不去维护和发展自己帝国的成功人士。毋庸置疑，有很多变量可以破坏或增强你的世界。我已经编写了一些基本的指令来帮助你在不断发展的博弈中保持领先。

Yesterday's Numbers

When we examine a company's accounting from the past, we calculate many ratios to compare against competitors and gauge the health and stability of the business.For example, what is the makeup of the customers? Does one client account for the majority of the sales? All that really matters, is how much profit was earned, not how much revenue was generated.

We can also determine if management has been accurate on their previous forecasts. I need to know if the company captains were responsible for the earnings or if they got lucky with unexpected income. Obviously, we would be more prone to invest in a company that has a track record of annually reaching its predictions. Past earnings are a precise indicator of the ability and skill sets of the management team.

Sometimes a company will start with a high profit margin, but competition or other factors will erode that profit percentage. Maybe in the quest to reach higher sales, the company will build inventory in order to meet future demand which can be a danger sign. Some businesses try to get away with an inventory upsurge by booking it as sales. Others do the buildup as a way to cut manufacturing costs. Still others do it because a major customer will demand that the company have a certain amount of inventory in stock in order to carry the product unimpeded in their stores.Inventory buildup to meet escalating sales is smart business, but no matter what the reason, you must discern the basis for the stock expansion.

Relying on past earnings is only one element of your evaluation. Consult those statistics as an analytical tool, not as a reason to invest. Financial statements can be complicated, so make sure to closely examine the data and ask comprehensive questions.

过往数据

当我们调查一家公司过往的会计核算时，我们计算出许多比率来与竞争对手比较，并评估企业的状况和稳定性。例如，客户的组成是什么？一个客户是否占据了大部分销售额？真正重要的是赚取多少利润，而不是产生多少收入。

我们还可以确定管理层对于过往的预测是否准确。我需要知道取得收入的原因，是出于公司领导层的能力，还是只是由于幸运而获得了意外的收入。显然我们更倾向于投资一家年度业绩达到预期的公司。过往的收入是管理团队的能力和技能的精确指标。

有时一家公司的初始利润率很高，但竞争或其他因素会侵蚀利润率。为了达到更高的销量，公司可能会增加库存，以满足未来的需求，这可能是一个危险的信号。一些企业试图通过将预订视同于销售来摆脱库存的激增，其他公司则是为了削减制造成本而增加库存，还有一些公司这样做，是因为一个大客户要求他们要有一定数量的存货，以便其商店可以随时取货。增加库存以满足不断增长的销售是明智的，但无论什么原因，你都必须清楚增加库存的根据。

依靠过往的收入数据只是评估的一个要素。要将这些统计数据作为分析工具，而不能作为投资理由。财务报表可能很复杂，因此务必仔细检查数据并提出全面的问题。

Know Your Competition

Throughout this read, I have harped on thoroughly scrutinizing your competitors to better understand whether to invest or pass on a prospective deal. To reiterate the most obvious, you must know your competitor's channels of distribution as compared to those of your targeted investment. Examine how easy it is for future competitors to enter these same channels and how much money they spend annually on branding and promotion. But the scrutiny doesn't end there.

One way to further explore the competition and learn the landscape is to purchase intelligence from third parties. There are groups who do this for a living and can gather reports that answer a myriad of inquiries. How to effectively surpass your competitors is always the million dollar question, so constantly monitor all contenders.

Sometimes being the market leader is not the best position. Being a quality alternative with a higher profit margin is a more desirable preference. If you are confronted with a situation where there is no competition, you must jam on the brakes and ask why this is the case.

Experience the competitor's product or service whenever possible. Look, compare, and review the product, the packaging, and their advertising campaign.

Also, learn how your competitors are using the Internet and social media, then implement an advantageous tactic for this crucial space and maintain it daily. Do you have an app and is it as effective as others? Do you have a campaign to make your app popular? Regardless of how good your product is, you must constantly remind the consumer.

There are two types of competition: Passive and head-on. Imagine someone is considering the purchase of a product where there are unlimited choices, like an exercise machine. Some equipment is very expensive while others are severely discounted. It is exigent for a company to target these consumers because some individuals just want to lose a few pounds while others want to maximize their physical conditioning with a high end treadmill. It is always easier to target a customer who is product specific.

了解竞争对手

在此文中，我一直不断重申要仔细检查你的竞争对手，以便更好地了解是否应该投资一项潜在的交易。要重申最重要的一点，你必须了解竞争对手的分销渠道，并与目标投资相比较。调查未来的竞争对手要进入这些渠道是否容易，以及他们每年在品牌及推广上花费多少。但检查并没有就此结束。

购买第三方情报，是进一步探索竞争对手，并了解竞争环境的一种方法。有些团体以此谋生，他们能够收集大量的调查报告。如何有效地超越你的竞争对手永远是价值百万美金的问题，所以要时刻监视所有的竞争者。

有时候，成为市场领军者并非最好的定位，成为有高利润的品质代言人，才是一种更可取的选择。如果你遇到一种情况，根本没有人和你竞争，你必须踩下刹车，然后问为什么会这样。

要尽可能去体验竞争对手的产品或服务。观看、比较、检查产品和包装以及他们的广告宣传。

同时要了解竞争对手是如何使用互联网和社交媒体的，然后在这一关键领域里实施一项有利的策略，并每天进行维护。你是否有一个应用程序？是否和其他公司的应用一样有效？你是否开展活动以使这一应用流行起来？不管你的产品有多好，都必须不断地提醒消费者。

有两种类型的竞争：被动的和主动的。想象一下，有人正在考虑购买一种产品，可能会有无数种选择，比如一台健身机，有些设备很贵，而另一些则有很大折扣。对于一家公司来说，急需瞄准这些消费者，因为有些人只是想减掉几磅体重，而另一些人则希望用高端的跑步机来强化健身。瞄准想要特定产品的顾客，总是更容易。

How do you convince the customer to purchase your product? Of course, a name brand can play a part in the decision making. And pricing always plays a role. Then there are those individuals who don't care what it costs, they just want the newest and best. Most consumers only have so much money to spend on a purchase.With such a broad spectrum, you must identify which of these types is more likely to buy your model. From there, calculate a budget to appropriately promote your product.

As much as I hate competition, I also love it. I despise the encompassing efforts and expenditures required to prove your product is superlative and the one that should be purchased. Yet, I love competition because it forces you to be creative and churn out a better product.

The demand for a product or service must be real and sustainable. Very few new products jump out of the box with immense sales. We are weary if there is no similar product already on the market, but revolutionary technology cannot be overlooked.

Let's look at two examples. The fax machine was available for over ten years before it became universally accepted. Then along came the Internet which had already been around for multiple years before it started to gain ground. It can be argued that the fax machine and electronically disseminated information facilitated the Internet's market acceptance.

FedEx President Fred Smith played an integral part in making the fax machine popular when he realized the impact it could have on his business, delivering packages. Hence, Mr. Smith brilliantly installed fax machines in all FedEx offices and launched a large marketing campaign to entice people to use his fax machines. This marketing strategy created public acceptance that the fax machine was an excellent alternative to sending paper mail. Before long, the price of fax machines dropped to affordable levels, and everyone had one in their homes and offices.

Another example is bubble wrap which was invented in 1957 as an alternative to wallpaper. This application was a complete and total failure. Next, the investors tried to convince the building industry to use it as housing insulation. For a second time, it was a complete failure. Then came a breakthrough idea; why not use it for packaging material to protect items being shipped. IBM became a customer which validated the product for protecting shipped items. Soon the product was purchased by everyone and became a huge success.

你如何说服消费者购买你的产品？当然，在作出决定时，品牌可以发挥作用，价格也总会起一定的作用，还有一些人不在乎花多少钱，他们只想要最新的和最好的。大多数消费者只有固定的资金用于购物。拥有如此广泛的顾客群体，你必须确定哪种类型的人更有可能购买你这款产品，并从中做出预算，以适当推广自己的产品。

尽管我讨厌竞争，但我也喜欢它。我鄙视那些为了证明自己产品最好、最应该被购买所需要的努力和花费。然而我喜欢竞争，因为它迫使你变得富有创造力，并努力推出更好的产品。

对产品或服务的需求必须是真实且可持续的。很少有打破桎梏的新产品会立即大量出售。如果市场上还没有类似的产品，我们就会感到厌倦，但革命性的技术是不容忽视的。

让我们看两个例子：传真机在已经存在了十多年之后，才被广泛接受。后来互联网出现了，也是已经存在了多年，才开始有些起色。可以说是传真机和电子传播信息促进了互联网被市场认可。

联邦快递（FedEx）总裁弗雷德·史密斯（Fred Smith）为了让传真机能流行起来，发挥了不可或缺的作用，因为他意识到这可能会影响他的快递业务。因此，史密斯先生英明地在联邦快递的所有办公室里都安装了传真机，并发起了一场大规模的营销活动来吸引人们使用他的传真机。这种营销策略让公众接受了传真机是发送纸质邮件的绝佳选择。不久，传真机的价格降到了可承受的水平，每个人的家里和办公室都有一台。

另一个例子是 1957 年发明的气泡塑料，作为墙纸的替代品。这个应用是一个彻底的失败。接下来，投资者试图说服建筑行业将其用作住宅保温材料。第二次又完全失败了。然后出现了一个突破性的想法；为什么不用它在运输时作包装材料以保护货物呢？IBM 成为其客户，证实了气泡塑料确实可以在运输中保护货物，不久后大家争相购买，气泡塑料取得了巨大的成功。

Today, the original bubble wrap company is a thriving business with many more products beyond plastic bubbles! The parent company has a four billion dollar market cap with bubble wrap accounting for 400 million dollars a year in sales. What a wonderful example of never giving up, but instead persevering and eventually finding extraordinary profits.

Know your competition by better knowing yourself. Once I interrupted a pitch presentation by pointing out that the competition "a competing company"had an advantage that would make creating new sales a challenge. The presenters replied, "We are glad you noticed that, and we agree with you." They explained their solution, and why they were seeking the current investment to launch this new feature which would overtake all competitors. Sure enough, the very next presentation slide addressed this exact problem. I was so impressed with their solution that I made the investment. Furthermore, the entire time I owned this investment, the management team was proactive with forward thinking, always anticipated problems, and always furnished ready solutions.

Have a strategy that keeps the competition at bay. Stay focused and never become complacent and you will be able to meet and exceed all challenges.

如今，原来的气泡包装公司已是一家蒸蒸日上的企业，拥有众多产品而不仅仅是气泡塑料！这家总公司拥有 40 亿美元的市值，其中气泡包装的年销售额为 4 亿美元。这是一个永不放弃的好例子，他们坚持不懈，最终获得了非凡的利润。

要通过更好地了解自己而了解你的竞争对手。有一次我打断了一场融资演讲，指出竞争对手“一家竞争公司”有一个优势，会使创造新品发布成为挑战。发言人回答说：“我们很高兴你注意到了这一点，我们也同意你的看法。”他们阐明了解决方案，以及为什么要寻求当前的投资来推出这一新的功能，该功能将超越所有的竞争对手。果然，在接下来的幻灯片演示中解决了这一确切问题。他们的解决方案给我留下了深刻的印象，我做了投资。此外，在我拥有这一投资的全部过程中，管理团队都积极主动进行前瞻性思考，总是能预见问题，并且总能提供现成的解决方案。

要制定一个能够规避竞争对手的策略。保持专注，永远不要自满，你将能够迎接并超越所有的挑战。

Anticipating Problems

As alluded to a number of times, one of the most crucial skills an owner or investor must have is the ability to foresee problems and have practical solutions in place before a crisis occurs.As an example, consider how you might anticipate issues if the minimum wage is increased:

- Can such a payroll raise cripple the already tight margins of your growing business?
- Can you increase prices to offset the increase in payroll?
- Can you find another way to reduce other costs?

Pricing is sensitive and sales will be lost if increases are done too rapidly. Remember, the customer does not care if your costs are rising; all they care about is what they must pay for the item. Some possible wage increase solutions would be:

- Reducing the workforce.
- Raising more capital.
- Looking into a cheaper quality of products or manufacturing methods.

In addition to employee issues, anticipate equipment problems. You may have old manufacturing machinery that could break down and must be replaced. Some factories keep the same equipment for decades and just continually replace parts. At some point, that machine will no longer be efficient, so you must be pragmatic about purchasing a new model which will do the same job ten times faster and also reduce your energy costs.

If you don't have money designated for new machinery, another option might be leasing or renting. A third option might be an equipment loan. Calculate the savings created by the updated machines and the amount of time to pay for them. Such a computation will likely convince you to discontinue repairing the antiquated machinery and immediately buy new versions.

预见问题

正如多次提到的那样，业主或投资者必须具备的最关键技能之一，就是在危机发生之前能够预见问题，并能找到实际解决方案的能力。举个例子，考虑一下如果最低工资增加了，你会如何预见问题：

- 对于发展中的企业，这样的工资增长是否会削弱已经吃紧的利润？
- 能够通过提高产品价格来抵消工资的增长吗？
- 能够找到另一种方法来降低其他成本吗？

定价是敏感的，如果增长得过快，会损失收入。要记住，消费者并不关心你的成本是否上升；他们唯一关心的是必须要为这一商品付多少钱。一些有可能应对工资增长的解决方案是：

- 减少员工。
- 筹集更多资本。
- 寻求廉价产品或低成本制造方法。

除了员工问题之外，还要预见设备问题。你的制造设备可能已经陈旧了，会随时损坏，且必须替换。有些工厂几十年来一直使用相同的设备，只是不断地更换零件。在某种程度上，这台机器已不能再高效运转，所以你必须务实地购买一个新机型，能以十倍的速度完成同样的工作，同时也能降低你的能源成本。

如果你没有准备好购买新机器的资金，租赁可能是另一个选择。第三种选择可能是设备贷款。计算出更新后的机器所节省出来的资金，以及为其支付还款所需的时间。这种估算可能会说服你停止修理陈旧的机器，并立即购买新款。

I can personally attest to the fiscal limitations of deficient manufacturing equipment. I owned a factory that could afford fifty new machines. While this was a large expenditure, the efficient equipment paid for itself in eighteen months! Our earnings soared due to the increased production and decreased down time.

Sometimes smaller manufacturers are so consumed with just surviving that they disregard innovative options to produce the same product. However, when you anticipate problems, such concentrated thinking can lead to efficient solutions and increased profits.

我可以亲自证明生产设备不足的财政限制。我曾拥有一家能负担50台新机器的工厂。虽然这是一笔很大的开支，但高效的设备在18个月内就已经自行付清了！由于产量增加和减少了停工时间，我们的收入大幅增加。

有时，规模较小的制造商会过于专注生存问题，以至于忽视了生产相同产品的创新方式。然而，当你预见问题的时候，这种集中思考会带来有效的解决方案并增加利润。

Resolving Problems

People often comment on how they cannot wait to reach a point in their lives where problems will be nonexistent. This is wishful thinking, but impossible as life will always create predicaments, big and small.

When I have a problem, which is often, I hope it surfaces early in the morning, so it can be resolved that same day. The sooner a difficulty can be dealt with, the sooner I can stop thinking about it and move on to more productive deeds.

A mentor once told me: "Do not convey a problem unless you have the solution." I later realized that was an impractical approach. Not everyone has an immediate answer to a dilemma. The reality is that until you are aware of the crisis, you are unable to resolve it.

I encourage others to inform me of impediments since it is my job, not theirs, to find the solutions. I appreciate when someone else sheds light on a problem and provides an answer, but just knowing the trouble exists is sufficient elucidation to take action. Usually if you catch an impending disaster early enough, there will be a manageable situation. The longer it takes to discover a problem, the more complicated it will be to solve along with increased chances of morphing out of control.

I am also grateful to people who advise me of a problem that they caused. Create an environment where workers feel free to admit when mistakes are made so setbacks are promptly fixed and never ignored. You don't want employees hiding predicaments. Taking responsibility is not easy for most employees and such behavior should be viewed as the mark of a future leader.

Sometimes it takes a long time to remedy a problem. Maybe there is a quick fix that can last until a permanent solution is completed. Consider these problems and solutions:

Scenario 1: What if an old machine breaks down, but another machine cannot be delivered for six months?Then have extra inventory of the repair parts needed, so there is less downtime until the new machine arrives.

解决问题

人们常常会谈论他们是如何期待能够达到生活中没有任何问题的境界，这是痴心妄想，根本不可能，因为生活总是会制造出或大或小的困境。

我经常会遇到各种问题，每当这时，我希望问题能在早晨出现，这样就可以在当天解决。越早解决问题，就能越早停止思考该问题，从而去做更有成效的事情。

一位导师曾告诉我："除非你有解决办法，否则不要将问题遗留给别人。"我后来意识到这是一种不切实际的做法。并不是每个人都能立即解答难题。现实是，除非你意识到该问题所带来的危机，否则你无法解决。

我鼓励其他人告诉我一些问题，因为找到解决办法是我的职责，而不是他们分内之事。我很感激那些能够针对问题给我启示并提供解决方案的人，但只要知道存在问题，就足以说明应该采取行动。通常情况下，如果你能及早发现一场即将到来的灾难，就可以控制局面。发现问题所花的时间越长，解决问题的难度就越高，同时也增加了失去控制的可能性。

我还要感谢那些坦白自己做错事的人。要创造一种环境，让员工在犯错的时候能够敢于承认错误，这样困难就能及时得到解决，而不会被忽视。你不希望员工隐藏困境。对大多数员工来说，承担责任并不容易，这种行为应该被视为未来领导者的标志。

有时需要很长时间才能解决问题。在找到永久解决方案之前，也许会有一个快速的解决方案作为权宜之计。考虑以下问题和解决方案：

场景 1: 如果一台旧机器坏了，但是另一台机器需要 6 个月才能送到，这种情况怎么办？那就贮备必要的维修零件，以便在新机器到来之前，减少停机时间。

Scenario 2: What if the skill sets of the employees are inadequate to operate the new machinery, but they are excellent workers and should not be terminated?Hire an outside trainer to teach the loyal employees how to properly use the newly acquired equipment or send them to vocational school.

Scenario 3: What about the problem with returned items? You can either write them off, try to modify them to become acceptable, or find another source to offset potential losses.

This last scenario reminds me of an electronics company we invested in that had tens of millions of products returned due to a competitor's enhanced version. We were aware of this potential dilemma, but the demographics fooled us into presuming that consumers would be slow to adapt to the improved product. That forecast turned out inaccurate as customers instantly stopped buying our product. We were overwhelmed as it would take three months before we could launch another product to compete. Even worse, we could not afford to write off this returned inventory. We diligently researched for a solution and found that some foreign markets still had a need for our older product. Not only did we save the company, but it turned into a small gain.

Bluetooth technology looked like an investment bonanza. Who would use wires when you could be wireless? Such innovation propelled Bluetooth to be quickly adopted by the manufacturing community. To their surprise, this technology was not immediately welcomed by consumers. The earlier Bluetooth devices were very expensive, the battery life was very short, and the quality was misunderstood by the general public who believed that wires produced better results. Slowly, Bluetooth became popular, but it took many years to be fully accepted by the general consumer.

Why was the Bluetooth adoption rate so slow? Revolutionary technology can often be confusing and not well received by society. In fact, it takes roughly seventeen plus years for consumers to become comfortable with new electronic devices. This can be for many reasons, including costs, uncertainty over benefits, questions of reliability, and more. Sometimes the only solution is to not give up and persevere, as with Bluetooth and previous examples. You can't always win in the anticipated time frame.

场景 2: 如果员工不具备操作新机器的技能，但他们非常优秀，不应该被解雇，这种情况怎么办？从外部聘请一名培训师，来教导忠诚的员工如何正确使用新设备，或派他们到职业学校学习。

场景 3: 如果出现产品被退回的问题怎么办？你可以将其报废；试着修复使其合格；或者找到另外来源来抵消潜在的损失。

最后一个场景使我想起我们曾经投资的一家电子公司，因为竞争对手推出升级版产品，造成我们数千万的产品被退回。我们已经意识到这种潜在的困境，但人口统计数据愚弄了我们，推断出消费者不会很快接受改良产品。这一预测结果是错误的，因为顾客立即停止了购买我们的产品。我们立刻招架不住，因为还要等 3 个月，才能推出另一款可以竞争的产品，更糟的是，我们根本负担不起报废这些退货。我们努力寻找解决方案，发现一些国外市场仍然需要老型号产品。我们不仅挽救了公司，而且还获得了微小收益。

蓝牙技术看起来像是一笔不错的投资。当你可以用无线的时候谁会用有线的呢？这种创新推动了蓝牙技术迅速被制造业接受。令他们惊讶的是，这项技术并没有立即受到消费者的欢迎。早期的蓝牙设备非常昂贵，电池续航时间很短，而且其质量也被普通大众误解，认为有线的效果更好。慢慢地蓝牙才流行起来，但历经多年才被普通消费者完全接受。

为什么蓝牙普及速度这么慢？革命性的技术往往会让人感到困惑，不容易被社会认可。事实上，消费者需要大约 17 年以上的时间才能适应新的电子设备。这可能有很多原因，包括成本、不确定的优势、可信度问题等。有时唯一的解决办法就是永不放弃和坚持不懈，就像蓝牙及以前的例子所证明的，你不能总是在预期的时间范围内取得胜利。

Growth Decisions

Decisions on how to grow a business are a perpetual component of running a company. Assume you receive an unsolicited offer to buy your company. What should you do? Carefully analyze the proposition and question whether your current management team is capable of growing the company to a greater size and valuation than the offered price. If that answer is "No," then give extensive consideration to selling out and moving on.Sometimes, such an offer will force you to reassess management and ultimately make changes that will expand your company.

Most pundits agree it was a mistake in 1985 for Apple to remove Steve Jobs and replace him with John Sculley. After careful review, I disagree and believe it was the correct move. Jobs was a brilliant entrepreneur, but did not understand the sophisticated organization necessary for Apple to sustain its growth.

Worse yet, most experts thought Sculley was a complete failure. Again, I disagree. Sculley was hired to increase sales and, in this area, he did fail. On the other hand, he did succeed at adding organizational elements to Apple's structure which prepared the company for the next expansion phase. By the time Steve Jobs was rehired, he was more mature and had become an exceptional leader by developing new skills in other ventures. As I mentioned earlier, it is often prudent to rehire former employees which can lead directly to a checkmate.

发展决策

关于企业如何发展的决策是经营公司的恒久组成部分。假设你收到了一个主动提出要收购贵公司的报价。你应该做什么呢？仔细分析这一命题，并反问自己，当前的管理团队是否有能力将公司发展到比报价更高的规模和价值？如果这个答案是“不”，那么就应该在深思熟虑后将其出售并继续前行。有时候，这样的提议会迫使你重新评估管理方法，并最终做出改变，从而扩大你的公司。

大多数权威人士都认为，苹果公司（Apple）在1985年将约翰·斯卡利（John Sculley），替代史蒂夫·乔布斯（Steve Jobs）的职务，是一个错误决定。经过细致的检查，我不同意这一观点，认为这是正确的做法。乔布斯是一位才华横溢的企业家，但他不理解苹果为维持其增长所必需的复杂组织。

更糟的是，大多数专家认为斯卡利完全失败了。再一次，我不同意。斯卡利被雇来增加销售，在这方面，他确实失败了。而另外，他确实成功地为苹果公司的结构添加了组织元素，为公司的下一个扩张阶段做好了准备。当史蒂夫·乔布斯被返聘回来时，已经变得更加成熟，并且通过在其他企业中发展了新技能，成为了一名杰出的领导者。正如我前面提到的，重新雇用前雇员往往是明智的，因为他们可以在博弈中直接引领我们实现制胜一击。

Ramping Up

Oddly, the most challenging part of an investment is attaining success too quickly. For a product, the manufacturing may not be able to scale up fast enough to meet the demand. If quantity can be met, then maybe quality becomes troublesome. Additionally, if manufacturing requires special raw materials, then the availability of these elements is critical. A scarcity of the assembly supplies may create long delays and dramatically increase the cost of production.

With manufacturing, it is important to identify a second and third supplier of raw materials should issues arise. Locate several industrialized plants that you can rely on before there are supply chain problems or if you require increased capacity. If you outsource and the volume is high, have at least one of your personnel monitor that factory twenty-four hours a day to assure quality control is maintained. Logistics are not just about shipping the end product, but also about having a broad based coordination structure. For example, how will you transport the purchased raw materials to the manufacturing plant? Trailer truck, freight train, air cargo, container ship, private courier?

There are a plethora of concerns when demand suddenly exceeds supply. Most people say this is a problem they'd love to have. That is a misnomer because a product that is not delivered to the market on a timely basis will either prompt a customer to buy something else or the delay will tarnish the reputation of the brand as unreliable.

Even when you are structured for the ramp up, things can still go wrong. Unforeseen problems can stem from a workforce strike, a natural disaster that damages your factory, logistical issues that arise for hundreds of different reasons, and so forth.I cannot stress enough the magnitude of being prepared, having solid options to action, reading instructive books, and hiring top level and experienced employees.

增 长

奇怪的是，投资中最具挑战性的部分是获得成功的速度太快。对于一种产品，可能无法迅速增加产量以满足需求。如果数量可以满足，那么质量就会变得不好把控。此外，如果制造产品需要特殊的原材料，那么这些元素的可用性则是至关重要的。由于装配供应不足，可能造成长时间的延误，并极大地增加生产成本。

在制造业中，重要的是要确定第二个和第三个原材料的供应商是否会出现问题。在出现供应链问题或需要增加产能之前，找到几家可以依赖的工厂。如果你将产品制造外包出去，并且数量很大，至少要派一名你的员工每天 24 小时监控工厂，以保证质量控制。物流不仅仅是运输最终产品，还包括建立一个广泛的协调结构。例如，你如何将购买的原材料运送到制造工厂？拖车、货运列车、空运、集装箱，还是私人快递？

当需求突然超过供给时，就会有很多事令人担忧。大多数人都说他们欢迎出现这种问题。这种说法不对，因为如果产品没有及时交付市场，要么会促使顾客购买其他产品，要么会损害产品声誉，被顾客认为该品牌不可靠。

即使你构建为增长的模式，还是有可能出现差错。不可预见的问题可能源于工人罢工、一场毁坏工厂的自然灾害、数百种不同原因导致的物流问题等。我无法充分强调准备工作的重要性，有扎实的行动方案、阅读有指导意义的书籍以及聘用高水平及有经验的员工。

Several decades ago, a product that we owned was selling vigorously. Then suddenly every disaster I mentioned above happened and worse. Large orders came in, but our company was not adequately prepared to succeed so quickly. We began losing the ground that we had so assiduously gained, and the reputation of our new brand was under scrutiny. Two significant sales channels, that had been multifarious to earn, were also in jeopardy. We swiftly hired top manufacturing consultants and an exceedingly experienced retiree to troubleshoot. With such crisis management and communication, we were able to tread water and survive the calamity.

In the end, the damage was done and the company had to be sold, but we did recover our investment. Had we hired such competent people earlier, we would have made billions over the next ten years. In fact, the new owner propelled the business into the largest of its kind in the world. It only took this one humbling lesson to adjust my thinking. Now we leave no stone unturned, including unexpected disasters, to insure all our investments are 100% prepared for a ramp up. Our vast, hands-on experience is the primary reason why investors trust our fund to earn them extraordinary returns.

几十年前，我们拥有的一款产品正在热销。然后突然间，我前面提到的每一种灾难都发生了，甚至更糟。大量订单进来了，而我们公司对于快速的成功没有充分的准备。我们开始失去千辛万苦获得的市场，新品牌的声誉也受到了严厉的质疑。曾经有两大非常成功的销售渠道，现在也岌岌可危。我们迅速聘请了顶尖的制造顾问和一个非常有经验的退休人员来解决危机。有了这样的危机管理和沟通，我们得以安全涉水并从灾难中幸存下来。

最终，损失已经造成，公司不得不出售，但我们确实收回了投资。如果我们之前就雇用了这种称职人员，在接下来的十年里就会赚到数十亿美元。事实上，新东家把公司推到了该类别中世界上最大的公司。只有这样令人羞辱的教训才会改变我的思维。现在我们想尽任何办法，包括意料之外的灾难，以确保所有的投资都能 100% 做好增长的准备。丰富的实践经验是投资者相信我们基金能够获得非凡回报的主要原因。

Debt Loans

When a company assumes debt, they are assuming risk. When taking out a loan, you incur an increased monthly burden to pay the interest until the principle is paid in full. Bear in mind, debt is a tool that can enable your company to grow and prosper as well as other purposes, such as:

- A lifeline until an equity investor can be located.
- A short term solution until sales increase or a gigantic sale ensues.
- Purchasing real estate, cash management needs, and other growth related necessities.

Debt is a double-edged sword that can quickly annihilate a company if it gets out of control. Lenders set a punctual pay back schedule and are not sympathetic to those who are tardy with payments. Bond holders are similar and can quickly cause a company to go into bankruptcy if payments are missed.

I believe in acquiring debt, but only when there is an emergency or a solid plan to repay it. Some companies will find it impossible to grow without incurring some debt.

If you need a loan, the process should be well organized. Be prepared to relate a believable, but not desperate, narrative in order to qualify for the loan. A proper loan presentation includes past financial results and future projections. Your capital needs must be compelling with strong, logical components.

When sourcing a loan, visit as many institutions as possible and not just your current company bank. Often a new bank will be ripe for your business and approve a loan.

Debt can also be obtained by other methods. A company can issue a bond, and there are many ways to structure such financing. Bonds have a maturity date and a coupon attached with the interest rate that must be paid for the borrowed money. On some bonds, such as zero coupon bonds, the interest is paid only upon maturity and all at once. Other types of bonds serve as an enticement and can be converted into common stock.

借 贷

当一家公司承担债务时，就承担了风险。当你贷款时，在本金全部付清之前，会因支付利息而增加每月的负担。要记住，举债是一种工具，它可以使你的公司发展和繁荣，以及达到其他目的，例如：

- 在找到股权投资者之前，它是一条救生索。
- 在销售额增加或随之而来的更大的销售之前，它是一个短期的解决方案。
- 是购买房地产、现金管理需求及其他增长相关的必需品。

债务是一把“双刃剑”，一旦失去控制，就能迅速消灭一家公司。放款人设定了一个准时的还款时间表，不会同情那些延迟还款的人。债券持有人也同样如此，如果没有及时还款，会导致借款公司很快破产。

我主张举债，但只在紧急情况下或有可靠的偿还债务计划时才会这样做。一些公司会发现不承担一些债务是不可能增长的。

如果你需要贷款，应该组织好这一过程。准备好一份可信但不过分的相关陈述，以获得贷款资格。一份正规的贷款报告要包括过去的财务业绩及对未来的预测。你的资金需求必须有说服力且富有逻辑性，以令人信服。

在寻找贷款的时候，要尽可能地多拜访一些机构，而不仅仅是公司目前所属银行。有时新的银行会正好适合你的业务，并能批准一笔贷款。

也可以通过其他方法获得借款。一家公司可以发行债券，有很多方式可以构成这种融资。债券会有到期日和附有票面利率的息票，必须支付。有一些债券，比如零息债券，利息只在到期时一次性付清。还有具有吸引力的其他类型债券，可以转换成普通股。

With bonds, you will have legal expenses and a commission to the investment house. Unlike a bank loan, the issuing of bonds is protracted and requires you and your legal counsel to complete various filings. Like an IPO, be prepared to devote an excessive amount of time away from your business until completion, which will add even more to your final costs.

A business can also take on leasing. Just about everything can be leased, and they are generally easier to acquire than other types of debt.

Another approach is Mezzanine financing, which is a hybrid of debt and equity financing that grants the lender the rights to convert to an ownership or equity interest in the company in case of default. In the event of non-payment, the Mezzanine piece will be paid after other senior lenders are paid.

Mezzanine financing is normally completed with modest due diligence on the part of the lender and little collateral on the part of the borrower. Mezzanine is treated like equity on a company's balance sheet. When securing Mezzanine financing, owners sacrifice control and upside potential due to some loss of equity and generally pay more in interest than with other financing alternatives.

There are many didactic books on bonds and debt financing. Outside firms like Goldman Sachs, Morgan Stanley, JP Morgan, etc. can be hired to manage the bond process or a more amalgamated approach.

Debt is usually undertaken by public companies to avoid diluting their common stock. But be cautious as some debt financings can end up diluting the company stock. With the exception of a convertible bond, taking on debt normally does not dilute common stock equity.

Even when you are repaying your debt on time, there are normally loan covenants like debt to equity ratios that must be kept at certain levels. Often paying on time is not enough to avoid your loan being called.

Before taking on any debt, understand all implications and assure that the debt you are about to add to the company balance sheet is the best alternative.

要发行债券，就要支付法律费用和投资机构的佣金。与银行贷款不同，发行债券需要很长时间，你和法律顾问要完成各种文件。就像首次公开发行一样，要准备投入大量时间，在完成之前会无暇顾及你自己的企业，这将会使最终成本增加更多。

企业也可以利用租赁这种方式。几乎所有的东西都可以租用，而且它们通常比其他类型的借款更容易获得。

另一种方法是夹层融资，这是一种债务与股权融资的混合体，在违约的情况下，赋予贷款人转换为拥有公司所有权或股权的权利。倘若公司不付款，夹层融资部分将在其他优先贷款人得到还款后而得到偿还。

夹层融资通常是在贷款人做适当的尽职调查和借款人的小额担保中完成的。夹层被视为公司资产负债表上的权益。在获得夹层融资时，所有者会因为部分权益的损失而牺牲控制权和上行潜力，而且通常会比其他融资方式支付更多的利息。

有许多关于债券和债务融资的说教类书籍。高盛（Goldman Sachs）、摩根士丹利（Morgan Stanley）、摩根大通（JP Morgan）等外部公司可以被聘用来管理债券过程，或采取一种更加融合的方式。

上市公司通常承担债务，以避免稀释普通股。但要谨慎，因为一些债务融资最终可能会稀释公司股票。除了可转换债券，负债通常不会稀释普通股权益。

即使你按时偿还债务，通常也会有贷款契约，如负债股本比率，必须保持在一定的水平。经常按时还款并不足以避免贷款被提前收回。

在承担任何债务之前，要了解所有的影响，并确保即将添加到公司资产负债表中的债务是最好的选择。

Corporate Espionage

The days of James Bond type spies are fading. However, the internal spy at a company is still a very real danger.It has become a thriving business to steal the secrets of others. The variety of secrets that are intercepted can be as simple as marketing plans or as complex as advanced technology.

Corporate espionage and the pilfering of ideas have gone on for years.However, today there are billions of dollars in profits at stake in the fields of biotech and software that must be protected. A stolen product can be revised to displace a larger competitor by making their product obsolete overnight and putting them out of business.

Sometimes a disgruntled employee departs and starts a competing business using his/ her former company's secrets. Other times, it might be an employee who is paid on the side to divulge product formulas. And occasionally, it is a real spy, an undercover employee!

I advised earlier the importance of protecting and backing up all records and files. The quandary becomes where to store such duplicate copies. Many enterprises are careless and often clandestine files are easy for insiders to steal during the backup process. There must be an unyielding plan in place to properly and securely store all company data from potential thieves.

Software is so sophisticated that crimes of this nature can be executed from remote locations. Local bank robbers are extraneous compared to the immense thefts made by Internet hackers. Even a low tech business must take steps to protect the identity of their clients. Your competitors would cherish the chance to steal your client list and sell their product or service to them.

Protecting against the rogue employee, who sells secrets to outsiders, is a daunting task. Many outside firms can assist you, but again beware as even external agencies could be the derivation of future espionage. For that reason, I advise hiring an outside source to help develop such a plan, but further caution controlling it internally.

商业间谍

詹姆斯·邦德（James Bond）式间谍的时代正在消失。然而，公司内部的间谍仍然是非常危险的。窃取他人秘密已经成为一桩兴旺的生意。被截取的各种秘密可以像营销计划一样简单，也可以像先进技术一样复杂。

商业间谍和窃取创意的行为已经持续多年。然而，如今在生物技术和软件领域，数十亿美元的利润正濒于危险，急需得到保护。偷来的产品可以通过改进，就能让本来的产品在一夜之间被淘汰，因而取代这个大的竞争对手，并使其失去业务。

有时，一个心怀不满的员工离开公司后，会利用其以前公司的秘密，开办一家竞争的企业。其他时候，可能是一名员工被他人收买而泄露产品配方。偶尔，会有一个真正的间谍，一个卧底雇员！

我之前曾劝告过关于保护和备份所有记录和文件的重要性。这个难题变成了存储这种副本的地方。许多企业都很粗心，内部人员往往很容易在备份过程中窃取秘密文件，必须制订一个强硬的计划来妥善和安全地存储所有的公司数据，以防潜在的窃贼。

软件非常复杂，这种性质的犯罪可以远程执行。与互联网黑客的巨额盗窃相比，本地银行劫匪便显得无关紧要了。即使是科技含量低的企业也必须采取措施，保护客户的身份资料。你的竞争对手会珍视这一机会，窃取你的客户名单，并将其产品或服务卖给你的客户。

防范那些向外界出售秘密的流氓雇员是一项艰巨的任务。许多外部公司可以帮助你，但你要再次小心，因为即使是外部机构也可能是未来间谍活动的来源。因此我建议雇用外部资源来帮助制订这样一个计划，但是要进一步注意内部监控。

If your new product causes a market disruption, then competitors may try to steal your ideas and sabotage your company. This happens regularly and is a growing problem that should concern every enterprise. After all, it only takes one breach to suffer irreversible damage. So protect yourself and your business from spies!

如果你的新产品造成市场混乱，那么竞争对手可能会试图窃取你的创意，并破坏你的公司。这种情况经常发生，而且是每个企业都应该关注的一个日益严重的问题。毕竟只需要一次破坏就会造成不可挽回的损失。所以要保护你自己和你的企业不受间谍之害!

Crisis Management and Communication

Every company will eventually face a crisis. Not all adversities can be prevented, so having a crisis management plan is imperative.

How does a company respond when an unexpected event occurs? For example, a fire or hurricane has just destroyed the factory and all raw materials. While the company may have a second source for the manufacturing, they do not have the cash to repurchase the raw materials. What specifics are covered by the company's insurance package?

As in any crisis, the company leaders must remain calm and project confidence and strength in the face of a disaster while simultaneously working for a solution. Above all you, as the principal, must exude composure for your employees, clients, investors, and customers to dissuade them from resorting to social media and chatting about the company's problems. Furthermore, you do not want competent employees jumping ship and pursuing new jobs due to uncertainty.

When a fire destroys a plant, it must be rebuilt which raises questions. Reassess the overall health of the company and develop an appropriate game plan to begin construction, move to a new location or take the insurance benefits and shut down. Depending on the scope of the business, having a crisis public relations campaign or "crisis communications" is essential from both an internal and external perspective for your factory to survive such a calamity. The integrity of a company is very much embedded in its perception.

The longer a business is in existence, the higher the chances such disruptions will happen. Maybe it will not be a natural disaster, but the sudden death of a company leader. Do you have a succession plan in place? If you do not have a predetermined arrangement, you should. Otherwise, instantly call a meeting and appoint a successor as soon as possible. I have observed publicly traded stocks taking huge dips as a corollary of a leader suddenly dying or resigning. At that point, immediate communication to both the workforce and the financial markets is critical.

危机管理与危机沟通

每个公司最终都会面临危机。并不是所有的灾难都可以预防，因此制订危机管理计划势在必行。

当发生意外事件时，公司将如何应对？例如，火灾或飓风刚刚摧毁了工厂和所有的原材料。虽然该公司可能有第二种生产来源，但他们没有现金重新购买原材料。该公司的保险计划涵盖了哪些细节？

在任何危机中，公司领导人必须保持冷静，在灾难面前要展现信心和力量，同时努力解决问题。最重要的是，作为领导人，你必须向员工、客户、投资者和顾客表现出沉着冷静的态度，劝阻他们不要使用社交媒体来谈论公司的问题。此外，你不希望有能力的员工因为不确定性而跳槽寻找新工作。

当一场火灾烧毁了工厂，就必须要重建，从而会引发一些问题：重新评估公司的整体状况并为开始施工制订一个适当的计划；搬到新地点；或者接受保险赔偿而关闭工厂。根据不同的业务范围，从内部和外部的角度来看，危机公关活动或“危机沟通”都至关重要，能够使工厂在这样的灾难中生存下来。一家公司的诚信根植于其理念中。

企业存在的时间越长，这种突发事件发生的可能性就越大。也许不是一场自然灾害，而是公司领导人的突然死亡。你有合适的继任计划吗？如果你没有预先做好安排，那真应该安排一下。否则就立即召开会议，并尽快指定继任者。我曾观察到由于一个领导突然死亡或辞职，而造成公开交易的股票大幅下跌的必然结果。在这一点上，与全体员工和金融市场的及时沟通至关重要。

Consider the analogy of the snowball effect. The small snowball, as it rolls down the hill, grows in size and turns into an avalanche. If a diminutive problem is not handled promptly and straight on, you may face the snowball effect in the near future.

细想一下雪球效应的比喻。小雪球从山上滚下来，越滚越大进而变成了雪崩。如果一个小问题没有及时处理而任其发展，你可能会在不久的将来面临雪球效应。

Misdirection

Misdirection and misinterpretation of numbers are so common that even the most scrupulous of investors can fall prey to this predicament. To avoid this pitfall, distinguish and examine the weighting of each component of the model. Use the misdirection as a guide to shift back in the right direction. Such reverse analysis can lead to increased profits. The use of models is only one indicator when making vital decisions.

Components can also be re-weighted at different points in time for ulterior purposes. As my college professor warned, "Be careful if you are relying on a statistical based model because they can be manipulated to arrive at the specific and intended results to prove a point."

Investment data is often skewed in order to make a case that is not valid. Indicators can be distorted to induce you to reach a preconceived conclusion and therefore make a bad investment decision. Similarly, trend analysis is far from accurate and can cause an investor to over invest in an area that is no longer in vogue.

In addition, measurement theories rely on strong assumptions for certain stats to present meaningful information. To put this in layman's terms, assumptions are guesses and far from scientific proof.

When appraising various models, you must use critical thinking in addition to the assumptions. For example, GNP (gross national product) is far from the exact measurement that the populace believes to be true. It is numerical analysis based on many contributing facts and suppositions.

I love business statistics, and we at Checkmate Investing realize that the use of all types of models and indicators are the best and only way to accurately assess potential investments.

误 导

对数字的误解及被其误导非常普遍，即使是最谨慎的投资者也会陷入这种困境。为了避免这一陷阱，要区分和检查模型中每个组成部分的权重。用误导来引导你转回到正确的方向。这样的反向分析可以导致增加利润。在作重要决策时，使用模型只是一个指标。

这些组成部分还可以在不同的时间点进行重新加权，以达到更进一步的目的。正如我的大学教授所警告的那样，“如果你依赖于一个基于统计的模型，那么要小心，因为它们可以被操纵，为证明一个观点而达到特定和预期的结果。”

为了做成一桩原本无效的投资，其数据常常被曲解。指标可以被扭曲，诱使你得出一个先入为主的结论，因此作出一个糟糕的投资决定。同样，趋势分析也很不准确，可能导致投资者过度投资于不再流行的领域。

此外，测量理论依赖于对某些统计数据的强大假设，来呈现有意义的信息。用通俗的话来说，假设就是猜测，远非科学证明。

在评估各种模型时，除了假设以外，还必须使用批判性思维。例如，国民生产总值（GNP）远远不是民众认为真实的精密测量。它是基于许多因素的事实和假设的数值分析。

我喜欢商业统计，我们在“将军投资”中认识到，使用所有类型的模型和指标是准确评估潜在投资的最好和唯一方法。

CHAPTER 9
Wall Street Options

第九章
华尔街的融资途径

Banks vs. Wall Street

There is a discernible difference between a bank loan and Wall Street money. A bank is unwilling to take risk; they only care about having their money returned on a timely basis. Before loaning money, they will scour your books and examine all details of your past financial statements, then clearly specify in the underwriting and loan documents that you are legally bound to repay the money on a predetermined schedule. To protect the loan, they will often require collateral, like property or other valuable assets. In the case of default, a foreclosure proceeding will be held and the collateral will be seized by the bank. Given that the borrowed money must be reimbursed, its cost will be much cheaper than from other sources.

Wall Street operates on a dissimilar plane. While they will review and audit your past financial statements, in reality, they care little about those numbers. Wall Street is concerned with future earnings and is, by and large, an investor looking for equity and upside, not an interest rate or a collateralized guarantee. Wall Street anticipates the next five years of projected earnings and whether the profit margins will grow or at least be maintained. If Wall Street is satisfied that the company can prosper, then the stock will increase in value and raising capital will be uncomplicated.

The key to success on Wall Street is to create a believable and achievable future earnings narrative that can be repeated over and over to attract investors. You might wonder why there are Wall Street listed companies that have zero earnings and lose significant money every year, but still retain huge market value. For example, a biotech stock may have a pending FDA approval. Wall Street investors know that when this company is approved, it will go from a losing operation to billions of dollars in profits overnight! This demonstrates how future projected earnings can add value to a stock far before it is actually realized.

Simply put, while banks do care about future earnings, past earnings and collateral are weighted the highest in the decision making process. In contrast, Wall Street only cares about the company's future earnings. In the end, Wall Street will profit more from a successful company.

银行与华尔街

银行贷款与华尔街资本之间有一个明显的区别。银行不愿承担风险；他们只关心自己的钱能否按时收回。发放贷款前，银行会彻查贷款方的账目，审计过往财务报表的所有细节，之后在承销和贷款文件里明确规定贷款方须按预先约定的时间还钱的法律义务。为了保障贷款的安全，银行还通常要求贷款方提供抵押品，比如房产或其他贵重资产。一旦违约，银行就会启动止赎程序，没收抵押品。由于贷款必须被偿还，其成本要远远低于其他资金来源。

华尔街的运作逻辑则不同。尽管他们也会审计融资方的过往财务报表，但实际上对这些数字并不太在意。华尔街更关心融资方的未来收益；大体上，华尔街作为投资方更看重融资方的股份及其股价上升潜力，而非利率或抵押担保。华尔街预测公司未来 5 年的收益，判断其利润率是否会上升或者至少持平。如果华尔街确信一家公司未来能够蓬勃发展，该公司的股票就会升值，融资也会简便一些。

在华尔街成功的关键是撰写一个可信又可行的未来收益报告，能够反复讲述从而吸引投资者。你或许想知道为何一些华尔街上市公司每年收益都为零，还大幅亏损，但仍维持着高市值。举个例子，一家生物科技上市公司可能在等待美国食品及药物管理局的一项审批，但华尔街的投资者们知道，一旦审批获得通过，这家公司一夜之间就能扭转亏损，盈利达到数十亿美元！这证明了预期收益是如何能够远在其被实现之前增加一只股票的价值的。

简言之，尽管未来收益也在银行的考量之内，但既往收益和抵押品仍是他们决策过程中考量的最重要因素。相比之下，华尔街只关心公司的未来收益。最终华尔街能从一家成功的公司身上获利更多。

Notes and Bonds

The issuance of corporate debt is customary in America. Companies often issue both notes and bonds that will normally have a fixed interest rate and a fixed maturity. The coupon or interest rate will usually be paid quarterly, semiannually or annually. The interest rate is influenced by many factors, such as the length of maturity, but sometimes the interest is paid in a lump sum at maturity.

The issuer of the note or bond is the corporation itself. The underwriting can be done in-house by the company or by hiring a third party. In the USA, corporate notes and bonds are guaranteed by the full faith and credit of the company and considered senior debt so, in most cases, are the safest investment in a corporation. Corporate notes and bonds are above common stock and most other types of debt when it comes to safety. There are all kinds of hybrid notes and bonds models such as zero coupon, callable features, floating interest rates, convertible, and much more.

Bonds can be unrated or rated by a hired rating agency. Many unrated notes and bonds are as safe as rated ones. The difference being, the corporation simply found it unnecessary to pay for a rating because they could easily sell it unrated.

A "participating note or bond" is a hybrid that allows the note holder to participate in the earnings of the corporation or some specific project in addition to the coupon of the bond and the payback of the principle at maturity. The holder receives the agreed upon coupon, then would also participate in the net earnings as a bonus. The participation can range from 10% to 50% of the net earnings of either the company or a specific group of investments made using the proceeds of the note or bond. The mechanics of the participation will be explained in an offering document.

If an investor buys common stock, he/she is in the lowest position of safety. With a participating note or bond, the investor gets the highest protection that can be obtained in the world of corporate investing and upside which is usually only reserved for common stock holders. Many investors find this type of bond attractive due to its safety and potential upside.

票据与债券

在美国，企业发行公司债很常见。企业常常同时发行票据和债券，通常具有固定利率和期限。利息一般按季度、半年或年度发放。影响利率的因素有很多，比如到期日的长短，但有时利息会在债券到期时一次性付清。

票据或债券的发行人为企业自身。承销可以由企业自主完成，也可以聘请第三方。在美国，公司票据和债券采用企业的信用做担保并且被视为优先级债，因此在大多数情况下，公司票据和债券是投资一家企业的最安全标的。公司票据和债券在安全性上要高于普通股和其他大多数种类的债务。市面上存在多种混合型票据和债券模式，比如无息债券、可赎回债券、浮动利率债券、可转换债券等。

债券可以不予评级，也可聘请一家评级机构进行评级。许多未评级票据和债券的安全性不亚于已评级的。评级与否的区别在于，如果企业能够容易地销售未评级债券或票据，他们会发现其实没有必要花钱进行评级。

“参与分红票据或债券”是一种混合型债券，允许持有者在获得票息和回收到期本金之外，参与分享整个公司或某些特定项目的收益。债券持有者获得商定的票息之后，还能参与分享净收益红利。分红可占到公司净收益的 10% 至 50%，或占到公司使用票据或债券所筹资金进行特定投资净收益的 10% 至 50%。分红机制会在债券销售文件中予以说明。

如果投资者购买普通股只能获得最低级别的安全性。而参与分红票据或债券能够让投资者获得企业投资领域中最高的安全性，并从企业的升值潜力中获得好处，这通常是普通股持有者的专属利益。由于其安全性和升值潜力，这种债券在许多投资者眼中颇具吸引力。

When purchasing a note or bond, the person or entity fills out a subscription agreement which is signed by an authorized corporate officer as acceptance of the investor. Then the purchase amount and paperwork are wired to a specified account. The administration of the bondholders can either be done in-house or by an external firm, and the annual audit of the company is another safeguard for the note or bond holder. Bonds are generally not liquid like common stock, but some have buyback provisions that can be instituted before maturity (with penalties attached). When purchasing a bond, it is best to hold it until the maturity date to fully benefit.

The selling process or underwriting of a note or bond issue should be quick, no more than 90 days, due to the maturity nature of the investment. There is also a maximum and minimum amount for the raise, and if the minimum is not raised, the money is returned to the investors. It is common to have multiple issues of notes and bonds at different points in time. For example Note #1, Note #2, etc. There is no limit on the number or amount of notes or bonds that can be issued.

购买票据或债券时，个人或机构需要填写一份认购合同。合同由企业授权一名业务主管签署，作为承兑凭证。然后将购买数额和文书电汇至一个指定账户。对债券持有者的管理既可由企业自主完成，也可由外聘公司完成。而公司的年审也是对票据或债券持有者的另一重保护。债券的流通性通常不及普通股，但一些债券会设置到期前的回购条款（附有惩罚措施）。为了最大化收益，购买债券的投资者，最好在到期前一直持有该债券。

由于投资具有到期性，票据或债券发行的销售或承销过程要快，不应超过90天。单次募资额度设有上下限，如未能达到最低募资额，募集资金将退还给投资者。通常，一家企业可在不同时点多次发行票据和债券，比如，某公司先后发行1号票据和2号票据。票据或债券可发行的总数或总额并无限制。

Special Purpose Acquisition Company (SPAC)

SPAC's are publicly traded buyout companies that raise collective investment funds in the form of blind pool money or "Blank Check." A SPAC will use an initial public offering (IPO), which is held in a trust, for the purpose of completing the acquisition of an existing private company in a targeted industry. The purpose of the SPAC is to effect a merger, share exchange, asset acquisition, share purchase, reorganization, or a business combination transaction (one or more similar businesses combined).

Shares of a SPAC are sold in relatively inexpensive units that include one share of common stock and a warrant conveying the right to purchase additional shares or partial shares. The warrant portion of the unit is intended to provide investors with an extra compensation "incentive." For example, if the per unit offering price in the IPO is $10, the warrants may have an exercise price of $12.50 per full share. But the warrants only become exercisable if the SPAC completes a business combination transaction, then shortly after the IPO, the warrants and common stock trade separately.

For nominal consideration, the SPAC's sponsors acquire founder shares, sometimes referred to as the "promote," which can result in 20% ownership of the SPAC's outstanding common stock upon completion of the IPO. The founder shares are subject to a lockup restriction for one to two years following the business combination. Sometimes the lockup will have an early release clause that will be triggered if the trading price of the post business combination company's stock reaches certain benchmark prices or upon an extraordinary transaction.

特殊目的收购公司

特殊目的收购公司（SPAC）是一种公开上市的收购公司，以“盲资公司”或“空白支票公司”的形式募集集体投资基金。SPAC 通过首次公开发行（IPO）来完成对目标行业中一家现存私人公司的收购，其募资由一家信托持有。SPAC 的目的是实现兼并、换股、资产收购、购股、重组或企业合并交易（一家或多家相似企业的合并）。

SPAC 的股份以相对便宜的组合形式出售，每份组合包括一股普通股和一份带有购买额外股份或偏股权利的认股权证。组合中认股权证的设置是为了给投资者带来额外的报酬“激励”。举个例子，如果 IPO 组合发行价为每份 10 美元，认股权证的行使价可能为每股 12.5 美元。但认股权证只有在 SPAC 完成一次企业合并交易后才能够被行使。在 IPO 完成后不久，认股权证和普通股则分开进行交易。

作为象征性报酬，SPAC 的发起人将获得创始人股份，有时该股份也被称为“激励股权”，在 IPO 完成时该股权可以转换为 SPAC 流通股的 20%。这部分创始人股份在企业合并完成后，会有一至两年的禁售期。有时禁售也会附带一项提前出售条款。如果合并后公司股票的交易价格达到了某些基准价格或者该合并为一项非常规交易，那么提前出售条款将被触发。

The founder shares are intended to provide value to the SPAC team, which typically does not draw any salary or take any management fees from the SPAC until a business combination transaction is completed. In order for the SPAC to pay expenses associated with the IPO, the SPAC's sponsors will likely purchase warrants from the SPAC. This purchase price is at least equal to their fair market value in a private placement that closes concurrently with the closing of the IPO. These warrants are substantially identical to the public warrants. If the SPAC does not offer units, then the sponsors characteristically purchase shares of common stock at the IPO price in order to allow the SPAC to pay these expenses.

An amount equal to at least 100% of the gross proceeds of the IPO raised from public shareholders is placed into a trust account administered by a third party trustee. The IPO proceeds are not permitted to be released from the trust account until the closing of the business combination or the redemption of public shares. At the closing of a business combination, public shareholders may redeem their shares for a pro rata portion of the cash held in the trust account. The balance of the trust account is released to the company to be used in the business combination transaction and for working capital purposes.

If the SPAC fails to complete a business combination in the required timeframe, all public shares are redeemed for a pro rata portion of the cash held in the trust account. The proceeds in the trust account generate interest income, some of which may be used for the SPAC's expenses until it completes a business combination transaction.

The amount that a SPAC raises in its IPO is on average about one quarter to one third of the expected enterprise value of its business combination target. If the SPAC needs to raise more capital to complete the transaction, this may come from the sale of additional equity by the SPAC. This will dilute the percentage ownership of the sponsors' founder shares.

In order to maintain the 20% promote, a SPAC may implement a separate class of stock which creates the effect of anti-dilution. The SPAC may also raise debt in connection with a business combination transaction.

创始人股份的设立旨在为 SPAC 管理团队提供利益，而管理团队在企业合并交易完成前通常不会从 SPAC 领取薪水或收取管理费。为了让 SPAC 支付 IPO 的相关费用，发起人一般都会从 SPAC 购买认股权证，买入价不低于这些认股权证在与本次 IPO 同期结束的一轮定向增发中的公允市价。这些认股权证与公开出售的认股权证极其相似。如果 SPAC 不以组合发行形式筹资，那么发起人一般会以 IPO 发行价格购入普通股，使得 SPAC 能够支付 IPO 的相关费用。

SPAC 要将来源于公众股东的 IPO 募资总额（比例至少为 100%）放入一个由第三方受托人管理的信托账户。除非企业合并交易完成或公众兑现股份，IPO 募集资金不允许从信托账户中取出。企业合并完成后，公众股东可以将所持股份按照一定比例兑换成信托账户内的现金。信托账户的余额会发放给公司，用于企业合并交易以及作为营运资金。

如果 SPAC 未能在规定的期限内完成企业合并，所有公众股份都会按照一定比例兑换成信托账户内的现金。信托账户内的资金会产生利息收入，其中部分收入可用于 SPAC 的费用支出，直至其完成一项企业合并交易。

SPAC 在 IPO 中募集到的资金平均约占到其合并目标企业估值的 1/4 至 1/3。如果 SPAC 需要募集更多的资金来完成交易，可以通过增售股份来实现。但这会稀释创始人股份所占的比例。

为了维持激励股权 20% 的占比，SPAC 可以单独设置一类产生反稀释效应的股票。SPAC 还可以发行与企业合并交易相关的债务。

The IPO process of a SPAC IPO is recorded using a registration statement on Form S1 and is conducted in the same manner as an IPO for any other company. Most SPACs will qualify as emerging growth companies under Section 2(a)(19) of the Securities Act of 1933, as amended (the Act). Consequently, under Section 6(e) of the Act, most SPACs may submit a draft registration statement to the Securities and Exchange Commission (SEC). This draft is confidential and for nonpublic review by SEC staff prior to the public filing. However, the initial confidential submission and all amendments must be publicly filed with the SEC no later than fifteen days before the date on which the SPAC conducts its road show for the offering.

The SPAC has no operating business to disclose or discuss in the registration statement. Therefore, the SPAC instead focuses on its structure and business combination strategy. If the SPACintends to concentrate on a particular industry, then that will be discussed as well.

The SPAC has no real operations or assets, so the financial statements and the "Management's Discussion and Analysis of Financial Condition and Results of Operations" section are not significant. As mentioned, the primary asset of a SPAC before the IPO is its management team. Accordingly, the "Management" section of the registration statement centers on the disclosure of its leaders' background and experience. At the time of its IPO, the SPAC must state in its registration statement that it has not identified any business combination targets.

Because the SPAC is a shell company, it is subject to certain restrictions and limitations under the federal securities laws. After completing the IPO and before it accomplishes a business combination, the SPAC must identify its shell company status on the cover of its periodic reports under the Securities Exchange Act of 1934, as amended. A SPAC cannot use a Form S8 to register any management equity plans until sixty days after completing a business combination. Holders of SPAC securities may not rely on Rule 144 under the Act for resale of their securities until one year after the company has filed current Form 10 information with the SEC reflecting its status as an entity that is no longer a shell company.

SPAC 的 IPO 流程使用 S1 表上的注册申报文件来记录，处理方式与其他所有公司的 IPO 一致。根据修订后的《1933 年证券法》（以下简称《证券法》）第 2（a）（19）条，大多数 SPAC 属于新兴成长型公司。因此，根据《证券法》第 6（e）条，大多数 SPAC 公司可以向美国证监会（SEC）递交一份注册申报文件草案。这份草案在公开申报前会保密，仅由 SEC 工作人员进行非公开审查。但最初的保密草案和所有修订本向 SEC 公开申报的日期，不得晚于 SPAC 招股路演前的 15 日。

在注册申报文件中，SPAC 不披露或讨论营运业务信息。因此，SPAC 会着重阐述自身公司结构和企业合并战略。如果 SPAC 的合并意向集中在某一行业，那么此项议题也会在注册申报文件中予以讨论。

SPAC 没有实际运营的业务或资产，所以财务报表和"管理层对财务状况和运营成果的讨论与分析"这一部分并不重要。如前所述，SPAC 在 IPO 前最主要的资产是其管理团队。因此，注册申报文件中的"管理层"这一项会着重披露公司现任领导的背景和经历。在 IPO 时，SPAC 必须在注册申报文件中表明公司尚未确定任何企业合并目标。

由于 SPAC 是一个壳公司，因此其受到联邦证券法规的某些约束和限制。根据修订后的《1934 年证券交易法》规定，SPAC 在完成 IPO 之后和实现企业合并之前，必须在其定期报告的封面上注明其壳公司的身份。企业合并完成之后的 60 日内，SPAC 不得使用 S8 表来注册任何管理层持股计划。只有在 SPAC 向 SEC 提交了当前 10 表的相关信息，表明目前主体身份已不再是一家壳公司的一年之后，SPAC 的证券持有者才可以依照《证券法》第 144 条规则转售所持证券。

Upon the closing of the IPO, most SPACs choose to list their securities on the NASDAQ which has appropriate listing requirements. For example, the initial business combination must be with one or more businesses having an aggregate fair market value of at least 80% of the value of the SPAC's trust account. It must complete a business combination within thirty-six months from the effective date of its IPO registration statement, or such shorter time as specified in its registration statement. If public shareholders vote against a business combination or if no vote is held, they must have the right to convert their shares of common stock into a pro rata share of the aggregate amount concurrently in the trust account.

Upon and after the listing, a SPAC must have at least 300 round lot shareholders (holders of at least 100 shares). At the closing of a business combination, the SPAC must meet NASDAQ's initial listing requirements, even if the SPAC is the continuing public company.

During the process leading up to the business combination and until the closing of the IPO, the SPAC cannot hold substantive discussions with a prospective entity. Following the IPO, the SPAC can begin to search for a target business. If the SPAC is unable to complete a business combination within a specified timeframe set forth in its organizational documents, then the SPAC is dissolved and must return all money in the trust account to public shareholders within twenty-four months after the closing of the IPO. And the founder shares and warrants will be worthless.

If a SPAC is running out of time, it may seek a shareholder vote to extend its lifespan. With any such vote, the SPAC's organizational documents usually offer public shareholders the right to redeem their shares for a pro rata portion of the cash held in the trust account.

The proceeds from the sponsors' warrant (or stock) purchases are not placed into the trust account, but instead used to pay the IPO expenses and other costs until the SPAC completes a business combination. The proceeds in the trust account generate interest, some of which may also be used to pay expenditures. If such amounts are insufficient, the sponsors may also make loans to support the SPAC's operations.

IPO 完成后，大多数 SPAC 选择在上市要求较为合适的纳斯达克证券市场上市。比如在上市要求方面，要求参与首次企业合并的一家或多家企业的公允总市值不得低于 SPAC 信托账户资金额的 80%。SPAC 必须在 IPO 注册申报文件生效之日起的 36 个月内，或注册申报文件中所规定的更短期限内完成一次企业合并。如果公众股东投票反对某项企业合并，或者没有举行投票，他们必须获得相应权利，能够将所持普通股按照一定比例兑换为信托账户内的现金。

在上市期间和上市完成之后，一家 SPAC 必须拥有至少 300 位整数股股东（至少持有 100 股的股东）。完成一项企业合并时，即便该 SPAC 已经获得上市公司身份，仍必须满足纳斯达克证券市场的首次上市标准。

企业合并准备期间以及直到 IPO 完成之前，SPAC 都不得与潜在目标主体进行实质性商谈。IPO 完成之后，SPAC 才可以开始搜寻目标企业。如果 SPAC 无法在其章程性文件中规定的期限内完成一次企业合并，那么 SPAC 将会被解散并须在 IPO 完成之后的 24 个月内将信托账户内所有资金退还给公众股东。届时创始人股份与认股权证也将不具有价值。

如果 SPAC 在规定期限内来不及完成合并，可以通过举行股东投票来决定是否延长公司的生命期。通过此类投票，SPAC 的章程性文件通常会为公众股东提供相关权利，让他们可以将所持股份按照一定比例兑换为信托账户内的现金。

发起人购买认股权证（或股票）所缴纳的资金不会纳入 SPAC 的信托账户，但会在 SPAC 完成企业合并之前用于支付 IPO 的费用以及其他成本。纳入信托账户内的资金会产生利息，部分利息收入也会用于支付费用。如果这些资金不够开销，发起人也可通过举债来支撑 SPAC 的运营。

After entering into an agreement for a business combination, the SPAC must offer each shareholder the right to redeem their shares in conjunction with the transaction. They must also prepare and circulate to its shareholders a document containing information on the transaction and the target company, including audited historical financial statements and pro forma financial "Projections." This document is normally in the form of a proxy statement for a shareholder vote, which also is filed with the SEC and is subject to SEC review.

A SPAC may also conduct redemptions by filing tender offer documents with the SEC instead of a proxy statement. The funds from the trust account are primarily used to complete the business combination and to pay for the redemption of shares from any shareholders that have elected to redeem their shares.

If a shareholder vote is held, the voting standard is delineated in the SPAC's organizational documents. At the IPO, the management team agrees to vote its founder shares and any public shares acquired during or after the IPO in favor of the proposed business combination. Any public shareholders can redeem their shares of common stock for a pro rata portion of the trust account at the time of the closing of the business combination, whether they vote for or against it. Often, the agreement relating to the business combination contains a condition requiring a specified amount of cash to remain after the SPAC satisfies all redemption requests.

The vote of the shareholders is governed by the federal proxy rules because the SPAC is a public company. Unless it is a foreign private issuer, the SPAC must file with the SEC in compliance with Regulation 14A, subject to SEC review and comment. A key consideration in preparing this proxy statement is disclosure of financial and other information of the business combination target that complies with applicable SEC requirements (including Regulation 14A, Regulation SK and Regulation SX). The same information is required if the SPAC instead conducts redemptions in accordance with the SEC's tender offer rules. Once the SPAC completes a business combination, it becomes an ordinary public operating company, with applicable rules due to its former status as a shell company.

If the business combination does not receive a majority vote or fails to be completed, the SPAC may search for another business combination target, as long as the specified timeframe for completion has not ended.

签订企业合并协议后，SPAC 必须给予所有股东相关权利，使其能够在该交易中将所持股份兑现。SPAC 还必须准备并向股东分发一份包含交易和目标公司信息的文件，包括目标公司经过审计的历史财务报表和预计财务报表。这份文件通常以股东投票委托书的形式向 SEC 申报并接受其审查。

SPAC 还可以通过向 SEC 递交要约收购文件而非股东委托书来进行股份兑现。信托账户内的资金主要用于完成企业合并，以及支付任何选择兑现的股东所持有的股份。

如果举行股东投票，SPAC 会在章程性文件中就投票标准进行说明。在进行 IPO 时，管理团队同意使用创始人股份及所有在 IPO 期间或完成之后买入的公众股份来行使投票权，以支持完成所提议的企业合并。任何公众股东都可以在企业合并完成时将所持普通股按照一定比例兑换成信托账户内的现金，无论对于合并投赞成票还是反对票。通常情况下，企业合并相关协议都会包括一个条件，即要求 SPAC 在满足了所有股份兑现申请后留出一定数额的现金。

由于 SPAC 为上市公司，其股东投票需遵守联邦委托法规。除非 SPAC 的主体身份为外国私人发行人，否则必须按照 14A 条例向 SEC 申报，接受 SEC 的审查和评议。准备此类股东委托书的一个重要考虑因素是对企业合并目标的财务及其他信息的披露要符合 SEC 的适用要求（包括 14A 条例、SK 条例和 SX 条例）。如果 SPAC 选择依照 SEC 的要约收购规则进行股份兑现，也需要披露同样的信息。SPAC 完成一项企业合并之后将变成一家常规的上市公司，鉴于其之前的壳公司身份，需要遵守相关规则。

如果企业合并未能获得多数股东投票或交易未能完成，只要规定的完成期限未到，SPAC 可以寻找其他的企业合并目标。

A SPAC offers the opportunity to raise a significant amount of cash in the public markets to complete a business combination transaction because investors will have liquidity as opposed to raising a similar amount of cash in the non-liquid private markets. The management team's compensation, which is most likely its founder shares, is an outright ownership position as opposed to the "carried interest" paid to private equity (PE) fund managers who earn a percentage of profits, but do not receive outright equity. After the business combination, the management team also has the chance to profit due to an increase in value derived from its warrant position.

But beware, there are also many negatives to the SPAC:

- It can take up three years to complete a transaction.
- An elongated completion time or dissolution means the money has earned little or nothing.
- As the timeframe lessens, the SPAC sponsors may become desperate and choose a poor target that will not perform well in the public markets.
- The complex nature of the SPAC can be a breeding ground for future lawsuits.
- The formation of a SPAC is expensive and time consuming.
- It can be difficult to get analyst coverage.
- There can be management conflicts and issues.

通过 SPAC，募资人可以在公开市场上募集到大量现金用于完成企业合并交易。相较于在不具备流动性的私募市场中募集类似数目的现金，SPAC 的投资者能够获得流动性。SPAC 管理团队的报酬——通常为创始人股份——即为对公司的直接拥有权。相应地，私募基金经理则是按照一定比例赚取利润，获得“附带权益”，但不获得直接股份。企业合并完成之后，SPAC 的管理团队还有机会从所持认股权证的升值中获利。

但需要注意的是，SPAC 同样存在诸多弊端：

● 一笔交易的完成时间可长达 3 年。

● 如果交易延期完成或公司解散将意味着资本回报很少，甚至为零。

● 随着期限的临近，SPAC 的发起人可能会孤注一掷，选择一个劣质的合并目标，该目标未来在公开市场上的表现不一定理想。

● SPAC 的复杂特性可能会引发日后的诉讼。

● SPAC 的发起过程成本高昂，耗时长久。

● 公司有可能很难获得分析师的关注。

● 有可能出现管理冲突和管理问题。

Reverse Merger

A reverse merger, also known as a reverse takeover or reverse IPO, is a way for private companies to go public. It's a simpler, shorter, and less expensive process than that of a conventional initial public offering (IPO).

With a traditional IPO, the company hires an investment bank to underwrite and issue shares of the soon to be listed public entity. Aside from filing the regulatory paperwork, the bank also helps to create interest in the stock and provides advice on appropriate initial pricing. The traditional IPO combines the going public process with the capital raising function. Alternatively, a reverse merger separates these two functions, making it an alluring strategic option for both corporate managers and investors.

In a reverse merger, investors of the private company acquire a majority of the shares of a public shell company, which is then combined with the purchasing entity. Investment banks and financial institutions prefer using shell companies because they can make the SEC registration process relatively straightforward and less expensive on the front end, prior to the transaction. To complete the deal, the private company trades shares with the public shell in exchange for the shell's stock, transforming the acquirer into a public company.

Reverse mergers allow a private company to become public without raising capital, which considerably simplifies the process. While conventional IPOs can take months or even a full year to materialize, reverse mergers can take as little as forty-five days to complete. This saves management a lot of time and energy, ensuring sufficient time is devoted to running the company.

Undertaking the conventional IPO process does not guarantee that the company will ultimately go public. Managers can spend hundreds of hours planning for a traditional IPO and it might still fail. If stock market conditions become unfavorable to the proposed offering, the deal may be canceled, and all those hours will be a wasted effort. Pursuing a reverse merger minimizes this risk.

反向兼并

反向兼并，又称反向收购或反向 IPO，是私人公司的一种上市方式。与常规 IPO 相比，这种方式更加简单，耗时更短，成本也更低。

选择传统 IPO 的公司会聘请一家投资银行来承销和发行即将上市主体的股票。除了向监管机构递交资料，受聘投行还要帮助这只股票创造利益，并就合适的发行价提供建议。传统 IPO 将上市过程和融资功能结合起来，而反向兼并则将这两项功能分开。无论是对企业管理人士还是对投资者来说，反向兼并都是一个颇具吸引力的战略选择。

在反向兼并中，私人公司的投资者购入一家上市壳公司的大部分股权，之后该上市壳公司再与收购主体公司进行合并。投资银行与金融机构更倾向使用壳公司，因为这样可以让交易之前的 SEC 注册过程相对简便，前端成本更低。要完成该类交易，私人公司需要与上市壳公司进行换股，以取得壳公司的股份，从而将收购主体转变为上市公司。

通过反向兼并，私人公司不需要募资就能上市，由此大大简化了上市流程。常规 IPO 可能要花上数月甚至一整年的时间才能实现，而反向兼并短至 45 日即可完成。这能为管理层节省大量的时间和精力，能够确保其将足够的时间投入到公司的经营中。

采用常规的 IPO 并不能确保公司能最终上市。管理人士可能花费了数百个小时来计划上市方案，但最终仍有可能功败垂成。如果股票市场环境对本次上市提议不利，交易可能会被撤销，之前所有的努力都会付之东流。而反向兼并则能将这种风险最小化。

Since a reverse merger is solely a mechanism to convert a private company into a public entity, market conditions have little bearing on the offering. Rather, the process is undertaken in order to attempt to realize the benefits of being a public entity. Private companies, with revenue of 50 million to several hundred million USD, are usually attracted to the prospect of going public.

The company's securities become traded on an exchange, and thus enjoy greater liquidity. The original investors gain the ability of liquidating their holdings, providing for convenient exit alternatives to having the company simply buy back their shares. The company has greater access to the capital market as management now has the option of issuing additional stock through secondary offerings. If stockholders also own warrants, which give them the right to purchase additional stock at a pre-determined price, the exercise of these options provides additional capital infusion into the company.

Public companies historically trade at higher multiples than do private companies. Increased liquidity means that both the general public and institutional investors have access to the company's stock, which can drive up prices. Management also has more strategic options to pursue growth, including mergers and acquisitions. They can use company stock instead of cash to acquire target companies. Finally, because public shares are more liquid, management can use stock incentive plans (stock options) in order to attract and retain employees.

Motivations for the merger must be understood. Managers must thoroughly investigate the public shell company to make sure it is clean and not tainted as well as examining the potential investors. A comprehensive understanding of any pending liabilities (such as future litigation) must also be reviewed.

If the public shell's investors sell significant portions of their shares right after the merger, this can materially and negatively affect the stock price. To reduce or eliminate such a risk, lock ups (clauses in a merger agreement designating required holding periods) are often included.

Investors of the public shell should also conduct reasonable due diligence on the private company, including its management, investors, operations, financials, environmental problems, safety records, and possible pending liabilities.

由于反向兼并仅仅是一套将一家私人公司转化为上市公司的机制，市场环境对其影响十分有限。确切地说，采用反向兼并就是为了实现作为上市主体的利益。收入在5000万美元至数亿美元之间的私人公司往往对于上市充满了向往。

由于上市公司的证券可以在交易所进行交易，因此拥有更大的流动性。原有投资者能够将所持有的股份变现，从而退出方式变得方便多样，不会仅局限于公司回购股份这一种方式。上市公司也能够在市场上获取更多的资本，因为管理层可以选择进行二次发售，发行更多的股票。如果股东也同时拥有认股权证，即有权按照预先约定的价格增持股份，那么这些期权的行使可以为公司注入更多的资本。

一直以来，上市公司的市盈率都要高于私人公司。流动性增加意味着大众投资者和机构投资者都能买到公司股票，因此该公司的股价会被推高。公司管理层也拥有包括并购在内的更多的战略选择来追求公司的成长。他们可以使用公司股票而非现金来收购目标公司。此外，由于公众股的流动性更高，管理层可以使用股票激励计划（股票期权）来吸引和留住员工。

必须要明了反向兼并的动机。管理层必须对上市壳公司进行彻底调查，确保其背景干净，没有污点，另外还要审查潜在的投资者。对于一切未偿债务（如未来的诉讼）也必须全面了解。

如果上市壳公司的投资者在兼并完成后立即抛售大部分持股，这将对股价造成严重的负面影响。为了降低或消除这一风险，兼并协议中常常会包含禁售条款（指定股份的持有期）。

上市壳公司的投资者也应对私人公司进行合理的尽职调查，调查内容涵盖管理层、投资者、公司运营、财务状况、环境问题、安全记录以及可能存在的未偿债务。

One drawback to reverses mergers is they are often thinly traded and can be hard to sell. Smaller businesses are not always acclimated to be a public company and, even though now listed, might not attract much attention and demand for their stock will be minimal. There may be a lack of operational and financial scale which may not educe analyst coverage from Wall Street. For a company's shares to be of interest to prospective investors, the company itself should be operationally and financially sound in addition to presenting a plausible plan with achievable future earnings projections. Regardless of the method, extensive exposure of the listed company's upside is imperative for the stock price to realize its potential.

Managers are often inexperienced in regards to the regulatory and compliance requirements associated with being a publicly traded company. As a result, managers must devote more time researching and applying administrative concerns rather than running the business. Such companies would be wise to hire employees or consultants with relevant compliance experience to expedite and assure the process. After a reverse merger, managers should have everything in place to ensure that the company has the administrative infrastructure, resources, road map, and cultural discipline to meet these new requirements.

反向兼并存在一个弊端，即其股票的交易量少，股票可能较难出手。不是每一家小型公司都能适应上市公司这一身份，而且尽管已成功上市，小型公司可能也吸引不到太多关注，投资者对其股票的需求也极少。由于业务和财务都缺乏规模，公司也可能无法获得华尔街分析师的关注。而如果一家公司的股票想要吸引潜在投资者，除了需要展示可行方案，表明能够获得未来预期收益之外，还要确保公司在运营上和财务上相当健全。无论采取哪种方法，要想让股价尽可能上涨，大量宣传该上市公司的利好消息都至关重要。

由于管理人员往往对于上市公司的相关监管和合规要求经验不足，因此他们必须投入更多的时间来研究和处理行政事宜，而这会挤占用来经营业务的时间。针对这一情况，明智的做法是聘请有相关合规经验的员工或顾问来加快和确保相关流程的顺利进行。完成反向兼并之后，管理人员应确保一切就位，保证公司具备必需的行政架构、资源、路线图和企业文化来满足这些新要求。

Alternative Public Offering (APO)

An alternative public offering is the combination of a reverse merger with a simultaneous private investment of public equity (PIPE). It allows companies an alternative to an initial public offering (IPO) as a means of going public while raising capital.

What differentiates an APO from a reverse merger is the simultaneous PIPE raise. A PIPE is when a publicly traded company sells its stock to investors in a privately negotiated transaction. The stock is normally sold at a discount to current market value, and investors are acquiring unregistered "restricted" stock. The typical PIPE investor is an institutional entity such as a hedge fund or mutual fund. PIPEs are usually completed by investment banks who act as "Placement Agent" in the transaction.

An APO is a quick transaction compared to an initial public offering (IPO). At the closing of an APO, the public shell and private company sign documents to complete the reverse merger. They file a Form 8K, which is the required public disclosure of transaction, and a registration statement of the PIPE shares with the Securities and Exchange Commission. At that point, funds are released from escrow, and the company will issue a press release announcing the completion of the transaction. The company's newly valuated stock now begins trading.

A company can close an APO in as little as 30 to 90 days. It is then funded and has exactly the same SEC disclosure requirements as an IPO. Approximately 3 to 4 months after the completion of the APO, the company's registration statement should clear comments and "go effective" with the SEC. When this is accomplished, the company can submit its application to obtain a listing on whichever exchange they choose. Listing approval for the exchanges, such as moving from the OTC to the NASDAQ, will take about one month, and then analyst research coverage begins and the company focuses on IR efforts, non-deal road show, conferences, etc.

融资型反向收购

融资型反向收购（APO）是一种同时进行反向兼并和私人投资公开股票（PIPE）的融资形式。对于公司而言，这是除了 IPO 之外的另一个既上市又募资的选择。

APO 与反向兼并的区别在于前者可同时进行 PIPE 融资。PIPE 指一家上市公司通过私下磋商交易将股票出售给投资者。股票售价通常要低于现行市价，而投资者买入的是无记名“限制性”股票。PIPE 投资者通常为机构主体，比如对冲基金或共同基金。PIPE 通常由投资银行完成，后者在交易中扮演“承销商”的角色。

与 IPO 相比，APO 的交易周期短。APO 结束时，上市壳公司和私人公司会签署文件来完成反向兼并。他们会向 SEC 递交 8K 表，按照相关规定公开披露交易信息，也会递交 PIPE 股份的注册申报文件。与此同时，第三方托管账户将会放款，公司也会发布新闻稿宣布该交易的完成。这之后该公司经过重新估价的股票才开始交易。

APO 交易完成的时间很短，一般为 30 天至 90 天。公司在交易完成之后收到融资，而 SEC 对其信息披露的要求与对 IPO 的要求完全一致。APO 交易完成约 3 个至 4 个月后，公司递交的注册申报文件应该完成对 SEC 相关评议的清理工作，并开始在 SEC“生效”。这一步完成之后，公司可申请在选定的交易所挂牌上市。上市申请（比如申请从场外交易转至纳斯达克证券市场）的审批大概需要 1 个月的时间，接着分析师开始发布研究报告，公司也会集中精力处理投资者关系、举行非交易路演、召开会议等。

At the conclusion of an APO transaction, a company has received equity funding and has a base of institutional investors. The business has the sponsorship of an investment bank and is exchange listed with analyst coverage. There is now a true market value for the company which is positioned to raise additional capital in PIPE transactions.

Companies choose to become public through an APO for several reasons. The public shell company already has shareholders, so after the APO is completed, the formerly private company already meets the requirements for NASDAQ with 300 shareholders. A company that goes public through an IPO must sell its stock to a large number of shareholders in order to meet these same requirements which necessitate a broad marketing and road show process. Unlike an IPO, there is no public disclosure required until the transaction closes. Customers, suppliers, employees, and press are unaware until closing. With an IPO, a company must publicly announce its intentions and file with the SEC at the beginning of the process.

The APO model owes much of its success to the involvement of the Investment Bank. In a traditional reverse merger, anyone could simply buy a shell and go public whether or not they had sufficient financial performance to justify being a public company. With an APO, the investment bank would not raise capital for a company that it did not believe would be successful in the marketplace. This is why the APO has such a high success rate. The investment bank also brings research, trading, and liquidity to the company's stock after the transaction closes. Investment banks find the APO process appealing because they can receive the same fees for raising the capital as they do in an IPO, but in a much shorter period of time and to a significantly smaller number of investors.

PIPE investors are attracted to the APO because they can buy stock at a negotiated discount to the projected public market value of a company. In addition, because the company completed a reverse merger and is now public, there is a guaranteed exit (liquidity) defined upfront if they wish to get out. After a company completes an APO, potential investors will be inclined to invest in additional PIPE raises for the company because the public company has had SEC disclosures from day one including audited financial statements, Sarbanes-Oxley, 10Qs, 8Ks, etc.

APO 交易完成时，公司获得了股权融资，拥有了一批机构投资者，同时得到了投资银行的支持，成为了有分析师关注的交易所上市公司。这一切使公司获得了真正的市场价值，具备了通过 PIPE 交易获得更多融资的能力。

公司选择 APO 上市有以下几个原因。首先，由于上市壳公司已经拥有了股东，因此在 APO 完成之后，参与兼并的私人公司就已经满足了纳斯达克证券市场关于上市公司必须拥有至少 300 个股东的规定。而选择 IPO 上市的公司为了满足同样的要求必须向大量股东出售股票，这需要大范围的市场营销和路演工作。另外与 IPO 不同，在 APO 交易完成之前，公司不用向公众披露任何信息。在交易完成之前，公司的客户、供应商、员工和媒体均不知晓。但如果选择 IPO，公司必须从一开始就向公众披露意向并向 SEC 提呈。

APO 模式的成功很大程度上要归功于投资银行的参与。在传统反向兼并中，任何人都可以直接购买一家壳公司上市，其财务表现不与上市资格挂钩。而在 APO 交易中，投资银行要确信一家公司能够在市场上取得成功，否则不会为其募资。这是 APO 成功率如此之高的原因所在。投资银行还会在交易完成之后为公司股票提供研究、交易和流动性服务。投行之所以认为 APO 具备吸引力，是因为在该过程中他们所收取的费用与在 IPO 中相同，但前者所涉及的周期要短很多，面向的投资者数量也少许多。

PIPE 投资者之所以会对 APO 感兴趣，是因为他们可以通过商定的折扣，以低于公司预期公开市场价格买入该公司的股票。此外，由于公司完成了反向兼并且已上市，投资者如果想要退出，完全可按照预先设定好的退出（流动性）通道成功退出。公司完成 APO 之后，潜在投资者会倾向参与该公司额外的 PIPE 募资，因为新的上市公司从起初就已经具备了 SEC 所要求的信息披露，包括经过审计的财务报表、《萨班斯—奥克斯利法案》框架下的申报、10Q 表、8K 表等。

Private Investment in Public Equity (PIPE)

A private investment in public equity is a private investment firm's or another qualified investor's purchase of stock in a company at a discount to the current market value. The purpose of a PIPE is to raise capital faster than alternatives. In a traditional PIPE, common or preferred stock is issued at a set price to raise capital for the issuer. A structured PIPE issues common or preferred sharesof convertible debt. This financing technique is more efficient than secondary offerings, due to fewer regulatory issues with the SEC. PIPE's are generally used for small to medium size public companies that may have a difficult time accessing more traditional forms of equity financing.

A publicly traded company may utilize a PIPE when securing funds for working capital, expansion or acquisitions. The business obtains funding within two to three weeks, rather than waiting several months or longer, as with a secondary stock offering.

In a standard PIPE agreement, investors purchase stock in a private placement. Registration of the new shares with the SEC becomes effective within a month of filing. PIPE investors may purchase stock below the market price as a hedge of protection against the price devaluing.

A traditional PIPE agreement lets investors purchase common stock or preferred stock that is convertible to common shares at a predetermined price. If the business merges with another company or is sold in the near future, investors may be able to receive dividends or other payoffs. Because of these benefits, traditional PIPEs are usually priced at or near the stock's market value.

With a structured PIPE, preferred stock or debt securities convertible to common stock are sold. If the securities contain a reset clause, new investors are shielded from downside risks. The negative is that existing stockholders are exposed to dilution in their share values. For this reason, a structured PIPE transaction may need stockholder approval.

私人投资公开股票

私人投资公开股票（PIPE）是指一家私人投资公司或其他合格投资者以低于当前市价的折扣价购买一家公司的股票。PIPE 的目的是以最快速度融资。在传统型 PIPE 交易中，发行人通过以预定价格发行的普通股或优先股来融资。而在结构型 PIPE 交易中，发行人发行可转为普通股或优先股的可转债。这种融资手段的效率比二次发售更高，因为 SEC 对其监管要求更少。对于可能难以获得传统股本融资的中小型上市公司，一般会采用 PIPE 方式融资。

上市公司可利用 PIPE 为营运资本、扩张或收购募资。所募集资金在两三周内即可到位，而不必像二次发售那样要等上几个月甚至更久。

在标准型 PIPE 协议中，投资者通过定向增发认购股票。新股在 SEC 的注册可在申报后一个月内生效。PIPE 投资者可以通过折扣价认购股票，作为对股价下跌风险的对冲保护。

在传统型 PIPE 协议中，投资者可以购买普通股或是购买能够按照预先约定价格转为普通股的优先股。如果公司不久后与其他公司合并或出售，投资者还可能得到股利分红或其他收益。因此传统 PIPE 的定价通常等于或略低于股票市价。

而结构型 PIPE 出售的是可转为普通股的优先股或债券。如果这些债券包含重置条款，新的投资者可免受下行风险的冲击。但其负面影响是现有股东所持股票的价值有可能遭到稀释。因此结构型 PIPE 交易可能需要股东的批准。

Private Equity Funds

A private equity fund is raised and managed by investment professionals. Generally, a single private equity firm will manage a series of distinct private equity funds and will attempt to raise a new fund every three to five years as the previous fund becomes fully invested. The funds from investors can be traditional, where all the investors invest with equal terms, or asymmetric, where different investors have different terms. Private equity funds are designed for the bigger investors such as institutions.

Most private equity funds are structured as limited partnerships and are governed by the terms set forth in the limited partnership agreement (LPA). The fund will have a general partner (GP) (maybe Co-GP's) that raises money from institutional investors. These investors are known as limited partners (LPs) in the fund.

The partnership is usually a fixed-life investment vehicle that ranges from five to ten years and there are often extensions. For example, a 5 plus 2 fund has a life of five years, but can be extended for two more.

An annual "management fee" is paid by the fund investors to the fund manager to cover operations for the private equity firm's investment. This can range from 1% to 3%.

Profits will be proportionally allocated between Limited and General Partners. First, this distribution or waterfall includes a preferred minimum rate of return. For example, 3% to 10% might be set. This minimum return must be achieved before the General Partner can receive any carried interest, which is the share of the profits paid to the GP above the preferred return. The split is usually 70% to 80% to the Limited Partner and 20% to 30% to the General Partner.

A fund's manager has almost total discretion to make investments and control the affairs of the fund. However, the Limited Partners do have certain restrictions and controls that may limit the type, size, geographic focus of investments, and how long the manager is permitted to make new investments.

私募基金

私募基金由投资专业人士发起和管理。一般情况下，一家私人股本公司可管理一系列独立的私募基金，并且每3年到5年，一旦有基金满仓，就会设法发起一只新的基金。资金的募集可以采用传统方式，即所有投资者具有相同的条款，也可采用不对称的方式，即不同投资者有不同的条款。私募基金为机构投资者等大型投资者所设计。

多数私募基金都采用有限合伙制结构，依据有限合伙协议（LPA）中所设立的条款进行管理。基金要有一位普通合伙人（GP），有时也可能拥有多位共同普通合伙人（Co-GP's），负责从机构投资者那里融资。而这些投资者则称之为基金的有限合伙人（LPs）。

这种合伙关系通常具有固定期限，从5年到10年不等，且常常会延期。举个例子，一只"5加2"基金的期限为5年，但到期后可以延长2年。

基金投资者每年向基金管理者缴纳"管理费"，用于支付私募公司的投资运营成本。这笔费用的缴纳比率为1%至3%。

投资利润会按比例分配给LP和GP。首先，该利润分配（也叫"分配瀑布"）包括一个优先最低回报率，比如可设定为3%至10%。这一最低回报率必须首先得到实现，之后GP才可以获得附带权益，即GP获得的超出优先回报部分的利润占比。分配比例一般为LP占70%至80%，而GP占20%至30%。

私募基金管理人在投资和基金事务管理方面拥有几乎绝对的自主权。不过，LP也拥有某些限制和控制权，可以限制投资的类型、规模、重点地域，以及基金管理人进行新投资的间隔时限。

Investments in various companies are known as "portfolio companies" and are funded with the capital raised from Limited Partners. Some private equity funds make it a practice to co-invest with other funds. In addition, many private equity funds may also use debt with their investment strategy.

A number of private equity investment transactions are highly leveraged by using debt as part of the scheme to invest. A "leveraged buy-out" (LBO) is used when such an investment practice is undertaken. The cash flow from the portfolio company usually provides the source for the repayment of such debt. In most instances, debt is incurred from commercial banks or mezzanine funds.

The acquisition price of a portfolio company is based on a multiple of the company's historical income. Considerations include earnings before interest, taxes, depreciation, and amortization (EBITDA). Private equity multiples will vary according to the portfolio company's industry, the size of the company, and other factors.

A private equity fund's goal is to eventually exit the investments that are transacted. Exit can be created through a listing, distribution of assets, or a sale to another organization, like a merger or acquisition. Private equity funds are designed for investors who can afford to have capital protracted while generating high passive returns.

对多家公司的投资通常被称为“投资组合公司”，其资金来源于LP。一些私募基金采用与其他基金进行联合投资的业务模式。此外，许多私募基金还可能会在投资战略中使用债务。

许多私募投资交易使用债务作为投资计划的一部分，可获得较高杠杆率。此类投资业务通常会用到“杠杆收购”（LBO）。在此类业务中，债务的偿还资金通常来自投资组合公司的现金流。大多数情况下，债权人为商业银行或夹层基金。

投资组合公司的收购价格基于公司历史收入与一个倍数的乘积。考虑因素包括税息折旧及摊销前利润（EBITDA）。私人股本倍数会根据投资组合公司所在的行业、公司规模以及其他因素变化而定。

私募基金的目标是在完成交易后最终退出投资。退出途径包括上市、资产分配或出售给其他机构（比如并购）。私募基金的目标投资者可获得高额的被动回报，但要能够承受漫长的资本回收期。

CHAPTER 10

Checkmate Summary

第十章
“将军投资基金”概要

As founder of the Checkmate Investment Fund, I've attempted herein to succinctly recapitulate valuable lessons I learned during three decades of investment experience, both domestically and internationally. I've also included my perspective on how to become wealthy, attain happiness, and live a gratifying life.

Success is a balanced matrix of many elements working together in unison. Continually improve yourself and work on both qualitative and quantitative skills. Also develop a network of relationships, including a circle of trusted friends and a reliable team of dedicated employees. Properly aligning your priorities is the secret sauce to creating ubiquitous ROI's while also retaining a content and peaceful life.

Everything works holistically. For example, it is difficult to build lifelong business relationships and preserve intimate friends if you permit your temper to interfere and tarnish your character. Instinct and intuition are inherent, but diligent analysis is also mandatory. Work conscientiously, but also take care of your mental, physical, and emotional health and eat nutritiously, exercise regularly, relax habitually, and maintain a positive attitude.

My approach to life and investing combines the superlative aspects of American and Chinese culture. I am American by birth, but have spent many years conducting business in China and coordinating investments between the two dominant countries. I believe that by merging the best interests of America and China, there are many benefits for all concerned.

If you want a Checkmate in your life and investments, then apply the lessons presented in this book. Many of the concepts may seem simple when viewed as individual pieces, but with each subsequent reading, you'll absorb the overall effect through osmosis. I also advise additional research on any topics of interest to broaden your acumen.

Success is more than merely a person's financial wealth. True wealth is enjoying both business riches and personal happiness. Success is more than merely having an abundance of money. Recently I was chatting with a Chinese friend named Emma on how important balance is in the process of making money. I told her that the idea of spending every waking moment seeking money was a poor approach to life. She gave me an interesting analogy. She told me that people have two hands. One hand can be for earning money and the other should be used for health, family, learning and other things. I loved this explanation as it clearly defines the balance we should all be seeking.

作为“将军投资基金”的创始人，我想在这里简要概括一下，在这30年的国内外投资经验中，所学到的宝贵经验。我还把关于如何致富、获得幸福及美满生活的观点也包括其中。

成功是一个平衡的矩阵，是许多元素齐心协力的结果。要不断提高自己，提升定性与定量技能，也要发展人际关系网络，包括可以信赖的朋友圈子和可靠敬业的员工团队。适当调整你的优先顺序是创造无处不在的投资回报的秘诀，同时也能拥有美满和平静的生活。

一切事物的运行都是相互联系的整体。例如，如果你纵容自己的脾气干扰和影响性格，那么就很难建立终身的商业关系和维持亲密的朋友。本能和直觉是与生俱来的，但勤于分析也是必不可少的。认真工作，但也要关爱自己的心理、身体和情绪健康，营养膳食，定期锻炼，经常放松，以及保持积极的态度。

我对于生活和投资的理解结合了美国和中国文化的精粹。我出生在美国，但多年来一直在中国开展业务，并在两个主要国家之间协调投资。我相信，通过将美国和中国的最佳利益结合起来，会使所有相关方面受益匪浅。

如果你想在生活和投资中能够“将军”制胜，那么就把这本书里的经验教训应用到你的生活中。很多概念如果像一枚棋子一样，单独看待都很简单，但是随着每次后续阅读，你就会通过渗透来吸收整体效果。我还建议可以对任何感兴趣的话题进行补充研究，以开阔思路。

成功绝不仅仅是个人拥有财富。真正的富有是要享受商业财富和个人幸福。成功绝不仅仅是拥有大量的钱财。最近，我和一位名叫艾玛（Emma）的中国朋友聊起，在赚钱的过程中保持平衡的重要性。我告诉她，如果人们每天睁开眼睛就只想着怎样挣钱，这种生活方式太糟糕了。她做了一个有趣的比喻。她说人们都有两只手。一只手可以用来赚钱，另一只手应该用于健康、家庭、学习和其他方面。我喜欢这个解释，因为它清楚地定义了我们都应该寻求的平衡。

A Few Thoughts on Time

The study of time can be a powerful tool on your journey to success. In fact time management is learned skill that most successful people have mastered and use on a daily basis. It is a common belief that time is not your friend. While this is generally true there are instances when time can be on your side. Have you ever lost someone you love through a breakup or divorce? The pain can be so intense and severe that all you can do is to think of ways to get the person back into your life. Your thoughts are consumed with strategies to win back your departed love. But as time goes on, the pain subsides and you think less and less about the person. Eventually you move on with your life and you recognize that person is gone if not forgotten. It is a healthy process or we would be paralyzed with grief.

On the other hand, the misuse of time can be a disaster for both your personal and business life. Every minute you lose will add up to many days over the course of a year. Earlier, in Chapter Two, we explored the annual loss of time that will be realized from a daily commute of two hours. This two hour daily commute will cost you almost 480 hours each year. Furthermore, driving is a stress builder a distraction that adds no value to your life. Ask yourself what, besides driving is stealing your time? How much better can your life be if you had this time back?

I have noticed that many people are squandering time simply by inefficient management. A well planned schedule each day can free up many hours. To explore this, over the course of one month chronicle your use of time by recording your activities as the day progresses. Also note which of these times were the least productive, enjoyable or rewarding. At the end of the month you will be able to find many hours that could be better used for family, exercise, learning, professional development, or even enjoying your favorite hobby. So much can be gained from this simple exercise. Actually the time you find can be life changing.

I put these comments last in the book to reinforce the importance of how we invest our time. Once time is gone you will never get it back. Use your time wisely and you will experience a better personal life and a more successful business future.

关于时间的几点思考

对时间加以研究能够使之成为你走向成功的有力工具。事实上，时间管理是许多成功人士都掌握并每天使用的技能。人们普遍认为时间不是人类的朋友。虽然一般来说这是正确的，但也有实例能证明时间会对人们有所帮助。你是否曾经因为分手或离婚而失去过你爱的人？这种痛苦异常强烈和严重，你所能做的就是想方设法让这个人重新回到你的生活中。你冥思苦想各种对策，以赢回逝去的爱。但是随着时间的推移，痛苦逐渐消退，你对那个人的思念也越来越少。最终你会继续自己的生活，并会意识到，对于那个人，你即使没有忘记，也已远去。这是一个健康的过程，否则我们会因悲伤而一蹶不振。

另外，滥用时间对于你的个人生活和事业都将是一场灾难。你失去的每一分钟都会在一年的时间里累积成很多天。之前在第二章里，我们探讨过从每日通勤车程两小时中形成的年度损失。这两小时的每日通勤车程一年中会花费将近 480 小时。此外，开车会造成压力，是对生活毫无价值的分心。扪心自问，开车除了会偷走你的时间外，有何益处？如果能把这段时间找回来，你的生活会变得多美好？

我注意到许多人只是因为管理不善而浪费时间。计划周详的每日时间表可以省出许多小时。为了探索这个问题，可以在一个月里，记录下每天各种活动所用的时间。还要注意这些时间段中哪一段是效率最低的、令人愉快的或有益的。在月底时，你将能够找到更多的时间，可以更好地用于家庭、锻炼、学习、职业发展，甚至可以享受你最喜欢的业余爱好。从这个简单的练习中可以得到很多。实际上，你找回的时间可以将生活改变。

我把这些评论放在书中最后部分，以强调我们如何投入时间的重要性。时间一去不返。明智地利用时间，你会体验到更好的个人生活和更成功的商业前景。

APPENDIX

附　录

You will find in this section multiple checklists to help you in your business and personal life. At Checkmate Investing we use checklists for every step of our investing process. These checklists are not meant to be complete but instead a starting point. The purpose of this section of the book is to teach you the importance of detail and process. Often, when organizing a task, steps are taken out of order.

By using checklists you will be sure to not forget to go back and complete all elements of the task. Some of the attached checklists only scratch the service such as the IPO going public checklist. The actual checklist for going public is an entire book in itself.

You will also want to add your own items to the checklists. We always recommend using professionals such as consultants, accounts, lawyers, engineers, etc. and each of these professionals will have their own checklists.

You will find a good sampling of checklists in this section of the book. You can also go to "The Checkmate Investing" app and you find many additional checklists that are not in this book. Once you get in the habit of using checklists you will find that you will enjoy greater success across the board. In the world of investing every detail means something and every step of the process is important. By using checklists, you will find greater success than you have known in the past.

本部分提供了多个清单，可在业务和个人生活方面为你提供帮助。在“将军投资”，我们针对投资过程中的各个步骤采用了相关清单。这些清单并非完整信息，而仅作为一个出发点。本书该部分的目的在于说明细节和过程的重要性。在组织一项任务时，通常人们采取的步骤是杂乱无章的。

通过使用清单，你一定不会忘记完成全部任务内容。一些随附清单只说明了服务项目，如 IPO 上市清单，而实际公开上市清单本身就可以是一整本书。

此外，你还可以在清单中添加自己的项目。我们始终建议雇用顾问、会计、律师、工程师等专业人员，每位专业人员都将有自己的清单。

你可以在本部分中看到很好的清单样本，还可以通过“将军投资”应用软件查看本书中未涵盖的更多其他清单。一旦你习惯于使用清单，会发现很享受由此带来的全面巨大成功。在投资界，每个细节都有某种意义，过程中的每个步骤都具备重要性。通过使用清单，你会得到比过去更大的成功。

Checklist for seeking Angel Investors

Intellectual Property Checklist

Checklist for "Clear and Clean" IP Rights

Pitch Deck Checklist

Checklist for Obtaining a Loan

Checklist for Crowd Funding

Checklist for Developing an App

Checklist for App Store Optimization (ASO)

Checklist for Websites

Checklist for Initial Public Offering (IPO)

Checklist for Franchise Investing

Checklist for Mergers and Acquisitions

Fundraising Tips for Startups

Checklist for Life

扫一扫即可查看及
下载附赠投资必需清单

关于寻求天使投资者的清单

关于知识产权的清单

关于“明确清晰”知识产权的清单

关于融资演讲稿的清单

关于获得贷款的清单

关于众筹的清单

关于应用软件开发的清单

关于应用商店优化（ASO）的清单

关于网站的清单

关于首次公开发行（IPO）的清单

关于特许经营投资的清单

关于兼并与收购（并购）的清单

创业筹资技巧

关于生活哲学的清单

扫一扫即可查看及
下载附赠投资必需清单

Glossary

Angel Investor is an affluent individual who invests in early stage or start-up businesses in exchange for an equity ownership interest.

Market Size refers to the number of potential buyers and/or sellers of a product or service in a particular market.

Target Customer refers to the specific group who are likely to buy a product or service.

Intellectual Property refers to protection of creations of the mind, which have both moral and commercial values.

Exit Strategy a planned approached to terminating a situation in a way that will maximize benefit and/or minimize damage.

Patent refers to an exclusive right granted by the government for a limited time for an invention.

Trademark refers to a recognizable symbol, phrase, design, or expression that identifies products or services as originating from particular source, e.g. originating from a particular company.

Copyright refers to a legal right to protect the original expression of ideas, such as copyrights on music, video, books, etc.

Trade Secrets refers to confidential information that provides a business advantage and include a formula, a business practice, a manufacturing process, a design of a manufacturing machine, a method, or even a compilation of information.

Pitch Deck refers to a brief presentation used to sell an investment opportunity.

Competitive Landscape refers to an analysis identifying a company's primary online and offline rivals.

Financial Projections is a forecast of business revenue and expenses.

Crowdfunding refers to the raising of capital from a large number of people.

词汇表

天使投资人是富有的个体，投资于早期阶段的企业或新的创业公司，以换取股权权益。

市场规模是指某一特定市场上某一产品或服务的潜在购买者和/或销售者的数量。

目标客户指可能购买产品或服务的特定人群。

知识产权是指对具有精神财富和商业价值的智力成果的保护。

退出策略是有计划的以一种使利益最大化和/或损失最小化的方式来结束的策略。

专利指的是政府在有限的时间内授予的一项专有权。

商标是指通过可辨认的符号、短语、设计或表达来识别产品或服务源自特定来源，例如来自特定公司的产品或服务。

版权是指保护原创思想的合法权利，例如音乐、视频、书籍等。

商业机密是指能够提供商业优势的机密信息，包括一个配方，一次商业实践，一个制造过程，一个制造机器的设计，一种方法，甚至是一个信息的汇编。

融资演讲稿是指用来出售投资机会的简短介绍。

竞争环境指的是一项分析，确定一家公司的主要在线和线下竞争对手。

财务预测是对企业收入和支出的预测。

众筹是指从大众中筹集资金。

APP Store Optimization refers to increasing the visibility of an APP, which typically includes optimizing the ranking of an APP in an APP store.

Search Engine Optimization refers to increasing the visibility of a website by obtaining a high-ranking placement in the search results page so it can increase sales.

Content Strategy refers to a series of plans for the creation, consumption and management of content.

LOI refers to a letter of intent, which summarizes the assumptions, main points of business proposal before a formal agreement is signed.

MOU refers to a memorandum of understanding, which is a non-binding document that outlines the terms of an agreement between two parties.

Working Capital is a measure of both a company's efficiency and its short-term financial health. Working capital is calculated as Working Capital= Current Assets – Current Liabilities.

Quality of earnings describes the amount of profit from core operations rather than accounting methods, extraordinary situation or earning managements.

Capital Budget is a process used by companies for future development, access to greater compensation, and to make expenditure plan.

Intellectual Property Litigation refers to lawsuits related to patents, trademarks, copyrights, and trade secrets.

Technology in-license refers to a legal agreement to license technology to for a product or service, often in the context of licensing technology for additional research and development.

Partnership Agreement is between two or more individuals who join as partners to form and carry on a for-profit business.

Acquisition Agreement refers to the process when one company acquires another.

Power of Attorney is a legal document that allows you to appoint a person or organization to manage your affairs if you become unable to do so.

Equity Finance Agreement is the process of raising capital through the sales of shares in an enterprise.

应用商品优化指的是增加应用软件的知名度，这通常包括优化应用软件在应用商店中的排名。

搜索引擎优化指的是通过在搜索结果页面中获得靠前位置来增加网站的知名度，从而使其增加销售量。

内容策略指的是内容的创建、消耗和管理的一系列计划。

意向书指的是一份合同草约，它概括了在正式商业计划协议签署之前的假设和要点。

谅解备忘录是一份不具约束力的文件，它概述了协议双方的条款。

营运资本是衡量一家公司的效率和短期财务状况的指标。营运资金本计算方法为：营运资本 = 流动资产 – 流动负债。

收益质量描述的是核心业务的利润额，而不是会计方法、特殊情况或盈利管理。

资本预算是企业用于未来发展、获得更大补偿和制订支出计划的过程。

知识产权诉讼是指与专利、商标、版权和商业秘密相关的诉讼。

技术许可是指得到产品或服务技术授权的法律协议，通常是在技术许可的背景下进行额外的研究和开发。

合伙协议由两个或两个以上的个体组成，以合作伙伴的形式进行营利性的业务。

收购协议是指一个公司收购另一家公司的过程。

委托书是一份法律文件，允许你指定个人或组织，在你不能自行完成的时候，处理事务。

股权融资协议是通过出售企业股份筹集资金的过程。

Non-Competition Agreement is a written legal contract between an employer and employees. It lays out binding terms and conditions about the employee's ability to work in the same industry and with competing organizations upon employment termination from the current employer.

Collective Bargaining Agreement is the process of negotiating the terms of employment between an employer and a group of workers.

Net Operating Loss is a negative profit for tax purposes. It usually occurs when a company's tax deductible expenses exceed its taxable revenues, making the company unprofitable.

Golden Parachute is a contractual provision that provides an executive with a substantial package upon termination, usually in the event of a takeover or merger.

Statute of Limitations is a law, which sets out maximum time that parties have to initiate legal proceedings from the date of an alleged offense.

Hart-Scott-Rodino is an antitrust statute that authorizes the FTC and the Antitrust Division of the Department of Justice to evaluate the potential anticompetitive effects of certain merger and acquisition transactions.

D & O Insurance refers to Directors and Officers Liability Insurance.

Intellectual Property Insurance refers to insurance to defend against common intellectual property lawsuits, such as patent lawsuits, copyright lawsuits, trademarks lawsuits, etc.

E & O Insurance refers to errors and omissions insurance, which shields you and your employees when clients accuse you of making mistakes that cost them money.

Employee Liability Insurance is insurance protection against claims for damages resulting from sickness or injury sustained during the course of work.

Umbrella Policies is extra liability insurance coverage that goes beyond the limits of the insured's home, auto or watercraft insurance. It provides an additional layer of security to those who are at risk for being sued for damages to other people's property or injuries caused to others in an accident.

竞业禁止协议是雇主和雇员之间签订的书面法律合同。它列出了关于雇员在与现任雇主终止雇佣关系后，在同一行业及竞争企业工作权限的条款和条件。

劳资协议是在雇主和员工之间协商雇佣条款的过程。

经营净亏损是纳税后的负利润。通常发生在公司的可抵扣税款超过其应纳税收入的时候，使公司无利可赚。

黄金降落伞是一种合同条款，可以在被接管或合并的情况下，为高管提供一系列实质性的保障。

诉讼时效是一项法令，规定当事人从被指控的罪行发生的日期开始，必须提起诉讼的最长时间。

哈特·斯科特·罗宾诺改进法案是一项反垄断法案，授权美国联邦贸易委员会和司法部反垄断部门评估某些并购交易可能产生的反竞争影响。

董事责任保险是指董事和官员责任保险。

知识产权保险是指针对常见知识产权诉讼的保险，如专利诉讼、版权诉讼、商标诉讼等。

职业责任保险是指过失和疏忽责任保险，当客户指责你因失误而浪费其钱财时，可以保护你和你的雇员。

雇员责任保险是指在工作过程中因疾病或受伤而造成的损害索要赔偿的保险。

个人庇护保险是指超出了被保险人的住宅、汽车或船只保险范围之外的额外责任保险。为那些因在事故中造成他人财产损失或他人受伤，而被要求赔偿者提供了额外的安全保障。

Index 索引

E

F

G

H

I

J

K

L

Acknowledgements

I want to thank everyone who has touched my life as from each I have learned much. In addition I want to thank the people listed below for their contribution to this book as advisors and editors.

Thomas Paschall – Tom is my partner and co-founder of Checkmate. Tom was previously a senior corporate and project finance attorney at the prestigious Wall Street law firm Milbank Tweed. In the past Tom has enjoyed a wide range of success including being a principal in one of the most successful alternative energy funds partnered with Panasonic Corporation of North America. That fund was one of the fastest growing in the United States. The return Tom has produced for Checkmate in Energy Technology, Biotech and other areas is among tops in the fund business. Tom's list of his accomplishments are too large to list. The truth is Tom is the most brilliant person I have ever met. He is a balanced person who can always keep things in perceptive. When it comes to deal structure and balancing risk versus reward Tom is always wise and prudent. I want to thank Tom for his input and friendship.

Michelle Wang – Michelle is a long term friend. She is a wise woman. I choose Michelle as the primary Mandarin translator due to her way of thinking. She is a balanced person who is in touch with both life and business. She is very organized and responsible and I want to thank her.

Bobb Hopkins – Bobby is a long-term friend and associate. He is a superb writer having written 26 full length feature films. Bobby is also a business man having produced multiple movies and TV shows. Bobby tells me he learned much editing this book and I want to thank him for his outstanding efforts.

致　谢

我要感谢这一生中每一位触动到我的人，我从他们那里学到了很多东西。另外，我要感谢下面列出的人士，他们作为顾问和编辑对本书作出了贡献。

Thomas Paschall——汤姆（Tom）是我的合作伙伴，也是“将军投资”（Checkmate）的联合创始人。汤姆曾是华尔街著名律师事务所美邦律师事务所（Milbank Tweed）的高级企业和项目财务律师。在此之前，汤姆获得了广泛的成功，包括成为与北美松下公司（Panasonic Corporation of North America）合作，最成功的替代能源基金之一的负责人。该基金是美国增长最快的基金之一。汤姆在能源技术、生物技术和其他领域对“将军投资”（Checkmate）的回报，在本基金业务中名列前茅。汤姆的成就清单很长，不胜枚举。事实上，汤姆是我所见过的最聪明的人。他是一个平衡的人，总能对事物保持敏锐的洞察力。当涉及交易结构和平衡风险与回报时，汤姆总是明智而谨慎的。我要感谢汤姆的帮助和友谊。

王梅（Michelle Wang）——Michelle 是我多年的好友，非常聪颖。我之所以选择 Michelle 负责汉语翻译工作，是鉴于她的思维方式，她在生活和事业中能够保持平衡，做事有条有理，尽职尽责，我要感谢她。

Bobb Hopkins——鲍比（Bobby）是我的长期朋友和伙伴。他是一位出色的作家，曾写过 26 部完整的故事片。鲍比也是一个商业人士，他制作了多部电影和电视节目。鲍比告诉我，在编辑本书时，他学到了很多，我要感谢他的杰出努力。

Dr. Edward Van Gieson - His assistance on the intellectual property sections were most valuable. Dr. Van Gieson is an intellectual property attorney in Silicon Valley. In addition to his legal education, his education includes a Ph.D. in electrical engineering from Cornell University. He has worked at top Silicon Valley law firms as a patent attorney. His clients have included Fortune 500 companies, entrepreneurs, and many high tech clients.

Edward Van Gieson 博士是美国硅谷一位极具天赋的专利律师，其在知识产权方面的帮助极具价值。除了法学学位，他还毕业于美国常春藤联盟康奈尔大学并获得了电子工程博士学位。他具有在硅谷顶尖律师事务所工作的经验，其客户包括世界 500 强公司、企业家及很多高科技客户。

The End

I hope you have enjoyed reading this book. It was written as much about investing in life as about investing for monetary gain. Everything you do is an investment of some type: money, education, health, and a myriad of every day choices that require your time, effort, and energy.

Life is like a game of chess, whether personal or in business, we will always encounter difficulties and often hesitate to make the next move. When challenges are encountered it is best to be far-sighted, knowledgeable, prepared and invincible. In the game of life, everyone's resources are limited. To realize success we need to constantly learn and improve ourselves. With practice a person can learn to optimize their finite resources into infinite possibilities. In the end this process will be the catalyst to making an intelligent rational decision and produce a checkmate to win.

At every turn in life, we ask "Why?" The answers are all based on having faith, continually improving yourself, being productive, keeping perspective, and giving to others. To achieve this inner balance, it is imperative to appreciate others' points of view. Show them respect, be pleasant, smile often, make them feel comfortable in your presence, and always be responsible, punctual, prepared, and truly learn to care about their needs as well as your own. Never raise your voice in anger or become jealous of another person's success or become vindictive as trying to get even is always a waste of time and energy. Forgive others, learn to apologize and learn to accept apologies, be proud of your accomplishments, count your blessings, and be disciplined, but never robotic as being open minded and spontaneous is as important as compassion and empathy which must always emanate from the heart. Avoid gossip and sarcasm, stay diplomatic.

结束语

真心希望你能喜爱本书，其中描写对于生活的投资如同为了货币收益的真实投资一样，都会终有所获。你从事的每件事都是某种投资：钱财、教育、健康、无数日常选择，这些都会需要投入时间、努力和精力。

人生如同博弈，无论在个人生活还是生意场上，我们总会遇到困难重重、举棋不定的时刻，每当此时，我们多么希望自己能高瞻远瞩、知识渊博、万事俱备、战无不胜。博弈中每个人的资源是有限的，要想成功需要平时不断学习、提高自身，将有限的资源优化组合成无限的能量，最终确定目标，一举制胜。

每当处于人生的转折点，我们总会问“为什么？”所有答案都建立在拥有信念的基础上，要不断改善自身、提高效率、保持观点、给予他人。要达到这一内在平衡，我们必须欣赏他人的观点，尊重他人、和蔼可亲、笑口常开、令人愉悦，并且要有担当、能守时、有准备，学会像关心自身需求一样关心他人需求。不因生气而高声，不嫉妒他人成就，也不心存怀恨，因为试图报复他人会浪费时间和精力。原谅他人、学会道歉、接受道歉、为自身成就引以为豪、常怀感恩、遵守纪律，但不机械刻板，因为心胸开阔、真情流露和慈悲悯人、感同身受一样重要，均出自内心。避免闲言碎语、讽刺嘲笑，要善于交际。

Never be swayed by peer pressure, but accept inspiration from others and wisdom from mentors. Be open to suggestions, but prior to making any decision, take a deep breath, slowdown, and listen. By believing in yourself, you, too, will inspire others and generate the opportunity to become a mentor. Even if you do not always succeed, you will always learn from trying new endeavors. Don't let the fear and embarrassment of failure inhibit your integrity. It is normal to have doubt, but never give up. Be a self-starter, think good thoughts, accept responsibility, make the most of every opportunity, and never make decisions out of desperation.

Lastly, stay loyal to your family, your health, your goals, and honor your commitments.

不受来自同伴压力的影响，但要接受来自他人的灵感和导师的智慧。接受建议，但在作出决定之前，做深呼吸、放慢动作、仔细聆听。相信自身，你同样能够激励他人，并不断积累最终成为他人的导师。即使你不总是成功，也能够在不断尝试新的努力中学到很多。不要让失败的恐惧和尴尬阻碍你的诚信。心存有疑虑很正常，但要永不放弃。要做事主动、思想积极，勇于承担责任，充分利用每一次机会，不在绝望中作出决定。

最后，要忠于家庭，关注健康，心怀目标，履行承诺。

图书在版编目(CIP)数据

一击制胜：华尔街金牌投资人的99条忠告：汉英对照／(美)江柏德(John M. Probandt)著. --北京：法律出版社，2018

书名原文：Checkmate Investing：Three Decades of Investment Tips, Philosophy and Wisdom for Creating Wealth and a Happy Life

ISBN 978-7-5197-2482-5

Ⅰ.①一… Ⅱ.①江… Ⅲ.①金融投资-基本知识-汉、英 Ⅳ.①F830.59

中国版本图书馆CIP数据核字(2018)第164504号

一击制胜：华尔街金牌投资人的99条忠告(汉英对照)
YIJI ZHISHENG：HUAERJIE JINPAI TOUZIREN DE 99 TIAO ZHONGGAO(HANYING DUIZHAO)

[美]江柏德(John M. Probandt) 著

责任编辑 赵明霞
装帧设计 马 帅

出版 法律出版社
编辑统筹 法商出版分社
总发行 中国法律图书有限公司
开本 710毫米×1000毫米 1/16
经销 新华书店
印张 28.5
印刷 三河市兴达印务有限公司
字数 528千
责任校对 李景美
版本 2018年10月第1版
责任印制 胡晓雅
印次 2018年10月第1次印刷

法律出版社／北京市丰台区莲花池西里7号(100073)
网址／www.lawpress.com.cn
投稿邮箱／info@lawpress.com.cn
销售热线／010-63939792/9779
举报维权邮箱／jbwq@lawpress.com.cn
咨询电话／010-63939796

中国法律图书有限公司／北京市丰台区莲花池西里7号(100073)
全国各地中法图分、子公司销售电话：
统一销售客服／400-660-6393
第一法律书店／010-63939781/9782
西安分公司／029-85330678
重庆分公司／023-67453036
上海分公司／021-62071010/1636
深圳分公司／0755-83072995

书号：ISBN 978-7-5197-2482-5
定价：99.00元
(如有缺页或倒装，中国法律图书有限公司负责退换)